The Lean Toolbox

for

Service Systems

by
John Bicheno

Lean Enterprise Research Centre, Cardiff
Business School
and
University of Buckingham

Production and Inventory Control, Systems and Indu
Engineering Books
PICSIE Books
Buckingham, England
2008

Published by

PICSIE Books
Box 622
Buckingham
MK18 7YE
Telephone and FAX : +44 (0) 1280 815023
www.picsie.co.uk
email: picsiebook@btinternet.com

ISBN 978-0-9541244-4-1

British Library Cataloguing-in-Publication Data
A catalogue record for this book is available from the British Library.

Printed in the United Kingdom by Lightning Source UK Ltd

For Joel and Erin

Acknowledgements

Many have contributed to my journey into Lean and Lean Service.

Eric Hall and Val Bolitho started me off. My eternal thanks. Peter Checkland introduced me to Systems – an unexpected delight. George Davidson of Toyota inspired. Roy Marcus added entrepreneurial flair, and changed my direction. VS Mahesh continues to influence and inspire all those he teaches, including me. Peter Hines gave support and opportunity. Simon Elias and Sarah Lethbridge moved us cheerfully forward. Claire Gardner supported. John Seddon and Richard Davis continue to share their groundbreaking material most generously. Christian Hansen was patient as we learned and re-learned together. Kate Mackle has been a beacon of clarity. John Darlington keeps me on the ground by reminding about the bottom line. A whole generation of Buckingham Service Management students, and the first MSc Lean Service class in Cardiff thought that I was teaching them, but the reverse was true. Others who deserve special mention include Viktor Peters, Alex Speciale, Deba Correia, Neil Dewfield, James Carr, Bjarne Olsen, Joakim Hillberg, and Stuart Panton and his team of Peter, Mo, and Paul. And last but not least, Sally – my patient and gentle critic and counsel.

Errors, of course, are mine. I still have lots to learn.

Foreword

John Bicheno has a well-deserved reputation for an encyclopaedic knowledge of tools and techniques for performance improvement. In this compendium he extends his repertoire to service organisations. There are more tools here than you may use in a lifetime; it is a jamboree of things to do that will appeal to managers.

But what to do? It is not a question of which tool do I use but what problems do I have, and do I understand my problems? Taiichi Ohno's favourite word was 'understanding'. To understand problems and thus realise opportunities we have to learn how to study the work and learn how to avoid being misled by many of management's current assumptions about problems and their causes.

Ohno also insisted we should never codify method. Had his warning been heeded we might have avoided the misguided attempts to apply the tools developed in manufacturing to service organisations. The well-publicised failures have damaged the reputation of 'lean' and put back the opportunity for significant improvement. This compendium is a timely contribution, steering service organisations away from misguided advice. We should remember that Ohno did not call his innovation 'lean' – he didn't want it called anything. He could, perhaps, foresee the folly of a label.

Ohno's contribution was a profound challenge to management's paradigm. He found counter-intuitive truths. I hope this book helps you find them too.

John Seddon
Managing Director, Vanguard Consulting
Visiting Professor, LERC, Cardiff University

CONTENTS

How to Read this Book

This book is aimed at a wide spectrum of service operations: from repetitive office tasks, through classic customer-facing operations such as hotels and health, to field service and to consulting and design.

The book also covers some conventional Lean theory.

The book is therefore not intended to be read from cover to cover.

I recommend reading those parts of Part 1 that you find relevant. Don't miss reading about 'Check' and Variability. Then have a look at the Mapping Flowchart. This covers several service sectors so you are unlikely to follow through all the branches. It should, however, give you an indication of sections that are of particular relevance. Read Part 2 and the material on Level 1 mapping. This is relevant to most service environments.

Finally select those tools from Part 3 that you consider most relevant. Keep in mind that there is quite a bit of overlap and interaction between the sections.

I hope you find the book useful.

Best wishes

John Bicheno

About Lean Service and The Toolbox

Introduction and Positioning

This book presents a set of core tools for Lean service operations. Particular attention is given to mapping tools in service.

A prime theme throughout the book is the emphasis on System. Tools without system can only be piecemeal and incremental, and will ultimately yield disappointing results. The systems approach to Lean service requires appropriate tools. Concept can only get you so far.

The book does not present core Quality and Six Sigma tools or philosophy, except where they integrate with mapping tools. Quality and Six Sigma tools are described in the companion book *Six Sigma and the Quality Toolbox*.

Nor does this book cover 'people aspects' of Lean service specifically. Most books on Lean do not delve much into Behaviour in Organisations questions – even though they are vital to Lean success.

The New Lean Toolbox (2004, second edition 2008) presents mainly the Lean manufacturing tools and philosophy. Although *The Lean Toolbox for Service Systems* aims to be self-contained with respect to Lean, there is nevertheless a continuum of manufacturing and service. It may be that concepts of scheduling, for example, which are fully described in *The New Lean Toolbox*, are only cursorily described in this book, and some readers may wish to refer to *The New Lean Toolbox* for a fuller explanation.

We are all in Service!

'Service' in this book is not just 'the office' or 'administration', which have been the focus of several publications, but is also service in wider situations which are not necessarily repetitive, where 'takt' time is not applicable, and where task times may be both long and variable. Service in this context could mean anything from a hospital to a university, from an administrative process to a consultancy, and from a warehouse to field service maintenance.

We should not, however, confuse 'service' with the service industry sector classification found in government publications and used by economists. For these people, there is a distinction between 'manufacturing sector' and 'service sector'. Today this classification seems of limited use. All manufacturing firms have service elements. Many 'service sector' organisations have manufacturing-like operations in that they produce regular outputs along value streams.

Instead, 'service' in this publication will be taken to mean the 'service concept' or 'product service bundle'. These are all the activities (both 'hard' and 'soft') that provide value to the customer along a value stream. So we will not be concerned with the making of 'hard' products – that is the focus of the many books on Lean manufacturing. However, the book will certainly be relevant to service activities within manufacturing companies.

The focus of the book is also on 'Lean'. The book is not about, but does overlap with
— general service operations management (for example by Johnston and Clark or Metters and Metters)
— services marketing (for example by Zeithaml, Bitner and Gremler)
— 'process management' (for example by Slack *et al*).

The book is about practical tools that can be applied immediately for real gains in service quality, customer satisfaction, and productivity.

A 'meta tool', to which several other Lean service tools will be attached, is value stream mapping. Value stream mapping is a well-established tool within Lean manufacturing. However, virtually all of the 'Acme Stamping' type of mapping, made popular by Rother and Shook, assumes short-cycle repetitive operations with minimal customer interaction. This is sometimes the case in some office processes, but in general has limited applicability within service. This book attempts to provide a set of tools, particularly mapping tools, which have wider applicability.

The Lean System

In manufacturing, Toyota has long had the idea that Lean, or TPS (Toyota Production System), is really about system. Unfortunately many would-be followers of Toyota ignored the system aspect and went piecemeal into tools and techniques – often with disappointing results. This is now slowly being corrected as managers realise the system dimension.

Then came service. There are now potentially two problems. The first is once again to repeat the manufacturing mistake and leap into tools, ignoring the system aspect. The second is to try to use manufacturing tools in a service context. As with the manufacturing experience, there will be some limited success despite these problems.

As Richard Davis of Vanguard has pointed out, much of what goes under the heading of Lean Service is merely trying to adapt the manufacturing tools derived from Toyota, instead of deriving what to do from the more fundamental, profound systems ideas that Ohno and Toyota used to develop TPS.

However, there still remains a misunderstanding about the term 'system'. Lean is NOT a technical system, it is a LEARNING SYSTEM. The tools are best regarded as tools with which to learn more about the system. So, taking a manufacturing example, kanban is not a tool or technical system for inventory reduction but a way of learning more about improvement. TPS can also stand for Thinking People System. This is even more appropriate in Lean service operations.

Jim Womack has an equation: Lean = Purpose + Process + People (LEI, 2006).

That equation is a good, quick summary of what this book is about.

And, 'while cost reduction is a natural consequence of "lean", it is not its purpose. The purpose of "lean" is to increase capacity by designing a system that optimally responds to customer demand' ('Watch out for the toolheads', Vanguard Education, 2006, www.lean-service.com/6-23.asp).

Value and Value Stream Focus

The concepts of Value, the Value Stream and Flow are the first three Lean Principles. These are the starting points of this book. The book is ultimately about improving customer value through focusing on value streams - the cross-functional sequence of activities that should be capable of giving the customer what is required, when and where it is required, without hassle. This requires the sequence of activities to flow without waste.

The concept of the Value Stream, so well described in Womack and Jones' *Lean Thinking*, is fundamental to Lean and has application in manufacturing and service. It is highly relevant to this book.

Of course, giving the customer a hassle-free experience is the first priority. Although this is still unfortunately relatively rare, customers expect it. It is a 'basic' (Kano) or 'qualifier'. Yet in administration, and particularly service, it is frequently no longer good enough to give basic service. 'Performance' must aim to delight. This book will attempt to give pointers.

Lean Service In Manufacturing; Lean Manufacturing in Service

Every manufacturing organisation is involved with service; most service organisations have some repetitive or transactional activities. Most publications on Lean mapping, even those that are ostensibly about administration, have to date focused strongly on the repetitive end. This book embodies the belief that mapping for service and administration requires a 'horses for courses' approach.

Service and administration are generally characterised by greater variety than repetitive manufacturing, certainly of the 'Acme Stamping' (Rother and Shook) variety. Mapping short-cycle repetitive manufacturing is well catered for by classic texts such as *Learning to See*. If you are fortunate (?) enough to have an administrative process with high repetition, dedicated resources, low variation between similar products, highly standardised tasks, and minimal customer contact, then certainly you should use 'Learning to See' mapping. Takt time will be relevant. However, most of the time repetitive manufacturing concepts like takt time will have little or no relevance in service.

Service mapping must also recognise that, unlike a manufacturing business, the 'lowest level' staff are at the front line of service and it is they who can make the difference between retained profitable customers and uncommitted unprofitable customers.

Thus the quotation that is sometimes heard about Toyota getting brilliant results from managing brilliant processes with average people while their competitors get poor results from brilliant people managing broken processes, needs to be treated with caution. That quotation may well be valid in manufacturing, but for outstanding service, you need BOTH good process AND good people, not average. Average must be brought up to good or above and mapping is a way to do this. The quote becomes even less valid as you move down the list of the three types of map used in this book. In fact, in creative processes you need the best people possible working in a good process. At this end of the spectrum, a reasonable process is required but truly creative processes will be mediocre with just average people. With services that depend on front line staff, the Toyota quote may actually be offensive. Beware.

How Do People in Service and Manufacturing Spend Their Time?

Everyone is in 'service', even if you are in 'manufacturing' or construction. One view is that almost everyone at work can be seen as spending their working day or working week doing a mix of the following activities:

- **Manufacturing or Construction**. This is the time actually making physical products, not planning or doing kaizen activities. For a person in a 'service industry' this percentage would be zero. But for a person in manufacturing, this time would seldom be 100% - certainly not 100% for a manager in manufacturing.
- **Field service or repair** (or 'break fix') operations. This is the actual time carrying out physical repairs, not travelling or planning. This percentage of time will often be zero for factory and office workers.
- **Runner activities**. These are activities that take place typically in an office every day and occupy most of the day. The office factory. For example, a person taking calls in a call centre every day, most of the day.
- **Repeater activities**. These activities occur regularly or semi-regularly. For example, an accountant consolidating the accounts once each month, a sales and operations planning (S&OP) meeting, or any regular meetings, running training periodically but regularly. Many service workers have a range of activities that are Repeaters, some done perhaps every day, others perhaps every year. Many creative activities such as design or advertising are like this – as are routine divorce cases or routine hospital operations or seeing patients.
- **Stranger activities**. These are the non-regular activities that are seldom repeated. Major projects or research, non-regular special tasks, complex managerial, legal or medical cases.
- **Waste activities**. These are activities that can be eliminated with very little negative impact. The classic wastes of transport, waiting, overproducing, and errors come to mind. Also included is failure demand (Seddon) – as a result of not doing something or not doing it right the first time.

Of course these areas are not mutually exclusive. Runners, Repeaters and Strangers (RRS), are not neat little boxes. Perhaps it is more useful to think of a continuum of activities.

The first of these (Manufacturing and Construction) is not the topic of this book. However, insofar as many manufacturing jobs will involve service activities, those service activities are the topic of this book.

Field service or repair will be discussed, but it is an area that overlaps with manufacturing, so readers working in this area will also find much of relevance in the manufacturing toolbox. As with manufacturing, many field service or repair jobs involve service aspects that will be discussed here.

Runners, Repeaters and Strangers is a well-established classification concept relevant to manufacturing scheduling. In manufacturing it is the products that are so classified. In service it is the activities. In manufacturing RRS provides a guideline into layout and scheduling. In service, RRS may be relevant to layout but it is particularly relevant to the way work is organised.

When thinking about Lean service, an early step is to estimate the extent of each category with your service group or field. Note that this does not imply that your type of service will fit into just one of these categories.

Structure of the Book

Part 1 covers the inter-related concepts of The Systems Approach and Lean Philosophy as they apply to service.

Part 2 covers a classification for Lean Service and gives approaches to mapping in various types of service situation. There is no one single mapping tool which is applicable to all service. Mapping is subservient to the idea of system but is a way of understanding the end-to-end value stream and of helping to keep the big picture in mind. Mapping as presented here is a three-level approach.

Part 3 covers the essential Lean service tools. Some, for example Total Productive Administration, may be considered approaches in themselves.

Part 1: Lean in Service

What is Lean Service?

Lean Service is System

The essence of Lean is the Systems Approach. Systems thinking is holistic. As Peter Checkland, UK Systems guru – someone who is more widely recognised in Japan than in his home UK – says, 'the systems approach seeks not to be reductionist'. 'Seeks' because it is quite hard to keep the end-to-end system in view when almost the whole business world, and the whole academic world, is organised by function.

Ohno said, 'All we are trying to do is to reduce the time from order to cash'. Note the systemic nature of this statement. Lean is not about manufacturing or service but about the system that brings both of these together. Toyota is a 'systems' company rather than a manufacturing company. Toyota learned their systems craft from, among others, Deming. Ohno saw economies of flow rather than economies of scale.

The great, and hugely entertaining, systems thinker Russell Ackoff, Emeritus Professor at Wharton, talks about resolving problems by discussion, solving problems by fact-based tools approach, which is better, and dissolving problems by understanding the purpose of the system and using innovative thinking, which is best of all. Non-Lean practitioners resolve 'inefficiencies', beginner Lean practitioners solve problems by removing waste, but the experienced Lean practitioner improves the whole system. Ackoff also says that a system is more about INTERACTIONS than ACTIONS. In healthcare, for example, it is interactions between many professionals that count towards the success of a patient's recovery. In office systems it is the handoffs and rework loops that make the difference.

The systems approach means the focus should be on the organisation or entity as a whole before paying attention to the parts. This is a very hard thing to do for most managers and other workers who have been brought up and educated in vertical silos. That is why, in this book, the first port of call is to try to understand the system as a whole. What is its purpose? A related focus is on the customer. Again, this is different from Lean manufacturing where the focus is on the object being made. This, in turn, was an important move forward from traditional mass production where the prime focus was on the efficiency of individual departments or machines. If we don't remain systemic we quickly get into the 'push down, pop up principle' where we solve one problem and then another emerges because we have sub-optimised. That has been the problem in many service operations: in call centres call productivity improved but complaints rose; in hospitals imposing targets on A&E waiting, ambulance drivers were driving around the car park so the measured queue would not build; in offices the implementation of ERP has often meant a slowdown in reaction time, and so on. In healthcare it is sometimes pointed out that increasing the human lifespan is good overall, but increases the load on hospitals which must cater for more ever-older patients. Another way of saying this is 'Systems bite back'.

Water is a liquid at normal temperatures. Its constituents, oxygen and hydrogen, are gases. You can never understand the properties of water by studying oxygen and hydrogen. Likewise Lean and Lean tools. Lean is a system – it is more than the sum of its components. Systems are in constant interplay with their environment – it is not obvious where the boundary is, what should be outsourced, the extent to which customers and suppliers are involved. Systems adapt continuously but at a faster rate when threatened, like ant colonies (true kaizen culture). Systems evolve, as bugs develop immunity to insecticides. It's a question of how to recognise and kill off inappropriate tools while developing new and stronger ones.

Another analogy is the human body. Layout, supermarkets and buffers provide the skeleton; pull systems and information flows are the circulation system; vision and strategy are the eyes and brain; control, deployment and measurement come from the nervous system; quality and improvement come from the muscular system; and energy and getting rid of waste come from the digestive system. The body needs them all for 'simple, slim and speedy' Lean (to quote Katsuaki Watanabe, Toyota President). So it is not surprising that TPS stands not only for Toyota Production System but also for Thinking People System.

Pfeffer's book *What Were They Thinking?* gives numerous examples of top management from major corporations adopting practices that could be termed 'non-systems thinking'. (Pfeffer does not use the term 'systems thinking'.) Examples are top-down announcements of cutting staff or wages when a company gets into financial trouble, or driving staff with forces such as threats and rewards. These practices ignore the impact on the system in favour of short-term 'solutions'. They prove ineffective for the organisation, even disastrous, sometimes immediately and almost invariably in the medium term – although, unfortunately, not always disastrous for the executive himself. Systems bite back.

Lean Service is 'Customer First'

Watanabe also says that Toyota's core principle is 'The Customer First'. But this again is a systems service view because Watanabe means both external customers and internal customers, suppliers and dealers. He also has in mind a dream for the end customer: a car that can make the air cleaner, that cannot injure people, that prevents accidents from happening, that can make people healthier the longer they drive, that can excite and entertain, and drive around the world on one tank of gas.

It would be arrogant to say that this book has all the answers. It does not. But in service you can try to remain holistic by recognising that the common purpose of everyone, top to bottom, is to improve the experience of the customer – be that 'customer' an insurance claimant, a hospital patient, an air traveller, a client consulting a solicitor, or an aircraft receiving maintenance. Everyone needs to support the end service – so you have the picture of the inverted triangle with the front line at the inverted base and top management at the apex situated at the bottom.

Customers have rising expectations. That is another point that makes service different from manufacturing, which has specifications and hence clear defect targets like Six Sigma. In service, expectations rise and specifications are not easy to set, so the system must be designed to adapt and improve continually – otherwise it will be seen as failing.

Lean Service is Process

The Lean Thinker does not think in terms of 'optimising' functions or departments, but in terms of end-to-end value streams made up of the integration of marketing, sales, design, engineering, manufacture, distribution, and service. Note that the office is only a small part. These value streams are tied together by information. The closer to the customer, and the quicker the response, the better. This means a different type of organisation – a different structure, different measures, and different careers. Jim Womack identifies the 'perfect process' as one where every step is valuable, capable, available, and adequate, and where all steps are linked by flow, pull, and levelling.

Beware the 'Halo Effect'. Does culture drive performance or performance drive culture? The former is often assumed, but

Rosenzweig points out several prominent instances where the reverse is the case. This has even misled several prominent researchers and authors, some of them in the Lean field. If it is process that drives performance, then process is even more important than we thought. But then Deming said that a long time ago.

Lean Service is not Tools!

There is a danger that Lean is thought of as a box of tools to be cherry-picked. The problem is that it is an end-to-end value stream that delivers competitiveness. Tools are cause and effect – actions not interactions. No doubt some tools used individually give good results. A wonderfully designed office cell serving a morass of poorly controlled inventory is waste. A 5S programme without follow-through into flow is largely waste. Kanban working in a situation of unlevelled demand can be waste. And so on. Even if all these were sorted out through good value stream mapping and a well-directed kaizen programme, Lean may still fail to deliver its true potential. Ohno did not have a Lean toolbox. He had in mind a vision of where he wanted to be. The system first, THEN the necessary tools.

Lean Service is Value

Yes, Lean practitioners do go after waste. This is appropriate given the high levels of waste in most value streams. But chasing waste is ultimately a zero sum game that can only lead to decline in the long run, unless the advantages that Lean brings are translated into growth. The Toyota system is about growth, innovation and opportunity – not just waste reduction. Although there will always be another layer of waste to address, the more experienced practitioners need to return to Value – to the first and second Lean principles of customer and value stream. Like the Quality concept of quality of design and quality of conformance, waste elimination or prevention is but one half of the total picture. Rethinking the value side is at least as important.

Don't manage cost; manage value. When value increases, the cost will decrease. This message is from Deming, from Toyota, from Feigenbaum, from Seddon, and from many others.

Lean Service is Muda, Muri and Mura

Womack and Jones began their book *Lean Thinking* with the words, 'Muda. It's the one Japanese word you really must know'. The Lean world was sensitised to waste as a result. But Toyota talks about three 'Ms' – Muda (waste), Muri (overburden), and Mura (unevenness). Knowing about all three gives a more complete understanding of Lean. The three are interlinked.

Overburden is to do with excessive loading of people or machines; unevenness is to do with flow that is not smooth, but also with excessive variation. The three interplay, as we shall see, and are arguably even more relevant in service. Ohno said

Activity = Work + Waste

so reducing the waste frees up resources to do an even better job with the customer. And of course it should be more about waste prevention than waste elimination. Johnson and Bröms believe that the focus on elimination of waste is misleading, and argue that it is the subtle avoidance of waste while creating balanced flow, which is the key. This is just like the total quality concept of trading the costs of prevention against the costs of inspection and internal and external failure. Spend more on preventing failure and less on defects and inspection so you can 'have your cake and eat it' – better service with reduced cost through systems thinking.

Muda, of course, is waste – or, more correctly, it is non-value adding activity. Muri causes waste by 'overburdening' people and machines. First, people: if people are to be partners in the process, if they are to be willing participants in improvement, if they are to produce good quality work and to be responsible for that quality, they should not be stressed or overworked. They must enjoy good 'quality of worklife' at the workplace, so the ergonomics (temperature, lighting, vision, comfort, lifting, risk of repetitive strain) must be as friendly as possible. Safety must be paramount. This enables 'bring your brain to work' and 'hire the whole person' to be possible. Second, machines: although a little less relevant in service, machine overburden means making no allowance for maintenance, downtime or variation. Third, people and machines together: this book makes reference frequently to the problem of queues and variation.

Queuing theory tells us that if the 'utilisation' of people or machines (defined as the ratio of the average arrival rate to the average service rate) is above about 85%, we will be in trouble. Poor service will be inevitable. This is overburden. Overburden begins at less than 100% utilisation because of variation. This phenomenon is much more important in service where variation is greater than in manufacture. A later section is devoted to this topic.

Mura is unevenness. Swift flow is not possible with uneven demands. Queues and lead time will build up. Extra staff and inventory are required to meet peak demands. Of course customer demands are not entirely even – but consider two things. First, do not amplify the unevenness by your own policies, such as end of month reporting, quantity discounts, and the like. Second, encourage customers to demand more evenly and suppliers to deliver more evenly – often to mutual advantage. Does the supplier really want to deliver in bulk? Does the customer really want a six-month supply of toothpaste? Can you move closer to your customers to understand their true longer-term requirement - thereby enabling your own operations to be smoothed in terms of working hours, leave and so forth? Buffering and postponement will often be necessary.

Perhaps Mura is the root problem. Unevenness causes overburden, which in turn causes many other forms of waste. Periods of peak work cause stress to people and may cause lack of maintenance for machines, and high utilisation will result in deadlines being missed. But Muda can result in Mura due to lead times being long and quality being uncertain. So in fact it is circular: Mura causes Muri causes Muda causes Mura, and so on.

Lean Service is Innovation

Here the question is what business and service opportunities does Lean create? Think of Vision Express and the one-hour pair of spectacles, think of home breadmakers, or South West Airlines breaking the rules of established carriers. In these examples the customer is primary. Waste reduction and value enhancement are for the customer, not the service provider. There may be no greater waste than cutting waste for the provider while increasing it for the customer. Stand back and look at the customer as the 'object' of one-piece flow. Line up the stages in process order so that the customer can benefit.

Lean Service is Revolution and Evolution

The Toyota Production System (TPS) grew through revolution and evolution. Revolution rejected the concepts of mass production and economies of scale, and steered the organisation. Evolution developed the details and the tools. When TPS began there were few Lean tools - most developed from first principles over several decades, but fitting in with the top-level concept. Lean ideas developed from first principles; Taiichi Ohno believed in developing managers by the Socratic method – asking tough questions rather than providing answers. This is in line with the practice of Hoshin Kanri or Policy Deployment, where top management sets the strategic direction (the 'what' and the 'why') but evolves the detail level by level by a process of consultation (the 'how'). In the reverse direction decisions are taken locally, only migrating upwards in exceptional circumstances. This is much like the human body's management system. So a top-level system that imposes the detailed (Lean) tools, but takes decisions that are in conflict with Lean, is precisely the wrong way around.

Lean Service is Distributed Decisions

Ohno saw the TPS ideal as minimising the amount of information and control, like the human body where much routine operation is decentralised and self-repair takes place locally. Excess information must be suppressed, said Ohno. Perhaps the greatest opportunity for Lean is not on the office or factory floor, but in simplification and decentralisation that enables whole swathes of overhead and administration to be eliminated.

Today large ERP systems with data warehouses are 'in'. Also 'in' are CRM systems. In the late 1990s and early 2000s many organisations moved in the opposite direction by implementing large centralised systems – at great cost and often with mixed results. Today's need is for fast-reacting distributed decision-making. There is a case for centralised strategic decisions, but not for centralised operational decisions. The Lean way is to resolve, even dissolve problems with schedules, with quality, and even some aspects of design and supply at a localised level, but still keeping the end-to-end value stream in mind. This is not only more effective, but also more human. You may want ERP for planning but probably not for execution. Similarly you may use cost accounting for planning, but not for execution. Organisationally, the essence of the Hoshin process is 'Nemawashi' (consensus building) and 'Ringi' (shared decision making).

Lean Service and Six Sigma

Lean and Six Sigma are no longer at odds, nor should they be. Lean is better at the big picture, at establishing the foundation, while Six Sigma offers a powerful problem-solving methodology through DMAIC. The Lean service value stream mapping tools are generally superior but synergistic with those used in Six Sigma, and many concepts and tools are entirely synergistic. To be sure, there are also doubtful practices in Six Sigma, as pointed out by one of the originators, Keki Bhote, formerly of Motorola.

But much of Six Sigma itself is waste! What can be done to reduce or eliminate that variation before it even arises should be a prime question. Why is Toyota not falling over itself to get after Six Sigma or, alternatively, how has it been able to achieve Six Sigma levels of performance without legions of black belts and statistical software?

Lean Service is Green

Recently we have seen that it is possible not only to be Lean and 'Green', but also, by focusing on the wastes of materials and energy, to be both profitable and attractive to customers. Pamela Gordon in *Lean and Green* has researched many examples of the successful adoption of the three 'Rs' (Reduce, Reuse, and Recycle). Hawkin points out the scandalous fact that about 99% of the original material used in the production of goods in the US becomes waste within six weeks of sale. Presumably other countries are similar. Surely this is the ultimate waste. But Hawken, Lovins and Lovins in *Natural Capitalism* give hope, giving examples of a carpet made from recycled material that lasts four times longer, is stain proof and can be water cleaned, or windows that remain cool at high temperatures and warm at freezing temperatures, thereby drastically reducing the need for air conditioning and central heating. Surely this is ultimate Lean.

Further Reading

Russell Ackoff, *Management in Small Doses; Ackoff's Fables; Beating the System; Management Flaws, Creating the Corporate Future* (to name a few!)

John Seddon, *Freedom from Command and Control*, Vanguard, 2003

Thomas Stewart and Anand Raman, 'Lessons from Toyota's Long Drive: HBR Interview with Katsuaki Watanabe', *Harvard Business Review*, July August 2007.

Louis Savary and Clare Crawford-Mason, *The Nun and The Bureaucrat*, CC-M Productions, 2006 (an excellent book on systems!)

James Womack and Daniel Jones, *Lean Thinking*, revised edition, Free Press, 2003

Jinichiro Nakane and Robert Hall, 'Ohno's Method', *Target*, First Quarter, 2002

Richard Schonberger, *World Class Manufacturing: The Next Decade*, Free Press, 1996

H Thomas Johnson and Anders Bröms, *Profit Beyond Measure*, Nicholas Brealey, London, 2000

Jim Womack, *The Perfect Process*, Presentation, AME Conference, Chicago, 2002

Paul Hawken, Amory Lovins and L Hunter Lovins, *Natural Capitalism*, Little, Brown 1999

Phil Rosenzweig, *The Halo Effect*, Free Press, 2007

Jeffrey Pfeffer, *What Were They Thinking?*, Harvard Business School Press, 2007

Acknowledgement

Discussion with Richard Davis of Vanguard Consulting, 2007

Thoughts on Customers and Lean

The first Lean principle is Value. Some thoughts relating to Service and Customers follow.

- Deming taught that approximately equal time should be spent on each of the Plan Do Check Act (or Adjust) stages. But very often very little time is spent on Plan, most time on Do, and minor time on Check and Adjust. How often does management go back and check their assumptions, really reflect on the difference between what was planned and what was achieved, and try to explain the difference, and how much time do they spend on 'holding the gains' by adjusting to the new standards? So Value is a cumulative process, using the scientific method.

- Similarly with the five Lean Principles. Although Womack and Jones did not say as much, there should be the assumption that approximately equal time is spent on each principle. Sometimes it is just a few minutes on Value, and the rest of the time on value stream mapping and preparing for flow – but not actually achieving flow. If you have in mind spending much more time on Value it may encourage you to:

  - Dissect customer demands – time series demand data can be taken apart – only a small proportion need remain unexplained.
  - Actually listen and speak to customers at Gemba, not relying on market surveys.

  Womack and Jones went further with Customer Thinking in *Lean Solutions* (see the next section).

- Understand the customer's 'need'. A 'need' is more stable than a 'want'. For example, does a customer want a hole (a 'need') or a drill (a 'want')?

- Ask how the savings and improvements made in a Lean implementation can be passed on to the customer. Cost, quality, delivery certainly, but that is only the start. What about new markets and new products that can be created?

- And what about the Customer's Customer? Help the customer to delight his customer. Thinking one stage ahead helps to encourage end-to-end thinking and to limit short-term thinking.

Helping the customer to look good with his customers is a path to sustainable relationships. It encourages true partnership.

- Disruptive Technology can help to break through to new customer insight. Clayton Christensen's theory of Disruptive Technology teaches that many companies, from booksellers to computer manufacturers and sailing ship owners, have been caught out by making all the right decisions with current technology but ignoring 'non-viable' startup technologies.

- Likewise TRIZ trends. A powerful TRIZ notion is 'Free, Perfect, and Now'. Many products and services are heading this way, so what is the logical end state? The ultimate is free, perfect and now. Is this possible? Surely not – but think of Google, of Skype, of the near eradication of measles – they are getting close. All good service should be challenged with this idea.

- Sometimes customers cannot talk – where the 'root' customer is a computer, a car, a house, or an object in general. What would that customer say to you if it could talk? Can you imagine yourself as a patient's heart, as an aircraft engine, as a house that has just been flooded, or an item of clothing? What are their needs?

- Finally, don't ever be complacent. Customers' values change. If you are top of the world (like Toyota), be in a panic because then there is only one way to go. Keep in mind the fate of all but two of the Fortune 100 biggest companies in the USA 80 years ago: they don't exist.

Throw out command-and-control targets which derive fundamentally from management interests and rewards, and replace them with customer-driven, preferably end-to-end measures, which are work-related. Targets are often bad news for service because they so often drive deviant employee responses rather than help the customer. Employees will sometimes cheat and take short cuts to achieve the manager's targets even though it may make things worse for the customer. Measures (not targets), however, can be good news where they are set up to identify problems in the system, not with the employee. 'Work-related' means measures that help the flow of work. Remember that measures motivate. Subjective measures are generally valuable only if they come from a customer – not from a manager.

Objective measures are much more useful. Let the customer, not the manager, 'keep the score'.

Further Reading

Clayton Christensen, *The Innovator's Solution*, Harvard Business School Press, 2003
Darrell Mann, *Hands-on Systematic Innovation*, IFR Press, 2004
Dean Spitzer, *Transforming Performance Measurement*, AmaCom, 2007

Seddon's Six Stages of 'Check'

'System' is the theme that runs throughout this book. But how do we understand the system? John Seddon's 'check' stage is a powerful orderly way to do this. Here we will use the stages of Seddon's check model, and discuss each one. The 'Vanguard Model for Check' derives from the Deming Cycle – Plan Do Check Act – but begins with Check. Seddon may or may not agree with the comments! In my opinion the six stages of 'check' deserve to be as widely known as the five Lean principles. This is especially the case in service. The six stages of 'check' are:

- **Purpose:** Purpose is the reason why you are doing the task. It is not 'Vision': Vision is where you want to be. It is often worth stating both Purpose and Vision. Ask, 'What is the purpose of the system from the customer's viewpoint?' It is an 'outside in' view, not an 'inside out' view. Deming says about an aim, 'It is important that an aim never be defined in terms of activity or methods. It must always relate to how life is made better for everyone'. This can also be applied to Purpose.

  This requires taking a 'helicopter' view. Of course there may be several customer categories. If you get a list of things you are probably not high enough in your helicopter. So first seek the overall purpose – then you can get into the lists. You may then decide to home in on the most relevant item on the list – the system or sub-system of immediate concern. So you will get statements such as

  - 'To pay deserving clients as quickly and easily as possible'
  - 'To ensure a hassle-free air travel experience from A to B'
  - 'To equip participants with practical Lean Thinking skills'.
  Note: the purpose must have a verb and a noun.

  Why define Purpose? It is simply an opportunity to stand back and consider why the organisation exists, without getting into organisational functions or departments, an attempt to avoid sub-optimisation, to remain holistic. The Purpose statement should lead to the critical measures that enable a judgment to be made on whether the purpose is being achieved.

  Finally, to quote Seddon, 'While cost reduction is a natural consequence of "lean", it is not its purpose. The purpose of "lean" is to increase capacity by designing a system that optimally responds to customer demand' ('watchoutforthetoolheads', Vanguard Education, www.lean-service.com.6-23.asp).

- **Demand:** Having defined the purpose of the system, now you can consider the demands that are placed on the system by customers. Seddon uses the very powerful concepts of Value Demand and Failure Demand. Value Demand is demand that is in line with the purpose. It is what the system is there to do, what it exists to serve – 'it represents the demands customers make for things they want'. <u>Failure demand, by contrast, is 'demand caused by a failure to do something or do something right for the customer'</u> (Seddon). A demand is any customer action that triggers work in the system. Seddon's Failure Demand is monitored at the system boundary or Moment of Truth (MoT). To find out how much Failure Demand there is, it is necessary actually to monitor a sample of demand by listening to calls, going through correspondence, picking up front line requests at incoming points such as reception, call centre, or points of contact between customers and consulting engineers or workmen.

  You should never ASK the customer about his or her requirements. Rather you should LISTEN to the demands they place on the system. Categorise – find the 'Top 10' demands. Don't worry, at least initially, about the rest.

  Why do this? To understand how much work is being loaded unnecessarily on the system, hence possibly overloading the system, with severe consequences on response times (generating even more failure), but also destroying the morale of workers who may see themselves as 'fire fighters'. Many a service system has believed itself to be overloaded with work, only to discover, as failure demand is reduced, that there is easily sufficient capacity. Understanding the true demand, and its variation, enables us to get into the crucial capacity question.

  This is not simply a question of 'Muda' or 'necessary non-value added' work. Activities such as 'waste walks' or mapping simply will not pick up the extent of failure demand. This is also not the same as Phil Crosby's cost of poor quality concept of failure costs, inspection costs, and prevention costs where all quality-related activities are classified into one of these categories – this is an 'inside-out' viewpoint.

The phrase Moment of Truth (see later section) is a powerful concept made famous by Jan Carlsson of SAS airlines. Moments of Truth are applied to every interaction between service provider and customer. This stage, Demand, is really an elaboration of the MoT concept but applied for system level understanding rather than at transaction level.

Preventable Failure Demand. There is not always a clear distinction between Value Demand and Failure Demand. In some so-called 'break-fix' systems, where demand is for field service repairs, demand for first-time service is value demand. But if the root causes of the problem were adequately tackled through design or preventive maintenance, the demand could be eliminated. It may be useful to distinguish this type of demand from other failure demand. Call it preventable failure demand.

- **Capability**: This sets out to answer whether the system is able to meet the load put on it in a stable, predictable way. Is it 'in control' or 'out of control' with respect to system performance? See the section on control charts for a deeper appreciation. To know whether the system is capable it is necessary to know the purpose and the critical measure or measures. The appropriate measures will have to be taken over a representative period of time. Note that the measure will almost always be an end-to-end measure from the customer's viewpoint. Develop a run diagram or control chart. A run diagram is also a powerful way to understand the system variation. Are there patterns in the variation, period to period, area to area, and how much between customers? If there happens to be a service level agreement (SLA), is the SLA being met? (Beware, SLAs are often arbitrarily set as targets by managers, and do not necessarily relate to the needs of the customer.)

  Why do this? Because if there are special causes at work which are destabilising the system, they need to be identified and eliminated. It is very difficult to improve a system which is unstable or out of control. You should also find out if there are patterns in demand and stability. The crucial question, 'Are the system and its people capable of meeting the demand?' should be answered.

- **Flow:** Now that there is an overall appreciation from the customer's viewpoint, begin to look at how value is delivered to the customer. Is there flow? Is customer flow smooth, swift, simple, steady, and slim? Note that we are concerned here with flow that meets the purpose – not just flow for the sake of flow.

Don't attempt to flow activities which should not be there in the first place (Failure Demand). And we are concerned with the customer. If there are stages that don't contribute to the purpose they should not be on the 'main line' of flow. Stalk and Hout's Golden Rule is, 'Never delay a customer value adding step by a non-value adding step'. Support activities should be done off-line, in parallel where delays don't bother the customer. Here we may note a pseudo-difference between manufacturing and service: manufacturing focuses on the flow of the object, service focuses on the flow of the customer. The ideas of Goldratt are also highly relevant – focusing on the bottleneck – to determine the overall rate of flow, and possibly on the Drum Buffer Rope methodology. See the section on Goldratt's five steps. However, remember a point of caution: Goldratt appropriately focuses on the bottleneck in a manufacturing system and protects the bottleneck by ensuring that it is never idle and there is always inventory to work on. In a service system, bottlenecks are certainly important but a queue of customers in front of the bottleneck would elicit more concerns than a queue of inventory. So we have to find ways in which we can BOTH maximise the utilisation of the bottleneck AND not delay customers. This leads on to another consideration: the reduction of variation. There is only one way both to maximise utilisation and to reduce the queue, and that is to minimise variation. So levelling demand becomes important, as does the reduction of unnecessary variation – through waste reduction and mistake proofing.

Why do this? Because flow is primary to customers – but you cannot understand flow unless you know purpose and capability. The crucial question is, 'What is preventing customer flow from being swift and perfect?'

- **System Conditions**: The system conditions are what cause the system to behave the way it does. It is the structure, the processes, the measures, the managers and maybe the people. Here, Deming's 94/6 rule is highly relevant: 94% of problems are caused by the system, only 6% by the people. See the section on the Red Bead Game, under Control Charts. So the first reactions should not be to blame the person, call for training, say that they are 'concrete heads', or to complain about 'the culture', but to look at the process or system conditions that are causing the malfunction. This may mean:

    - Looking at the structure – how many handoffs are there?

- Looking at the process – how contorted is it? How long does it take to respond? Are errors recognised? Can the people do anything about these errors or are they time or function restricted?
- Looking at the measures – do the measures support flow and help to improve the process, or are they primarily there to make management happy? Are the measures end-to-end or exclusively departmental? Is the aim to 'make the numbers' or to solve the customer's problem? Are they targets or measures? Does the costing system support rational behaviour, or is it output driven to cover variances?
- Do problems get passed on, or are they tackled at or near the source?
- Are the workers primarily focused upwards towards management or horizontally towards customers?
- Is the information system or ERP system capable of meeting customer requirements? Does it collect and distribute correct information?
- Is the information 'dirty' (a Seddon phrase)? How much 'dirty' (incorrect/incomplete) data is flowing in the system?
- Is the layout conducive to achieving the purpose? Look at the state of visual management, 5S, etc.

John Seddon believes that the most important of these is the measurement system. 'Tell me how you'll measure me and I'll tell you how I will behave', or, 'You get what you measure'. In his excellent book *Transforming Performance Measurement* Dean Spitzer makes a strong case that measures are the most important force for influencing the culture of an organisation. So do go through the existing measures systematically and critically, asking if each supports or works against Lean. You may recall the often-quoted statement about Toyota: 'We achieve brilliant results with average people working with brilliant processes rather than mediocre results with brilliant people working with broken processes'. This statement captures the right sentiment – but it is a manufacturing statement, and in service many more people are customer-facing so good people are needed too. But good people cannot be good without good managers, so…

- **Management Thinking**: This is the true 'culture' of the system, because the beliefs of the managers flow down into the people. A Toyota saying is that 'the shop floor is a reflection of the management'. In many organisations, you quickly realise whether the managers are primarily focused on satisfying their manager's (or 'corporate') purpose, or whether they are focused on the customer's purpose. That is what has happened in many hospitals, banks, and universities, which are often so focused on meeting targets that the customer is forgotten.

- You can get a view of management thinking by looking at the reward packages of both managers and staff. What are the rewards based on? Rewards, by the way, are invariably a problem in themselves – see Alfie Kohn in *Punished by Rewards*.
- To what extent are managers, and hence the organisation, target driven rather than measure driven? The right measures, particularly end-to-end measures, help us to understand the system, but targets encourage cheating and dysfunctional competition.
- You can get more insight by monitoring how much senior managers know about 'The Gemba'. See separate section.
- And managers' attitudes: Frank Devine talks about three groups of employees – the inner-directed, the watchers, and the 'limit testers'. The limit testers are always testing, but the watchers observe managers' reactions – if the limit testers get away with it then a negative feedback loop is established.

The Vanguard Model for Check sequence gives an excellent insight into the system status. A holistic, system design can now begin. Seddon calls this 'making the work work'. By keeping the total system in mind, the sub-processes can be mapped and improved.

Further Reading

John Seddon, *Freedom from Command and Control*, Vanguard, 2003
See also the Vanguard web site www.lean-service.com
Alfie Kohn, *Punished by Rewards*, Houghton Mifflin, 1999
Dean Spitzer, *Transforming Performance Measurement*, AmaCom, 2007

Systems Thinking

Service operations of whatever type are a system. A system is holistic, and needs to be thought of as a collection of interacting sub-systems. Touching one sub-system may have a direct influence on several other sub-systems, and an indirect effect on all. Elements include customers, staff, machines, information, and suppliers.

Eli Goldratt of Theory of Constraints fame says there are four characteristics which apply to all (human activity) systems:

- Every system has a goal, and there are necessary conditions which must be satisfied in order to achieve the goal.
- The system optimum is not the sum of the local optima.
- Only a few variables limit the performance of a system at any one time.
- All systems are subject to cause and effect.

Peter Checkland uses a useful series of soft-system concepts, known through the mnemonic CATWOE, to look at systems and sub-systems. They are particularly important in service, less so in manufacturing. They are:

- **Clients**: These are often customers, but the word customer is not always appropriate – for example in a hospital or prison. There may be several groups of clients, not all of them customers, and they may have different needs. A local authority may have to mediate between several groups such as shoppers, disabled, and business, all wanting parking privilege. Meeting the needs of clients is what the system or value stream is there to do. Thought needs to be given to the clients for whom the system is to cater – today's clients, tomorrow's clients, and should they be segmented.
- **Actors**: These are the participants in the system, other than the clients and owners. They may include employees, suppliers or volunteers. Some actors may not be subject to direct control but may be vital to the working of the system – for example, an internet service provider. Make a list.
- **Transformation**: What the system sets out to do. Usually the clients are 'transformed' in some way. So this stage is about identifying the need that should be satisfied. Try to remain in general terms – 'holes' rather than 'drills' – the former is the need, the latter presumes the solution, perhaps too early. List the inputs and outputs.

- **Weltanschauung**: This German word relates to the fundamental beliefs of the system, which often go unchallenged. 'Reducing cost is good', or 'Customers cannot be trusted' are examples. The weltanschauung may be obvious to the client, but not appreciated by the actors. As an example, some Eastern airline passengers put courtesy and respect ahead of on-time arrival. The other way around may be the assumption in the West. This is a very powerful concept worthy of consideration in every service mapping exercise.
- **Owners**: Who 'owns' the system? Again, this is not always obvious or official. Shareholders perhaps. But perhaps (some) managers or unions. These are influential groups, which can cause a system transformation to crash. They may overlap with the actors. The true aims of the owners must be appreciated, even if they are not stated in words.
- **Environment**: Where does the system boundary lie? What is within the system and what is in the environment? System boundary is a very important concept – see Loops, below. The system boundary may not coincide with organisational boundaries. So it merits very careful consideration: if the system boundary is ill-considered, the transformation will fail. The environment beyond the system boundary cannot be easily controlled but may have a major influence. The economy, the weather, demographics are examples. An attempt must be made to understand it.

To these classic CATWOE may be added:

- **Victims**: Are there 'victims' of the present value stream? Will there be 'victims' of the future value stream? An example is call centre working hours that create 'victims' out of the employees' families. If more flexible working arrangements can be found, the turnover of staff may drop. Remember Steven Covey's dictum 'win, win or walk away'. Keep trying to find a way in which everyone wins.
- **Beneficiaries**: Likewise, there will be beneficiaries – intended or not.

SIPOC

SIPOC, a tool from Six Sigma, stands for suppliers, inputs, process, outputs, customers. It is certainly useful to list the SIPOC categories at the outset of a project – particularly towards the manufacturing end of the spectrum. SIPOC is really a less powerful, less insightful, version of CATWOE. Nevertheless, it may be very useful to draw up lists under each of the five SIPOC categories. For example, for an employee recruitment process:

Suppliers	Inputs	Processes	Outputs	Customers
Potential employees Universities Budget holder HR Ad agency	Vacancies Job spec inc salary Budget Legal requirements Admin support Room	The detailed steps of the process	Appointees Rejects Feedback Training gaps to be filled	Manager Successful candidates Unsuccessful candidates Universities

This exercise may appear trivial but in several situations – for example, complex supply chains and 'fuzzy' open-ended design situations – the 'players' are not necessarily known. Just listing them is beneficial to understanding, and to clarifying the task ahead to all participants.

Five Lean Principles, Lean Solutions, and Systems Questions

In *Lean Thinking*, Womack and Jones renewed the message set out in *The Machine that Changed the World*, that Lean, at least in automotive, was literally Do or Die, but they also extended it out beyond automotive. These reflective authors have given manufacturing, and to an extent also service, a vision of a world transformed from mass production to Lean enterprise. The five principles set out are of great relevance. Reading the Introduction to *Lean Thinking* should be compulsory for every executive.

Beware, however. Stating the five principles that were developed for manufacturing and applying them to any service carries a risk. Also, they codify method – something that Ohno was very cautious about doing for Toyota.

Throughout *Lean Thinking*, Womack and Jones emphasised Lean Enterprise rather than Lean Manufacturing. In other words they were emphasising systems. But unfortunately the book became thought of as a manufacturing book, and the system message was missed.

In this section, while using Womack and Jones' five principles, some liberties have been taken, particularly in relating them to service. Some managers are upset by the five principles, believing them not to be feasible within their industry. But this is to miss the point, which is vision: you may not get there within your lifetime, but try - others certainly will.

The starting point is to specify **Value** from the point of view of the customer. This is an established marketing idea, that customers buy results, not products - a clean shirt, not a washing machine. Too often, however, manufacturers tend to give the customers what is convenient for the manufacturer, or deemed economic for the customer. Womack and Jones cite batch-and-queue airline travel, involving long trips to the airport to enable big batch flights that start where you aren't and take you where you don't want to go, via hubs, and numerous delays. How often are new product designs or service operations constrained by existing facilities rather than by customer requirements? Of course we have to know who is the customer: the final customer, or the next process, or the next company along the chain, or the customer's customer.

Then identify the **Value Stream**. This is the sequence of processes all the way from raw material to final customer, or from product concept to market launch. If possible look at the whole supply chain or, probably more accurately, the 'demand network'. Again, an established idea from TQM/Juran/business processing. You are only as good as the weakest link; supply chains compete, not companies. Concentrate on the viewpoint of the object (or product or customer), not the viewpoint of the department or process step. Think economies of time rather than economies of scale. The value stream should be mapped, and a whole section of this book is devoted to this topic. Focus horizontally, not vertically.

The third principle is **Flow.** Make value flow. If possible use one-piece or one-document flow. Keep it moving. Avoid batch and queue, or at least continuously reduce them and the obstacles in their way. Try to design according to Stalk and Hout's Golden Rule - never to delay a value adding step by a non-value adding, although temporarily necessary, step - try to do such steps in parallel. Flow requires much preparation activity. But the important thing is vision: have in mind a guiding strategy that will move you inexorably towards simple, slim and swift customer flow.

Then comes **Pull**. Having set up the framework for flow, only operate as needed. 'Pull' in service means short-term response to the customer's rate of demand, and not 'over producing'. In service it is often capacity that is pulled, not inventory or product. Think about pull on two levels: on the macro level most organisations will have to push up to a certain point and respond to final customer pull signals thereafter. An example is the classic Bennetton 'jerseys in grey' which are stocked at an intermediate point in the supply chain in order to retain flexibility, but also to give good customer service at low inventory levels. On the micro level, there is responding to signals, for instance when additional staff are needed at supermarket checkouts to avoid excessive queues. Attention to both levels is necessary. Of course, pull needs to take place along the whole demand flow network, not only within a company. So this ultimately implies sharing final customer demands right along the chain. Each extension of pull reduces forecast uncertainty.

Finally comes **Perfection**. Having worked through the previous principles, suddenly now 'perfection' seems more possible. Perfection does not only mean quality - it means delivering exactly what the customer wants, exactly when, without delay, at a fair price and with minimum waste. Beware of benchmarking: the real benchmark is zero waste, not what the competitors or best practices are doing. Remember that a human activity system, unlike a mechanical process, cannot be copied – because although the actions can be seen, the interactions are invisible. You can learn good practice, but you cannot duplicate and expect it to work the same way.

You will quickly realise that these five principles are not a sequential, one-off procedure, but rather a journey of continuous improvement. Start out today.

Lean Consumption and Systems Questions

Womack and Jones ventured further into Lean service, or what they term 'Lean Consumption', with their book *Lean Solutions* (2005). Here they set out six thought-provoking requirements. These are essentially high-level systemic questions. The questions are set out below, together with comments:

- **'Solve my problem completely'**. Not a solution to a half-baked requirement, but the end-to-end requirement. So not just selling a product but the whole package of installation and support, end-to-end. The whole of what Jan Carlsson calls the 'cycle of service' – pre, during, and post.
- **'Don't waste my time'**. Focus on customer flow. Think that the customer's time is not free, as is often assumed. So what is the cost of the patient having to wait for the doctor, or the housewife having to stay in to wait for a parcel delivery? What we are now beginning to appreciate through the work of John Seddon and his concept of the elimination of Failure Demand is that focusing on the customer's waste in fact benefits the whole system.
- **'Get me exactly what I want'**. Understand the real need, do not force a 'solution' on a customer. Believe it or not, customers are different – different groups or individuals have different needs. John Seddon would say that this requires a service system to provide what Stafford Beer called 'requisite variety'.
- **'Provide value where I want it'**, and **'Provide value when I want it'**. Again, customers are different, so different systems with requisite variety need to be designed. These three questions – what, where, and when – are in fact the essence of what Ohno was seeking to do with cars – to make it economic to build one at a time. So Lean service should aspire to the ability to serve one unique customer at a time economically – not to find mass solutions for the 'common herd'.

- **'Get me the solution I really want'**. This is in fact a never-ending and ever-expanding quest – see the comments by Watanabe above on what a future car should be. The question raises the very important point about where the 'system boundary' should be.

So these are essentially questions about Purpose – the starting point of any Lean service venture.

Further Reading

James Womack and Daniel Jones, *Lean Thinking*, Revised edition, Free Press, 2003
James Womack and Daniel Jones, *Lean Solutions*, Simon and Schuster, 2005

Value

Womack and Jones' first Lean principle is about understanding value; the second is about removing waste. Activities that do not contribute value are waste – either total waste or temporarily necessary non-value adding waste. So we need to understand these concepts a little more deeply. This section considers value, the following section considers waste.

Value enhancement is arguably more important than waste reduction, especially in service. Thus, for example in car servicing, it may prove highly effective to get the technician to 'waste his time' by talking to customers directly rather than through a service agent. And it may improve value to give a discount to those owners who do not avail themselves of a courtesy car.

Porter says: 'In competitive terms, value is the amount buyers are willing to pay for what a firm provides them. Value is measured by total revenue, a reflection of the price a firm's product commands and the units it can sell'.

From a Lean perspective, this is a little too simple. First, there is present value – what present customers are willing to pay for. This is the usual way of identifying waste. Then there is future value – what tomorrow's customers are willing to pay for, but today's may not. This is relevant in research and development and design. These represent different value streams – so you should not judge a current manufacturing stream in the same way as an R&D stream.

Similarly, there are today's customers and tomorrow's customers. And today's customers come in different categories – those that are very valuable, an intermediate set, and a third set that are just not worth having. Perhaps your products or services are inappropriately focused. So waste may be different depending on the customer group, for instance the pensioner chatting to a checkout attendant and a time-hassled businessman.

One straightforward interpretation of value is Perceived Benefit/Perceived Sacrifices (Saliba and Fisher). Benefits may accrue before, during, or after the event. Sacrifices may be in terms of cost, convenience, time, or exchange. There are probably upper bounds on sacrifices that a customer is willing to pay, and lower bounds on benefits – like Kano basics. Both are dynamic.

Zeithaml and Bitner talk about four meanings for value. First, 'value is low price'. For these customers, lowest price is best. This is the ultimate Lean – cut out all activities which do not directly contribute to the product or service in the short term. No frills. Second, 'value is whatever I want in a product or service'. This focuses on benefits, not price. This is the classic marketing approach – selling the experience of owning a top-brand pair of trainers rather than the shoes themselves. Or a drill company selling holes not drills. Here, the Lean company needs to understand its customers' requirements deeply – so 'wasted' market research or image creation may not in fact be waste. The classic marketing statement – 'We know half of our promotional activities are waste, but we don't know which half' – comes to mind. Third, 'value is the quality I get for what I pay'. Here expectations are directly linked to price – pay more, expect more. Having standby services or extra inventory may be expected because the price is so high. Fourthly, 'value is what I get for what I give' – all benefits against all sacrifices, not just money. A luxury car may be worth the price and the wait, but of course customer satisfaction may increase if the wait decreases.

In service, value is a Moment of Truth experience, the totality of all the experiences. So value is getting the exact product or service that you require, in the right quantity, at the right time, with perfect quality of course, and at the right price. Moments of Truth are multiplicative. An example is the cumulative effect of getting a car on which you compromise for colour, which is delivered a week late, with minor faults, and including extras which you don't want but for which you are asked to pay. The basic product is fine, but the total experience is poor.

Kano, speaking about quality, talks about 'Basics', 'Performance Factors', and 'Delighters' (see separate section). Much the same can be said about value. There are some activities that are basic to value – defect-free has become a basic in some industries. There is 'performance' value – lead time for example in some businesses – and 'delighter' value. Moreover, as in the Kano model, value is dynamic.

In services and in products there is a relationship between functionality and price. A customer may be prepared to pay more for better service. The relationship is not necessarily a straight line, however. Getting the balance right means staying above the functionality-price curve.

Further Reading

Michael Saliba and Caroline Fisher, 'Managing Customer Value', *Quality Progress*, June 2000, pp 63-69

Valerie Zeithaml, Mary Jo Bitner and Dwayne Gremler, *Services Marketing*, 4th edition, McGraw Hill, 2006

Manuel Fernandes, 'The Importance of Value for Business Strategic Management', *Value World*, Vol 30, No 3, Fall 2007

Waste (Muda)

'Muda' is Japanese for waste. Waste is strongly linked to Lean. But waste elimination is a means to achieving the Lean ideal – it is not an end in itself.

Waste prevention is at least as important as waste elimination.
Value is the converse of waste. Any organisation needs continually to improve the ratio of value adding to non-value adding activities. There are two ways to do this – by preventing and reducing waste, but also by going after value enhancement specifically.

Taiichi Ohno, father of the Toyota Production System, of JIT, and patriarch of Lean Operations, originally assembled the Seven Wastes, but it was Deming who emphasised waste reduction in Japan in the 1950s. Today, however, it is appropriate to add to Ohno's famous list, presumptuous though that may be. The section after next begins with Ohno's original seven, then adds 'new' wastes for manufacturing and service.

TPS refers to 'Muda, Mura and Muri'. Mura refers to unevenness. Muri refers to 'overburden' – loading a service operator with excessive work that results in delay and dissatisfaction. See the earlier section.

Type 1 and Type 2 Muda, Elimination and Prevention

Womack and Jones talk usefully about two types of waste.

Type 1 Muda is activities which create no value but are currently necessary to maintain operations. These activities do not do anything for customers, but may well assist the managers or stakeholders other than customers or shareholders. Type 1 should be reduced through simplification. It may well prove to be the greatest bottom-line benefit of Lean. Moreover, Type 1 Muda is the easiest to add to but difficult to remove, so prevention of Type 1 Muda should be in the mind of every manager in every function.

Type 2 Muda creates no value, in fact destroys value, for any stakeholder, including customers, shareholders, and employees. Elimination should be a priority. Type 2 tends to grow by 'stealth', or carelessness.

Waste Elimination is achieved, as Dan Jones would say, by 'wearing muda spectacles' (a skill that must be developed), and by kaizen - both 'point' and 'flow' varieties. Elimination is assisted by 5S activities, standard work, mapping, level scheduling and by amplification reduction. Ohno was said to require new managers to spend several hours in a chalk circle, standing in one place and observing waste. This should happen more frequently in offices, in warehouses, and in factories.

Waste Prevention is another matter. Womack and Jones talk about the eighth waste – making the wrong product perfectly – but it goes beyond that. Waste prevention cannot be done by wearing muda spectacles, but requires strong awareness of system, process, and product design. It is known that perhaps 80% of costs are fixed at the design stage. Of that 80%, a good proportion will be waste. System design waste prevention involves thinking through the movement of information, products and customers through the future system. For instance, questioning the necessity for ERP and the selection of far-removed suppliers from a total perspective, and removing layers in a supply chain. Process design waste prevention involves the avoidance of 'monuments', the elimination of adjustments, and working with future customers and suppliers to ensure that future processes are as waste-free as possible. For instance, incorporating flexible service workers in a flexible layout. Prevention involves much more careful pre-design considerations. It also involves keeping options open via 'mass customisation' and recycling considerations. Of course, pokayoke is a prime technique for defect prevention in service and manufacturing.

In my opinion, waste prevention is likely to assume a far greater role than waste elimination in the Lean organisation of the future – in the same way that prevention in Quality is now widely regarded as more effective than inspection and fault elimination.

Value Added, Non-Value Added; Avoidable and Not Avoidable; Organisation Value Added and Organisation Non-Value Added

In Lean manufacturing the terms 'value adding', 'non-value adding' and 'necessary non-value adding' are widespread, meaningful, and useful. Abbreviate these to VA, NVA, and NNVA. Value added activity is something that the customer is prepared to pay for. In some types of service, for example healthcare and holidays, the customer is certainly prepared to pay for activities, so VA, NVA and NNVA designations are useful.

In other types of service and administration, for example many clerical procedures, you may argue that the customer is not prepared to pay. Yet to call activities NNVA can be both unhelpful (since everything is NNVA) and demotivating to employees. How would you like to spend most of your life doing necessary non-value added work?

In such situations it may be more useful, and clearer, to talk about 'Not Avoidable' and 'Avoidable' work. A problem here is negative connotation, and the abbreviation NA can be confused with not applicable!

Yet another alternative is to refer to Organisation Value Added (OVA) and Organisation Non-Value Added (ONVA). Here it is probably not helpful to talk about Organisation Necessary Non-Value Added – so this will not be used.

Ohno's Seven Wastes

A section on the wastes should begin with a great big warning. Do not go out and look for the Seven Wastes or the service wastes, or whatever, as a checklist. Doing so IS waste! Instead, take time to think about the customer's needs and the purpose of the system – then identify your own appropriate kinds of waste that are preventing the system reaching its ideal state. You can use the lists that follow as a prompt or as a source of some possible ideas.

Ohno's Seven Wastes were originally for manufacturing. However, they do have application in many types of service. As ever, in translating manufacturing concepts to service – beware!

You can remember the Seven Wastes by asking, 'Who is TIM WOOD?' Answer: Transport, Inventory, Motion, Waiting, Overproduction, Over-processing, and Defects. This idea came from the Lean Office at Cooper Standard, Plymouth, UK.

In all these wastes, the priority is to avoid, only then to cut.

The Waste of Overproduction

Ohno believed that the waste of overproduction was the most serious of all the wastes because it was the root of so many problems and other wastes. In many types of service this remains true. Overproduction is making too much, too early or 'just-in-case'. The aim should be to make or do or serve exactly what is required, no more and no less, just in time and with perfect quality. Overproduction discourages a smooth flow of goods or services. 'Lumpiness' (i.e. making products or working in erratic bursts) is a force against quality and productivity. By contrast, regularity encourages a 'no surprises' atmosphere that may not be very exciting but is much better management.

Overproduction leads directly to excessive lead time. For example, processing and passing on files in batches rather than one at a time. As a result defects may not be detected early, products may deteriorate, and artificial pressures on work rate may be generated. All these increase the chances of defects. Overproduction also impacts on the waste of motion – making and moving things that are not immediately required

Yet overproduction is often the natural state. People do not have to be encouraged to overproduce; they often do so 'just to be safe'. Often this is reinforced by a bonus system which encourages output that is not needed. By contrast, a pull system helps to prevent unplanned overproduction by allowing work to move forwards only when the next work area is ready to receive it. Hamburgers are only made at a rate in line with demand and clerical operations are most effective when there is a uniform flow of work. The motto 'Sell daily? Make daily!' is as relevant in an office as it is in a factory.

Overproduction should be related to a particular timeframe – first reduce overproduction (or early delivery) in a week, then a day, then an hour.

The Waste of Waiting

The waste of waiting is probably the second most important waste. It is directly relevant to FLOW. In Lean we are more concerned with flow of service or customers than we are with keeping operators busy.

In an office, any time a customer or customer item is seen to be not moving or not having value added is an indication of waste. Waiting is the enemy of smooth flow. Although it may be very difficult to reduce waiting to zero, the goal remains. Whether the waiting is for the delivery of a spare part or of customers in a bank there should always be an awareness of a non-ideal situation and a questioning of how the situation can be improved. Waiting is directly relevant to lead time – an important source of competitiveness and customer satisfaction. However, beware: because an item or customer is moving it does not necessarily follow that value is being added.

A bottleneck operation that is waiting for work is a waste. As Goldratt has pointed out in his book *The Goal*, 'an hour lost at a bottleneck is an hour lost for the whole plant'. Effective use of bottleneck time is a key to regular work, which in turn strongly influences productivity and quality.

The Waste of Unnecessary Motions

Next in importance is probably the waste of motion. Unnecessary motions refer to both human and layout. The human dimension relates to the importance of ergonomics for quality and productivity and the enormous proportion of time wasted at *every* workstation by non-optimal layout. A QWERTY keyboard, for example, is non-optimal. If operators have to stretch, bend, pick up, move in order to see better, or in any way unduly exert themselves, the victim is immediately the operator but ultimately quality and the customer.

An awareness of the ergonomics of the workplace is not only ethically desirable, but economically sound. Toyota, famous for its quality, is known to place a high importance on 'quality of worklife'. Toyota encourages all its employees to be aware of working conditions that contribute to this form of waste. Today, of course, motion waste is also a health and safety issue.

The layout dimension involves poor workplace arrangement, leading to micro wastes of movement. These wastes are often repeated many, many times per day – sometimes without anyone noticing. In this regard 5S (see later section) can be seen as the way to attack motion waste.

The Waste of Transporting

Customers do not pay to have goods moved around unless they have hired a removal service! So any movement of materials is waste. It is a waste that can never be fully eliminated but it is also one which should be continually reduced over time. The number of transport and material handling operations is directly proportional to the likelihood of damage and deterioration. Double handling is a waste that affects productivity and quality.

Transporting is closely linked to communication. Where distances are long, communication is discouraged and quality may be the victim. Feedback on poor quality is inversely related to transportation length, whether in manufacturing or in services. There is increasing awareness that for improved quality in manufacturing or services, people from interacting groups need to be located physically closer together. For instance, the design office may be deliberately placed near to the production area.

As this waste gains recognition steps can be taken to reduce it. Measures include monitoring the flow lengths of paper through an office or the distance a customer needs to walk while catching a plane. The number of steps, and in particular the number of non-value adding steps, should be monitored.

The Waste of Processing (or Inappropriate Processing)

Inappropriate processing refers to the waste of 'using a hammer to crack a nut'. Think of a mainframe computer rather than distributed PCs, or a large central photocopier instead of distributed machines. But further, think of a large aircraft requiring passengers to travel large distances to and from a regional airport. Thinking in terms of one big machine instead of several smaller ones discourages operator 'ownership', leads to pressure to run the machine as often as possible rather than only when needed, and discourages general purpose flexible machines. It also leads to poor layout, which as we have seen in the previous section, leads to extra transportation and poor communication. So the ideal is to use the smallest machine capable of producing the required quality, distributed to the points of use.

Inappropriate processing also refers to machines and processes that are not Quality capable: in other words, a process that cannot help but make defects. In general, a capable process requires the correct methods and training, as well as the necessary standards, clearly known.

Note that it is important to take the longer-term view. Buying that large bottleneck 'machine' (photocopier? kitchen? hospital scanner? air terminal?) may just jeopardise the possibility of flow for many years to come, for both customers and employees. Think 'small is beautiful'. Smaller machines avoid bottlenecks, improve flow lengths, are perhaps simpler, can be maintained at different times instead of affecting the whole plant, and may improve cash flow and keep up with technology - buying one small machine per year, instead of one big machine every five years.

The Waste of Unnecessary Inventory

Inventory is relevant in many types of service. Although having no inventory is a goal that can never be attained, inventory is the enemy of quality and productivity. This is so because inventory tends to increase lead time, prevents rapid identification of problems, and increases space, thereby discouraging communication. The true cost of extra inventory is very much in excess of the money tied up in it. 'Push' systems almost invariably lead to this waste.

There are three types of inventory: raw material, work in process, and end items. The existence of any of these is waste, but their root causes and priorities for reduction are different. End items must sometimes be held to meet variation in customer demand, but excessive inventory is waste. It also represents risk of obsolescence. Raw material may be temporarily necessary due to supplier constraints – quality and reliability. WIP or distribution inventories need to move through the supply chain as fast as is feasible. A section in this book is given to inventory considerations.

The Waste of Defects

The last but not least of Ohno's wastes is the waste of defects. Defects cost money, both immediate and longer term. In Quality Costing the failure or defect categories are internal failure (scrap, rework, delay) and external failure (including warranty, repairs, field service, but also possible lost custom). Bear in mind that defect costs tend to escalate the longer they remain undetected. Thus a fault in a microchip discovered when it is made might cost just a few dollars to replace, but if it reaches the customer it may cost hundreds to replace using field service, to say nothing of customer goodwill. So, central themes of total quality are 'prevention not detection', 'quality at source', and 'the chain of quality'. The Toyota philosophy is that a defect should be regarded as a challenge, as an opportunity to improve, rather than something to be traded off against what is ultimately poor management. In service, 'defects' include a variety of types including product defects, errors made by the server, and errors made by the customer.

More recently, 'zero defections' has become a powerful theme, recognising that the value of a retained customer increases with time.

The New Wastes

These may be added to Ohno's original list, and are appropriate in service and manufacturing:

The Waste of Making the Wrong Product Efficiently

This is Womack and Jones' eighth waste. It is really a restatement of the first Lean principle.

The Waste of Untapped Human Potential

Ohno was reported to have said that the real objective of the Toyota Production System was 'to create thinking people' (TPS = Thinking People System). So this 'new' waste is directly linked to Ohno. The 1980s were the decade of factory automation folly. GM and many others learnt the hard and expensive way that the automated factory and warehouse that does not benefit from continuous improvement and ongoing thought is doomed in the productivity race.

Today we have numerous examples, from total quality to self-directed work teams, of the power of utilising the thoughts of all employees, not just managers. Human potential does not just need to be set free. It requires clear communication as to what is needed both from management and to management, it requires commitment and support, because uncapping human potential is sometimes seen as a real threat to first line and middle managers, and it requires a culture of trust and mutual respect which can be won, not by mere lofty words, but by example, interest and involvement at the workplace (Gemba). Basic education is also necessary. The answer to the question, 'What happens if I train them and they go?' should be, 'What happens if you don't train them and they stay!'

Examples: not using the creative brainpower of employees, not listening, thinking that only managers have ideas worth pursuing.

The Waste of Inappropriate Systems

How much software in your computer is never used, not the packages but the actual code? The same goes for MRPII, now repackaged as ERP or CRM systems.

The Lean way is to remove waste before automating, or, as Michael Hammer would say, 'Don't automate, obliterate!' The waste of inappropriate systems should not be confined to computers and automation. How much record keeping, checking, reconciling, is pure waste? Recall the categories of waste.

Recently, for example in the Three Day Car project, the waste of inappropriate systems was highlighted when it was found that typical new car order to delivery time is seven weeks, of which less than a week is for manufacture. It's the order processing system, not the shopfloor, which is the greatest barrier. Often, it's not the operations which consume the time and the money: it's the paperwork or systems. And we now understand a little more of the dangers of demand amplification, of inappropriate forecasting, and of measurement systems that make people do what is best for them but not best for the company. All this is waste.

Wasted Energy and Water

Energy here refers to sources of power: electricity, gas, oil, coal, and so on. The world's finite resources of most energy sources (except sun and wind) were highlighted in a famous report, 'The Limits to Growth', written by the Club of Rome in 1970. Their dire predictions have not come to pass, but nevertheless the true impact of unwise energy use on the world's environments is growing. Wasting these resources is not only a significant source of cost for many companies, but there is also the moral obligation of using such resources wisely.

There is little doubt that this form of waste will escalate sharply up the priority list in the years ahead. Reducing these wastes is likely to have greater and greater financial impact – and moreover enjoys the support of everyone.

Although energy management systems in factory, office and home have grown in sophistication there still remains the human, common sense element: shutting down the machine, switching off the light, fixing the drip, insulating the roof, taking a full load, efficient routing, and the like. By the way, the JIT system of delivery (now used by Tesco) does not waste energy when done correctly: use 'milkrounds', dropping off small quantities to several shops in the same area, or rationalise suppliers to enable the collection of mixed loads daily rather than single products weekly.

Several companies that have 'institutionalised' waste reduction, Toyota included, believe that a good foundation for waste awareness begins with everyday wastes such as switching off lights and printers. You get into the habit.

Wasted Natural Resources

A most severe, and ever-more important waste is that of wasted natural resources. Hawkin, Lovins and Lovins of the Rocky Mountain Institute estimate that 99% of the original materials used in production of goods in the USA becomes waste within six weeks of sale. Robert (Doc) Hall points out that almost everything we own is en route to the tip. Paper is a case in point – the 'paperless office' is still a dream, in part because it has been a low priority. According to Lycra Research 1.5 trillion pages were printed in offices in 2006. In the US each person uses 320 kg of paper annually. Xerox found that Dow Chemical had 16,000 printers, producing 480m printouts per year at a cost of $100m over five years. By contrast Easy Jet is a paperless company – almost. Conservation begins with awareness and measures.

Today conservation of materials is not only environmentally responsible, but is beginning to be profitable. To reduce the waste of materials a life cycle approach is needed, to conserve materials during design, during manufacture, during customer usage, and beyond customer use in recycling.

Seven Service Customer Wastes

Most of the above wastes are seen from the organisation's perspective. What about the customer's perspective? Perhaps an improvement programme should begin with the service customer wastes:

- **Delay** on the part of customers waiting for service, for delivery, in queues, for response, not arriving as promised. The customer's time may seem free to the provider, but when s/he takes custom elsewhere the pain begins.
- **Duplication**: Having to re-enter data, repeat details on forms, copy information across, answer queries from several sources within the same organisation.
- **Unnecessary Movement**: Queuing several times, lack of one-stop, poor ergonomics in the service encounter.

- **Unclear Communication** and the wastes of seeking clarification, confusion over product or service use, wasting time finding a location that may result in misuse or duplication.
- **Incorrect Inventory**: Out-of-stock, unable to get exactly what was required, substitute products or services.
- **Opportunity Lost** to retain or win customers, failure to establish rapport, ignoring customers, unfriendliness, and rudeness.
- **Errors** in the service transaction, product defects in the product service bundle, lost or damaged goods.

Fourteen Office Wastes

Office wastes are probably the most pervasive of all types of service waste. They are especially important in professional service functions such as accountancy, law, design and consulting engineering. Office managers need to foster an awareness of these office wastes among all staff, and be responsible for creating an environment where the wastes can be progressively eliminated. Office wastes are not driven out by imposing additional rules, measures and procedures, but by assisting, mentoring and questioning at 'Gemba'. The office wastes are given below. They are not mutually exclusive. Indeed, some are root cause of others. The list below can also be used with the later section on Total Productive Administration. All these wastes are, of course, particularly acute where there are bottleneck resources. The office manager's task, then, is to recognise and protect the bottleneck from these wastes.

- **Sorting and Searching**: Looking for documents or computer files that have been temporarily misplaced or poorly located.
- **Inappropriate Measurement**: Measures drive behaviour so inappropriate measures will drive inappropriate behaviour. Are the measures there primarily to improve the customer system or to mollify the boss? Measures take time to collect, so at best their collection and analysis are necessary non-value added activity. Adding another measure seldom helps the system, but will certainly add to the workload and may encourage cheating and shortcuts.
- **Underload**: 'Work will expand to fill the time available for its completion', said Northcote Parkinson. But worse, underload may encourage the imposition of additional work on already-busy people who are making a difference to the customer. This happens when underloaded managers dream up new forms, procedures and measures. Ohno said, 'Excessive information must be suppressed'.

- **Overload**: Toyota's word for this is 'Muri' or overburden. See the section on queuing to appreciate the disastrous consequences in cases where work is fully loaded or even almost fully loaded.
- **Inappropriate prioritising:** Stephen Covey talks about a two-by-two matrix of urgency and importance, and points out the tendency to do the urgent but not important, rather than the important but not immediately urgent. We all get caught with this, and the office manager's role must be to monitor and protect. Many office managers are the source of activities which are urgent but not important.
- **Interference**: A variant on inappropriate prioritising is interference – by emails, excessive socialising, dropping-in, and noise. One way around this is to set aside blocks of time where none of these activities is permitted.
- **Inappropriate frequency:** This is where activities such as meetings, reports, measures are performed more frequently than is necessary to achieve a good flow of work. Diminishing returns, or even negative returns, may occur with increasing frequency. This is perhaps a re-statement of Occam's razor: 'Entities should not be multiplied unnecessarily'.
- **Start up and End off**: Work moves too slowly at the beginning of the day, or even after breaks, and slows down or stops too early at the end. The cause may be inadequate information or instruction.
- **Mistakes, Errors or Lack of Appropriate Knowledge:** These result in failure demand and so are a major source of reduced capacity. Recall Deming's '94/6 rule': most problems lie with the system, not the person.
- **Misunderstanding or communication errors**: These are the root of many of the other wastes. See the later section on the 'Gaps Model' where four gaps are described: between customer requirements and manager's perceptions of requirements, between perceptions and standards or instructions, between standards and execution of the service, and between execution and what is promised about the service.
- **Sub-optimisation** or improving the parts but not the whole: This is the essential 'systems' problem. Seeking to improve individual parts can sometimes make the whole worse. Examples range from installing a new computer system to improve one part, to measuring the calls per hour handled by call centre staff.
- **Waiting**: Not customers waiting in a queue, but office staff waiting for decisions, for gate stages, for others, for information. The consequences are particularly severe for bottleneck resources, or elements along the 'critical chain'. See the separate section on this topic.

- **Inappropriate presence:** The waste of attending meetings or activities where no productive purpose is served by attending. Meetings should be short and focused, not long and general.
- **Inappropriate tradeoff:** Smith and Reinertsen have made the useful point that six tradeoffs are made either implicitly or explicitly between four objectives: development speed, product or service cost, product or service performance, and development programme expense. In most cases the tradeoffs are not even considered. This results in too much or too little time being spent on such important considerations.

A starting point for office waste reduction is awareness of these wastes. Even better is estimation or quantification, perhaps through activity sampling.

To reiterate: The job of an office manager or an administrator is not to 'check up' on these wastes, but to help to facilitate their removal. This is the concept of the inverted triangle, where managers support front line activities, and hence improve the service.

Further Reading

Taiichi Ohno / Japan Management Association, *Kanban: Just-in-Time at Toyota*, Productivity Press, 1985
George Stalk and Thomas Hout, *Competing Against Time*, The Free Press, New York, 1990
James Womack and Daniel Jones, *Lean Thinking*, revised edition, Free Press, 2003
Paul Hawkin, Amory Lovins and L Hunter Lovins, *Natural Capitalism*, Little Brown and Co, 1999
Dominic Rushie, 'Business Reports a Loss on Paper', *Sunday Times Business*, 19 Aug 2007
Preston Smith and Donald Reinertsen, *Developing Products in Half the Time*, (second edition), Van Nostrand Reinhold, 1997
Ronald Mascitelli, *The Lean Product Development Guidebook*, Technology Perspectives, 2007

Variability

Variation is the Enemy of Lean! Every Lean manager should know and understand that queue length or lead time is a function of arrival variation, process variation, and capacity utilisation. These are in fact 'Mura' and 'Muri', the root cause of much 'Muda'. This section examines the two types of variation or Mura.

There are two types of variability: customer-introduced variability and internal process variability.

Customer Introduced Variability

Frances Frei has described five types of customer-introduced variability. But Frei also makes the point that there is a tradeoff decision to be made. Don't assume that reducing variability is always the right thing to do. Some customers are willing to pay a premium for increased variability, such as increased menu choice, or for the service provider to help with form filling and clean up. Frei also believes that sometimes it is possible to achieve both low cost and variability accommodation – by, for example, segmentation of customers that gives only that narrow band of customers the right level of support. This is a potent thought. Here we concentrate on variability reduction.

Frei's five types are:

1 **Arrival variability:** Unfortunately customers, whether walk-in or call-in, don't arrive uniformly, and don't place demands on a service system uniformly. This effect has been widely studied in Queuing Theory (see the separate Box on this topic). It may be possible to influence the demand rate, for example by booking, but many service demands are uncertain, at least in the short term – for example appliance failure, burglary, or house leaks. Over longer periods, arrival rates may be predictable to some extent, for example seasonal car breakdown demands. Service providers should first of all record then study arrival rates. The better you can predict, the better your service offering and capacity management will be. So, break down the 'time series' (the pattern of arrivals) by seeking out:

    - Seasonal patterns
    - Patterns by month, by week, by day, by hour
    - Patterns by regular events such as public holidays, Christmas, festivals

- Relationships with major irregular events, such as flood, a celebrity visit, the launch of a new product
- Other drivers such as end-of-year buying by central and local government.

Begin by simply drawing a time series graph, dividing it into appropriate time segments, and then annotating special events. It maybe a good idea to draw a control chart with upper and lower limits at plus and minus three standard deviations.

If you can get short-term average rates – for example weekly breakdown rates – you will be able, very probably via the Poisson distribution, to calculate probabilities of x arrivals in y hours.

2   **Request variability**: This is the variability within a service arrival. For instance, customers arrive at a bank in a variable manner, but also have different numbers of transactions. You will know the frustration of standing in a queue at a bank behind someone paying in the weekend's cash takings.

It may be possible to manage request variability. Methods include

- Having a fast track queue such as the ones you see at supermarkets
- Prohibition of certain types of transaction at certain times of the day, for example, no transactions except emergencies at night
- Limiting choice to menu items.

However, request variability should be tracked. An easy way in many service situations is simply to keep a tally chart. Length of calls can be automatically logged. This is NOT to check up on staff!

Complaints and failure demand in general are an important source of request variability. Not to log these is a major failing. What percentage of front line complaints is recorded and passed on? Often quite low or even nil. Also, on an ongoing basis, get staff to record value demand and failure demand. Post these and discuss them regularly around a Communications Board. See separate section under Tools.

3   **Capability Variability**: This is to do with the customer. Not all customers have the same skill level. Some require much more guidance than others. Older people, for example, may require more time to resolve a computer problem than teenagers. Clearly, this source of variability is much more important in some settings than others. Contrast a doctor diagnosing a patient or a technician diagnosing computer problems with form completion or payment for parking. Of course, reading customer capability variability not only helps the customer, but also improves organisational productivity.

Yet in most service situations the competence of all customers and technology cannot be assumed. It may be a customer problem, or it may be a technology problem – for example, a failure to read a magnetic strip allowing exit from parking. Capacity must be allocated accordingly. But the need for resource capacity can be reduced by

- **Clear signage**: It's surprising how often customers or patients don't know where to go. Follow a sample of customers; don't assume it is obvious. This overlaps with 'Servicescape' (see the separate section). Amazing things can be done with good signs and paint.
- **Reduced choice** also limits customer capability variability. Reduced choice menus are one reason why Benihana is able to turn around satisfied restaurant customers so quickly. (See later section).
- **'Over the shoulder' analysis**: Quicken software became famous for its user friendliness – made possible by close observation of customer interaction with its software.
- **Key stroke analysis**: Analysing computer key strokes and loops has become a standard practice.
- **Standard Operating Procedures (SOPs) for Customers!** Why not put as much effort into guiding the customer as is put into guiding employees? If the wonderful photo-guided SOPs now found in industry were standard practice with customers, the level of errors and complaints would surely fall.
- **Quick help guides**: Another standard practice is to include a 'quick start' as well as longer guides in cameras, computers, and the like. Online help is also standard. How can the pop-up flag principle that guides computer users be adopted?

- **Call buttons**
- **Customer training**: Zara trains customers to make immediate buying decisions or lose out.
- And last but not least, **patient coaching** and **friendly explanation** pay off. Resist the temptation for an employee to do the work themselves, especially with a scowl, and more especially where the customer is likely to return.

Reducing customer variability requires effort. Track the rate of errors made by customers. Pareto. Redesign where necessary. This is frequently an unrecognised source of problems, which can persist for years.

4 **Effort Variability**: Effort variability measures the effort that a customer makes to complete the transaction. For instance, does he put the supermarket trolley away or leave it for someone else to collect? Does he place the tray and waste in the appropriate box at Burger King? Does he leave litter? Of course this may have an impact on cost, and inconvenience other customers.

- What can be done? Shaming and penalties are generally not the way to go. Appeal to his sense of community. Humour can work. Thank him for doing the right thing. But also make it easy and obvious.

5 **Subjective Preference Variability**: This is variation in customer opinion. One customer may appreciate a lot of personal attention, another may not. In high intensity situations it may be possible just to ask for customer preferences.

- Some hotels are making a virtue out of this variability by asking customers their preference in pillows, sheets, beds, and so forth. This may win customers but may also complicate scheduling.

Internal Process Variability

The last section dealt with external or customer variability. This section examines the management of internal variability. This links with 'The Hinckley Framework' for Quality improvement (see separate section). Internal sources are the '6 M's and an I': Man (or people), Machine, Method, Material, Measures, Mother Nature, and Information.

- **'Man' (or people) variability**: A major source of variability. People-induced variation occurs not only between people but also by one person over time. Means of managing people variation include:

  - **Standard Operating Procedures (SOPs)**: These can be quite negative, demotivating, and/or harmful. Please refer to the Standard Operating Procedures section. You certainly do not want scores of different SOPs to attempt to cater for every service situation. But you do want to get the vital few things correct. So pareto the variety, then again pareto the steps in the process. Recall the story of the call centre operator required to ask respondents three times irrespective of their reply. It is important to get through the requirements of the process, whether interacting with a legal client or taking a menu order. But spontaneity and personal interaction are important. So, outline only. Once again it is worth reiterating that SOPs can be a positive source of empowerment rather than something restrictive – like the military 'rules of engagement'. Note that SOPs are appropriate for every level in an organisation.
  - **A Checklist** of items which must be covered (the 'what'), but leaving the 'how' to the service deliverer.
  - **Training:** Airlines are very successful in getting cabin crew to smile and be cheerful. Positive attitude can be built.
  - **Contingency Plans:** Common 'what ifs' can be thought through in advance. What if a key member of staff is ill, what if there is an 'unexpected' surge of work, what if the computers go down, and of course Health and Safety – what if there is a fire?

- **Machine:** Machine variability reduction is dealt with by TPM (Total Productive Maintenance) procedures. Although TPM can be involved, for office machines simple regular maintenance checks often suffice. Place a board with tasks that need to be done, who is responsible for doing them, and a sign-off or tick box to show that they have been done. This is particularly important where customers use machines.

- **Material:** Consistency of materials can be achieved through policy on purchasing and procurement. A consistent corporate style gives a positive message.
- **Measures:** A big one! Discussed in a separate section. 'You get what you measure' and 'Tell me about rewards, and I will act to maximise my own personal benefit'. You had better believe it.
- **Methods:** Regularity and reinforcement are key. SOPs are the means of reducing variability, but need to be appropriate to the level of work. Build in checks, such as valid fields in data entry. And audit, but not with blame or punishment in mind. So much can be achieved with checklists, in every service organisation, irrespective of level. From Queen's Counsel to Clerk, get into the habit of building and maintaining checklists as a way of recording experience. The WWWDD - what went well, and what should be done differently.
- **Mother Nature:** You can't play God, but you can prepare contingency plans for likely events. Virus protection?
- **Information:** Standardisation of information and displays can play a huge role in Lean sustainability. Decide what is necessary, ensure as far as possible similarity throughout the organisation, and establish responsibilities for updating and looking at the information.

Gemba and Learning to See

'Gemba' is the place of action – often but not necessarily the workplace. But this Japanese word has taken on significance far beyond its literal translation. Taiichi Ohno, legendary Toyota engineer and father of TPS, said, 'Management begins at the workplace'. This whole philosophy can best be captured by the single word: Gemba.

Contrast the Gemba way with the traditional (Western?) way. The Gemba way is to go to the place of action and collect the FACTS. The traditional way is to remain in the office and to discuss OPINIONS. Gemba can be thought of in terms of the 'four actuals': go to the actual workplace, look at the actual process, observe what is actually happening, and collect the actual data.

Gemba is also a learning-to-see approach to daily work. As you walk around, question what you see. For instance:

- Is it really necessary to keep everything under lock and key? And at remote locations?
- Is it really necessary to fill in all those forms? Can they be pre-prepared? Why is it that at check-in or check-out there are so many keyboard strokes?
- Why are customers asked to sign next to the 'X' agreeing that they know all the conditions, when reading them through would take half an hour?
- Can customers (or patients) wait in more comfortable conditions? Why do they have to wait in line anyway? Can they not be called when needed?
- Why are there interruptions in the middle of the process, leading to start-up losses?
- If there was a 'near miss' don't just sigh with relief, try to put in place preventive measures.
- Is a one-stop procedure possible?
- What is the root cause of the problem? Don't just do a patch-up job, but ask if the cause can be eliminated.

None of these questions can be effectively asked or answered by managers sitting at their desks. A questioning culture is only possible if you are at Gemba.

So Gemba breaks away from the 'it's not my problem' and 'I only work here' attitude. It is the managers' fault if workers have such attitudes.

What can be done to empower employees to make immediate improvements?

Under Gemba, if your organisation has a problem or a decision, go to Gemba first. Do not attempt to resolve problems away from the place of action. Do not let operators come to the manager, let the manager go to the workplace. Spend time at the service counter. This is the basis of so much Japanese management practice: that new Honda management recruits spend time working in assembly and in stores, that marketers from Nikon spend time working in camera shops, that Toyota sends its Lexus design team to live in California for three months, and so on. Ohno was famous for his 'chalk circle' approach - drawing a circle in chalk on the factory floor and requiring a manager to spend several hours inside it while observing operations, noticing variation, and taking note of wastes. The West too has its devotees. John Sainsbury, who ran the supermarket chain in its heyday, could pass a shelf and see at a glance if prices were wrong. His retirement may account for the decline of a once-great chain. An open plan office, with senior management sitting right there with 'the troops', is Gemba.

Gemba is, or should be, part of implementation. How often is the Western way based on 'change agents', on simulation, on computers or information systems, on classroom-based education? These have a place, of course, but Gemba emphasises implementation by everyone, at the workplace, face-to-face, based on in-depth knowledge. And low cost, no cost solutions rather than big-scale expensive information or technology solutions.

Gemba is often combined with other elements: the Five Whys, Muda (or waste), Policy Deployment, Kaizen, 5S, Seven Tools, and it is a central part of Total Quality. Gemba is a common theme in all of these. So today we hear of 'Gemba Kanri', 'Gemba Kaizen', and 'Gemba TPM'. The word has already appeared in English and American dictionaries.

Finally, let us remind ourselves that Gemba is not a 'Japanese thing'. The Japanese learned it from the Americans – specifically the famous Hawthorne experiments at General Electric in the 1930s. One study concerned the effects of lighting on productivity. Turn up the lights, productivity improves. Turn up the lights further, productivity improves further. Now turn down the lights. What happens? Productivity improves! What was happening was that workers were responding not to lighting levels but to the interest being taken in them by heavyweight researchers. This became known as the Hawthorne Effect. But the West promptly forgot this lesson. The Japanese took it on. So, don't sit in your office looking at your Excel spreadsheet and imagine that you are improving productivity – that is management by looking in the rear view mirror. Instead, 'get your butt to the Gemba', and learn to anticipate problems.

Further Reading

Masaaki Imai, *Gemba Kaizen*, McGraw-Hill, New York, 1997

The Four Toyota Rules applied to Service

In a now classic article in *Harvard Business Review*, Spear and Bowen proposed the 'Four Rules of the Toyota Production System'. The article has become immensely influential. It was written following extensive research at Toyota. Stephen Spear claims that the four rules capture the essence or DNA of Toyota. Here, the four rules are interpreted for service.

Rule 1: 'All work shall be highly specified as to content, sequence, timing, and outcome'.

Some people from service take a quick read of this sentence before rejecting it outright, as being applicable only to manufacturing. This is unwise. The rule needs to be interpreted in a wider context. It goes right back to the days of F W Taylor and his 'one best way', and is the basis of Plan, Do, Study, Adjust. But in service, it challenges us to think about the current best known way, or ideal way, to carry out work and to minimise error. So, what is the best or ideal way to

- do a check-out at your hotel?
- greet a passenger joining a flight?
- produce an annual report?
- collect necessary data from a legal or financial client?
- start designing a component?
- do a ward round in a hospital?
- run a university course?

Many of these are simply not specified, or are specified in insufficient detail, to their detriment. In service, we certainly do not want to over-specify and destroy spontaneity, but under-specification is also bad. Think of the waste of duplication of a new employee having to 'learn the hard way' or not benefiting from the accumulated experience of predecessors. Note that in service we are not talking about restrictive, prescriptive, scripted, responses. But we are talking about the things that simply must be done, like a credit check, and must not be done, like serving meals in a ward while a medical round is taking place.
The rule also places the onus on management to see that specifications are developed. If there is a problem it is not good enough to say, 'You must try harder', or 'You must work more conscientiously', or 'We have a motivation problem'. Instead, the process needs to be examined to see why the problem arose in the first place and to prevent it happening again. If there is no standard method, this cannot be done.

So, 'Why did the patient get the wrong medicine?' or 'Why was the necessary spare part missing when the repairman called?' puts the emphasis on the process, not the person. This is pure Deming.

Rule 2: 'Every customer-supplier connection must be direct, and there must be an unambiguous yes-or-no way to send requests and receive responses'.

If there is a problem or issue, the single, shortest path of communication must be clearly known and used. In the West we like to reward problem solvers. This is OK as long as the problem is communicated and its solution built into the new standard. But, too often, the problem is solved but hardly anyone apart from the problem solver and perhaps his immediate manager knows about it. The next shift does not know, so when the problem recurs it is 'solved' in another way. Both shifts get rewards for 'initiative', but the fundamental solution remains in the head of the solver. In service, when a customer complains to the front desk, does the front desk person communicate it? Does it get to the source of the problem, or, indeed, to management? Or, more likely, does management sit in a fool's paradise thinking everything is great? Sometimes the communication route is too long – most people have played the children's game of sending a message around a circle. Sometimes the problem is communicated to a 'CRM' or 'maintenance MIS', leaving it to someone else to follow up. And please don't think that having an IVR (interactive voice recognition) system means that you have addressed Rule 2. Sometimes the problem is communicated through many informal networks, thus introducing the possibility of distortion and mischief. Communication channels need to be thought out the other way around - from bottom to top. Moreover, in service, information should flow ahead of the customer, so that the car for service, the patient, the new recruit, the student, is expected and prepared for prior to arrival.

Rule 3: 'The pathway for every product and service must be simple and direct'.

This is about clear value streams. And it is about the minimum steps in the stream. We do not want the spaghetti of the job shop in either manufacturing or service. Simplify the streams, the routings, the priorities. If at all possible, don't have a complex of different people and conflicting priorities that the customer must navigate through. Open that extra till as soon as required. In service, have you ever experienced multi-stage automatic telephone answering – and finally got through to a person (or worse, a machine) who couldn't deal with your 'unusual' request? Try a human. Better still, try a highly knowledgeable human at the first stage. So, value stream map it <u>from the customer's perspective.</u> And remember Stalk and Hout's Golden Rule: 'Never delay a value adding step by a non-value adding step'.

Rule 4: 'Any improvement must be made in accordance with the scientific method, under the guidance of a teacher, at the lowest possible level in the organisation'.

This is about all improvements being done under PDSA, even if it is only a small improvement. Without PDSA there is little learning. Put up a hypothesis of what you expect, carry out the work, then see if your hypothesis is correct. If it is incorrect, why is it incorrect, and what can you learn for next time? All changes must be tested and reflected upon. The 'lowest level' means both place and organisational level. So improvement must be done <u>at Gemba,</u> by <u>direct observation</u>, probably using the <u>Socratic method</u>. Direct observation is needed for understanding and anticipating problems – not managing by remote control via KPIs that come in too late to make a difference to the customer. The Socratic method asks why; it does not show how.

Spear and Bowen suggest that the rules are not learned by instruction, but by questioning. The rules are not stated. They are absorbed over time. Challenging questions involve going to Gemba and asking:

- How do you do this work?
- How do you know that you are doing it correctly?
- How do you know that the outcome is defect free?
- What do you do if you have a problem?
- Who do you communicate with?
- How do you know what to do next?
- What signals cue your work?
- Do you do this in the same way as others?

In fact, it is learning by the ongoing use of Kipling's six honest serving men, who 'taught me all I knew; their names are What and Why and When, and Where and How and Who'.

Bear in mind that 'it is not the quality of the answers that distinguishes a Lean expert, but the quality of the questions' (source unknown), and as Yogi Berra said, 'Don't tell me the answer, just explain the question'.

To summarise: TPS is not rules or tools. It is not <u>instinct</u> (instinct can't be learned), but <u>instinctive</u> – like the unwritten rules of a society.

Further Reading

Spear and Bowen, 'Decoding the DNA of the Toyota Production System', *Harvard Business Review*, Sept-Oct 1999
For a healthcare related perspective on the four rules see Stephen Spear, 'Fixing Healthcare from the Inside, Today', *Harvard Business Review*, September 2005
See also Cindy Jimmerson, *Review*, www.leanhealthcarewest.com, 2004

We are all Beginners at Lean Service

For me, two of the most powerful aspects of the Toyota system are Humility and Reflection. Humility means the possibility that we are wrong – we still have a long way to go along the path to Lean. Even Watanabe, Toyota Chairman, says that after 40 years with Toyota he still has much to learn. If that is true in manufacturing, it is even more true in service. Reflection is the ability – and time – to contemplate where we could have done better. Without these two the manager or consultant is simply an ignorant beast.

Nassim Taleb writes that the human mind suffers three ailments as it comes into contact with history. I feel that the same three ailments apply, or should apply, to Lean. Taleb's points are:

1   **The illusion of understanding** – when the true system is far more complex.
2   **The retrospective distortion**, or how we can assess matters only after the fact. We are all very wise when explaining failure after the event, much less so before the event. And we think we know the characteristics of success but are often proved wrong in the longer term – a point made by Rosenzweig. So we need to set out to learn and reflect, and have humility.
3   **The overvaluation of factual information, and the handicap of authoritative and learned people, particularly when they create categories**. We love facts on Lean achievement, like reduction in lead time and improvements in quality. While it is good and reasonable practice to collect these facts, beware. Deming said, 'The true facts you'll never know'. I can hear him now saying that. In systems there is often the 'push down, pop up principle' – have you ever noticed how the 'push down' is always reported, but less frequently the 'pop up'? And in this book I categorise quite a bit – I would be wise to take heed of Taleb, and so should you!

Further Reading

Nassim Nicholas Taleb, *The Black Swan*, Penguin Allen Lane, 2007
Phil Rosenzweig, *The Halo Effect*, Free Press, 2007
Jeffrey Liker, *The Toyota Way,* McGraw Hill, 2004. Liker devotes one of his Toyota principles to *Hansei* (relentless reflection).

Concepts of Lean Service

The following four figures taken together illustrate general philosophical points about Lean service and Systems. They give an idea of what a Lean service transformation will look like.

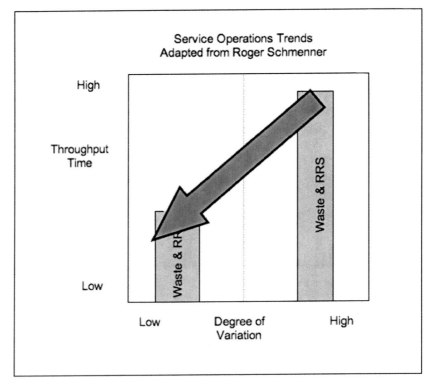

In the first figure the activities in a service area have been transformed. First, note that the diagram reflects a 'systems' view. That is, some activity groups now consume more time, others less, but overall much less time is required to do the work. This reflects Ohno's idea that Activity = Work + Waste. Notice that waste activities have been reduced. But this has not happened by 'taking out waste' or 'waste walk' activities. Such activities do take out some minor wastes, but the big hit is via transformation in thinking. Via, if you like, the 'Vanguard Model for Check' activity discussed in the first section. What has happened is that the activities have become more regularised. The Runner activities use about the same time, but the big move has been with Repeaters. More activities take place regularly. Greater repeatability drives down the error rate – by better processes, not necessarily by standardisation. There is better regular communication, perhaps around a Communications Board. As a result there is far less rework. The proportion of Stranger activities has also declined because more are done as part of a regular process. This has resulted from work reviews, feedback, checklists and systematic error reduction done every day.

The second figure also represents a systems view. Here more resources are put into 'up front' activities such as understanding customer requirements or moving skilled people forward. In these 'customer facing' stages, cost and time has increased. But the payoff is further downstream where there are now much reduced errors and rework. End-to-end time has been saved, even though times for earlier upstream activities have increased. The 'silo' view of measures and costing has been avoided.

In the third figure we see the Lean concept of pushing down decision making to an appropriately lower level. This is even more important in service than in manufacturing. In manufacturing it is good practice from a time perspective. In service it is good, if not essential practice, from both a time perspective and a customer perspective. Most people have experienced the annoying statement, 'I'll have to refer that to my supervisor'. But this is also too glib. In service it is the front line staff who make the difference, through numerous Moments of Truth, between excellent and poor service – irrespective of the service system design.

The fourth figure is an adaptation from Roger Schmenner, who maintains that there has been a trend among the best service companies towards what he calls 'swift, even flow' – surely a concise description of Lean. This is being achieved by two changes: reducing variation and reducing throughput time. Note that Schmenner is not talking about variation in the process but about a more focused service offering – solicitors specialising in conveyancing, hospitals specialising in specific areas, the emergence of a variety of fast food restaurants, and so on. Schmenner does not talk about waste and Runners, Repeaters and Strangers, but this is what has made the trend possible.

A Case of Failure Demand

In 2007 a leading UK bank advertised a financial product with a very attractive interest rate. Investors were required to complete an application form and existing account holders were required to have the investment funds available in their account. A large number of applications for investment followed. The office processing the applications was overwhelmed. Many applicants were still outstanding one month after completing the application form. Many enquiries were made - failure demand. Enquirers were told that the investment would be backdated to the application date. After six weeks many potential investors had taken their money out of their accounts. When these applications were processed the transaction could not be completed -failure demand - because the funds were not available. Letters were then sent out requesting re-application with sufficient funds - more failure demand, but this time internally generated. Many customers had already invested elsewhere.

A failure to resource the office adequately – or to monitor the flood of applications and adjust resources accordingly – led to a huge amount of unnecessary work as well as loss of customers – some probably permanently.

Caution: On Repetitiveness and Experience

Every service or administrative job, or customer that is dealt with, may seem to be unique. But almost every piece of service work has repetitive elements – for instance the stages of writing a report or conducting a meeting - even though the report or meeting is unique.

The late quality guru, Phil Crosby, spoke about 'Ballet, not hockey'. In a ballet, they rehearse, adjust and learn what works and what does not. Then they fix the performance and every show is the same, allowing for a degree of 'poetic license' and the possibility of using an understudy. In ice hockey, every game is different, even though the rules are followed. Hockey is fun, but is it good management? Hence, Crosby asked, is your company more ballet-like or more hockey-like? This is 'horses for courses' again, but in Lean we must attempt to be more ballet-like if possible. Ballet is, of course, a creative process but manages to have many transactional features. More 'ballet' is possible, even in hockey. Good ballet and good hockey (or football), like good service, has the right blend of repetitive elements that can be analysed, rehearsed, improved and fine-tuned, but still can be adaptive. There is the story of championship-winning golfer Gary Player who when asked about his luck said, 'Yes, I do have good luck, and you know what? The more I practice the luckier I get!' Similarly in good service – it's not luck, it's careful analysis, preparation and execution. In all these, mapping can help.

Don't be misled by the old story of 'I have 25 years experience!' Ask if, instead, the person has had one year 25 times.....

Further Reading

Roger Schmenner, 'How Service Businesses have Survived and Prospered', *Proc OMA – POMS Conference*, Como, Italy, 2003

Part 2: Service Mapping

A Service Mapping Framework

It is tempting to leap in and begin to map or 5S or do a kaizen event virtually on day one of a Lean implementation. This may be a reasonable, even good, thing to do in early days of Lean, for the sake of sending out a positive message to all levels of staff, top to bottom. I refer to this type of activity as 'Lean Light' as opposed to 'System Lean'. Lean Light can switch on the light, highlight the vast number of opportunities, enthuse the staff for a while, and may even teach a few Lean tools.

However, Lean Light does have its dangers: a piecemeal approach, a considerable risk of sub-optimisation, not much impact on the bottom line, and sustainability issues when staff at all levels begin to realise these points.

You may think you are doing great things by 5S activity up front. Perhaps you are. But you are more likely to be arranging deck chairs on the Titanic.

So, I would urge you to move to System Lean quite rapidly – although not necessarily at the very start of a Lean implementation.

For Lean Light, skip Level 1 as described below and move directly to Level 2 – but be aware of the risks. Remember, Lean Light is the mark of the inexperienced, though enthusiastic, Lean practitioner. It is much better to approach mapping on three levels as discussed below.

Level 1: This is the Big Picture or Systems view where the purpose of the system is understood. It should be more strategic, more senior manager led.
Level 2: This is the process value stream map level at which the end-to-end process is mapped in current state maps (note plural), and most often a future state map and action plan is proposed. In Level 2 four generic types will be presented.
Level 3: The detailed process activity map aimed at some sub-processes. This level is not always done, particularly for some types of value streams.

The three level concept is shown in the following figure. The Flowchart and accompanying text give an outline of the process.

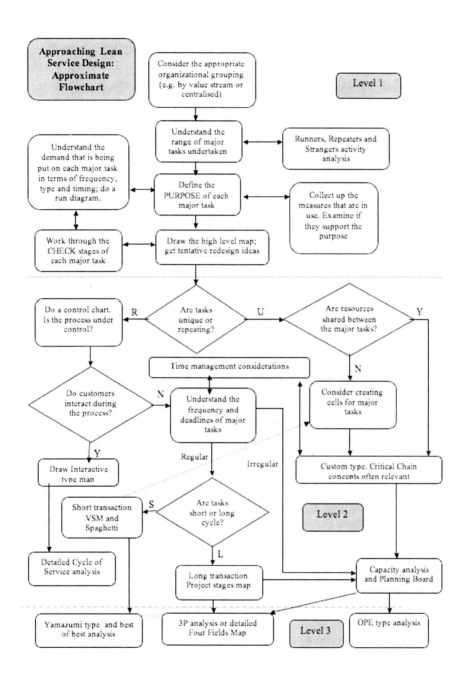

Approaching Lean Service Design: Approximate Flowchart

Consider the appropriate organizational grouping (e.g. by value stream or centralised)

Level 1

Understand the range of major tasks undertaken

Runners, Repeaters and Strangers activity analysis

Understand the demand that is being put on each major task in terms of frequency, type and timing; do a run diagram.

Define the PURPOSE of each major task

Collect up the measures that are in use. Examine if they support the purpose

Work through the CHECK stages of each major task

Draw the high level map; get tentative redesign ideas

Do a control chart. Is the process under control?

R — Are tasks unique or repeating? — U

Are resources shared between the major tasks? — Y

Time management considerations

Do customers interact during the process?

N — Understand the frequency and deadlines of major tasks

N — Consider creating cells for major tasks

Regular

Irregular

Custom type. Critical Chain concepts often relevant

Y — Draw Interactive type map

Level 2

Short transaction VSM and Spaghetti — S — Are tasks short or long cycle?

Detailed Cycle of Service analysis

L

Long transaction Project stages map

Capacity analysis and Planning Board

Yamazumi type and best of best analysis

3P analysis or detailed Four Fields Map

Level 3

OPE type analysis

The Lean Toolbox for Service Systems

69

Overview of the Lean Service Approach

This section gives an overview and relates to the flow chart. Detail on all the concepts follows in the various Level descriptions and in the Tools section. What is attempted here is an overview applicable to most administrative and service situations. The vast range of such situations means that the overview and flowchart can never be totally satisfactory. However, the intention is to provide general guidance and to raise a few relevant considerations.

Begin at what is here called '**Level 1**'. This is the big picture, the high level overview.

A starting point is to decide if the area you are working with should be centralised or decentralised. It is an organisation question that may not be relevant to all. Some offices and functions serve multiple product or service streams (in other words they are a central support function), while others are integrated with service delivery or manufacturing. If the former is the case, a good consideration is whether the function should be moved closer to the prime process. For example, should a call centre be decentralised to be closer to field service, or should accounting and planning be moved from a central function into a 'focused factory' located next to the shop floor? Or the other way round? This question is a vital one. You can proceed without answering the question immediately, but bear it in mind.

Then consider the range of tasks that are undertaken. Often there will only be one main task, like a call centre supporting field operations. Other times there may be a range of functions such as accounting, undertaking cash flow, credit checks, ledger, invoicing, measures, and so on. Of course there will always be secondary tasks, such as appraisals and training.

Have a look at the Runners, Repeaters, Strangers (RRS) concept. For example, are there Runners that take place all the time, and Repeaters that happen regularly but not continually? Do a Pareto of the activities. It is an important way to organise resources, and to prioritise analysis activity. You may come out with a two dimensional chart: main tasks against RRS categories.

Then attempt to define in concise terms the purpose or aim of each task or sub-system. Purpose should be from the customer's viewpoint, preferably end-to-end. The complete task. Look at the existing measures and ask if they support the purpose, or actually work against it. You are likely to find several measures that do the latter.

Once you have defined the purpose of the system, think, propose and discuss the ideal way in which the service should be delivered.

Keep in mind that the most effective thing you can do to improve the effectiveness of an existing system is to free up capacity. This enables response time to be improved and initiates a virtuous circle of improvement that steadily eliminates problems. And the most effective way of freeing up capacity is to reduce failure demand – demand that should not be there in the first place.

Understanding the demand on each task is critical. Major categories are Value Demand (first time demand) and Failure Demand. Quantify this. Often, listen directly to customers' actual words. Demand also needs to be understood in terms of frequency (load) and timing across an hour, a day, a month. A run diagram will be a powerful aid.

Having defined the main tasks, draw out a high level map for each task. Just the broad stages, no detail. An important consideration is, where is the 'system boundary'? As the map is drawn, carry out the 'Check' activities as defined by John Seddon. These Check activities are likely to refine the map and to re-quantify the demand situation. The outcome should be some tentative ideas on change. Perhaps some radical ideas. You are after high level wastes here. The detailed Seven Wastes are not really applicable at this level – it is broad level wastes which are of concern.

You will have got into some detail already, but now **Level 2** detail process analysis begins. An early point is to distinguish between unique and repeating tasks. This is not clear-cut. In service few tasks are ever the same, at least at the detail level. Dealing with complaints, bookings, repairs, reconciliations, property registrations, hernia operations, is repetitive, but designing a new building or defending a criminal case is not repetitive to the same degree. It is a judgment call.

Assuming repeating tasks, an early consideration is to use control chart theory to have a look at tasks that are 'out of control' and to explore the reasons. Maybe customer response goes walkabout when Joe goes on leave. List these 'system conditions' for future attention because they can have a devastating 'knock-on' effect.

Now look at whether customers interact during the process, or whether interaction takes place largely at the beginning and end. This is a fundamental distinction: where customers are involved the service needs to be more flexible. Customers are part of the process and the extent of their involvement is a consideration, they can make errors that are not fully under your control, and front line staff interaction is more critical. By contrast, in low interaction situations a staff member may never deal with an existing customer.

If the service is Interactive, the Service Blueprint or Cycle of Service methodology is a powerful approach. This looks at value enhancement primarily, efficiency secondarily. If the service is not Interactive but repetitive and where the tasks have regular deadlines and are generally short cycle, we call it Transactional in this book.

Both Transactional and Interactive approaches will benefit in a major way from the earlier Level 1 analysis. To 'jump in' directly to this stage risks sub-optimisation. You will never know what has been missed!

Where repetitive transactional activities are generally short cycle – say less than an hour - this would be the only area where some manufacturing-type value stream mapping MAY be applicable. Possibly the service is more of a 'service factory'. Cells may be relevant here, but are sometimes challenging to implement in service.

Long cycle activities are better dealt with by some project management concepts. Time management considerations are always important, but particularly so in what are called 'Custom environments' in this book.

Where tasks are unique, a question is whether critical resources (mainly people, sometimes facilities) are shared. By a 'shared' resource we mean the degree to which a person works alone or as part of a team. Perhaps no-one works completely alone, but it is the sequence dependencies that are the issue – to what extent critical resources are dependent on the completion of activities by others. Also of relevance is whether a critical resource works on several tasks simultaneously – perhaps a senior accountant, engineer or computer systems analyst whose expertise is required on several projects. Not good practice, but sometimes unavoidable. Where they are shared, sequencing and scheduling are simpler, but not necessarily very simple. Where they are not shared, the establishment of cells is easier. In Custom environments, 'Critical Chain' concepts are often helpful.

Level 3: the micro detail level. In repetitive environments, particularly short cycle, 'best of the best' analysis, and Yamazumi (capacity work balance) Board analysis is often useful. 3P type analysis is useful in several environments, but particularly in the Custom or project management type. Detailed Four Field mapping can be used to get right into the detail. In many professional service environments, Overall Professional Effectiveness (OPE) concepts can be very powerful.

Once again, beware of leaping into detail much too early. You risk shifting the deck chairs on the Titanic. Worse, you may completely 'turn off' staff by micro analysis, like silly 5S or time studies done way too early when 'everybody knows' that there is huge waste out there. This is not to say it is useless – ten seconds taken out of 50k activities per year is not trivial.

Sometimes you may stop work after Level 1. The insights and gains may be sufficient. It could be that you have taken out 50% of the time or waste. Similarly at Level 2. Take out the next 35%. Only then comes Level 3, for the last 15%. Not always of course – that is the challenge of Lean Service.

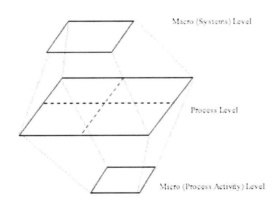

At the top level is the macro map, applicable in most service situations. This is the 'big picture' or Systems view. It is presented in the next section. Below that is found the mapping typology with the four types. This will be referred to as Process Mapping – although for two of the types, mapping in the usual sense of the word is less useful. Each of these four types is presented in a later section. Below that are 'micro' maps where, if necessary, the detail can be explored. The micro maps are the traditional 'industrial engineering' process activity maps or 'four fields mapping'. At the micro level, the '3P' process and concepts like Overall Professional Effectiveness are relevant in some situations. These are covered briefly in a later section. In many situations, but certainly not all, 'mapping' at all three levels is appropriate. However, such mapping may not be end-to-end. It is appropriate to map, or at least analyse, end-to-end at the macro level, but often mapping will only be partial if at all at the micro level.

All four types can be used to design and redesign a service delivery system. However, the Idealised and Custom types are applicable in specific design environments.

	Goals	Design or Structure	Management/ Measures
Organisation Level			
Process Level			
Job (Task) Level			

Another but similar view draws on Rummler and Brache (1990), who suggested a hierarchical improvement matrix, as shown in the previous table.

What is suggested in this book is that the 'System' or purpose be examined at the macro or organisation level, then the process level be explored in greater depth after the system purpose is understood, and then only in some cases the task or detailed job level be analysed.

However, the macro or systems level is not necessarily the organisation level. It may more commonly be a major grouping within the organisation. Levels 2 and 3 then follow appropriately. This is shown in the table below.

Organisation	Macro Level (Level 1: System) examples	Process Level (Level 2) examples	Micro Level (Level 3: Task) examples
Local authority	Housing, leisure services	Housing repairs, leisure centre management	Detailed visit process, swimming
Healthcare	A&E, patient operations (both end to end)	A&E patient flow, operation cycle of service	Detailed scheduling, ordering supplies
Bank	Personal banking, small business support	Account management, business advice	Opening an account, processing a loan
Consulting Engineer	Project management	Design	Preparing a contract
Field Service	Product support	Maintenance cycle of service	Ensuring correct parts

Level 1: System Considerations and Macro Maps

This section contains the stages necessary for macro service mapping and analysis. These basic concepts are applicable in every service situation and should precede the more detailed focused analysis undertaken in Level 2.

Acknowledgement

Parts of this section draw heavily on John Seddon's *Freedom from Command and Control*. However, the views presented here are not necessarily those of John Seddon.

Starting out on Lean Service Improvement

The methodology for Lean service improvement presented here starts at the System level. This is in marked contrast to almost all publications on Lean mapping, whether manufacturing or service, which generally start with the identification of families and then dive straight into process level mapping. Very little or no discussion is typically given about understanding the wider system. For example, see Keyte and Locher – a good book on what are here called 'service transactions' – and Drew, McCallum and Roggenhofer, whose Step 1 is 'Create value streams by grouping similar products or services'. Moreover, these books consider demand much later. This is acceptable in manufacturing but seldom in service.

A starting point in Lean service improvement is to identify the system of concern. Generally, at the macro level, this will be known. You will know that your concern is, for example, in Accident and Emergency or Field Maintenance. Where there is some uncertainty is with the system boundary – where the system of concern begins and ends. Note that this is different from the classic manufacturing value stream mapping approach, which breaks the overall area into families using a matrix of products or customers against major process steps – trying to identify appropriate groupings.

Looking at the system or big picture helps to avoid sub-optimisation. Or, as Stephen Covey advises, 'Start with the end in mind'.

The following procedure should be worked through by a high level team before actual Lean improvement begins.

Step One: Clarify the System

List and classify the major service delivery systems with which the organisation is concerned. These are the transformational processes that the organisation is primarily involved in delivering.

If you are lucky the area may have only one clear major activity that everyone works on all day, except, for example, when training, interviewing or appraising. But some administrative functions do several major tasks, such as an accounting function that does cash management, ledger, and payments. A university may do both research and teaching. If this is the case, these tasks or sub-systems need to be defined and clarified. The purpose of each needs to be defined. A useful way in is to use a matrix with tasks and Runners, Repeaters and Strangers, as shown.

	Major Task 1	Major Task 2	Major Task n
Runners	Sub process prime Sub process support		Etc
Repeaters	Sub process support	Sub process prime Sub process support	
Strangers			

If you know the system of concern you can skip over the following and jump straight to system boundary considerations below.

There are two types of system:

- **Primary (or Core)**: a series of activities which deliver customer value in terms of a product or service. In a hospital, a primary mission may be concerned with transforming a sick patient into a reasonably well patient. But this would have to be broken down into the main core systems such as A&E, adult surgical, and outpatient care. Generally, primary systems deliver value to real, external customers. Call centre activities, together with any related field service activity, are primary. A creative process such as design or research may best be regarded as primary, insofar as value is delivered to future external customers.

- **Support**: a series of activities which are necessary to support the prime systems. A support process does not generally deal with external customers. The recruitment process is an example. Do not get into an argument about support processes being value added or non-value added. To label support processes as 'non-value adding' can be demotivating, if not insulting. The distinction between primary and support is not always clear-cut. There are 'grey' areas between them – examples are invoicing and a university library. If in doubt classify it as 'support' because the doubt reveals that it is at least not in the front rank of prime customer value.

Begin by listing the primary systems.

- Carry out a ranking exercise that aims to arrange the processes in terms of importance to the current and future business. This can simply be done by voting on a one-to-five basis. A 'smarter' way is to do pair-wise comparison whereby every candidate process is ranked against every other on the basis of more important (+1), same (0) or less important (-1). Simply add up the point scores for each process.
- Rank the systems in terms of perceived ease of implementation.
- Plot the processes on a matrix showing importance against ease of implementation. You will often give priority to processes in the 'important/easy to implement' category.
- Discuss which systems should be considered for the first tranche of Lean improvement.

Then repeat the exercise with the support processes. There may be good reason to start a Lean improvement exercise with support activities, since you may want to develop some experience with mapping before getting into core processes. You may, of course, wish to do all the prime processes in an area together because they overlap so much.

At this stage you will want to select the team to do the exercise. A good team size is around eight, including an experienced facilitator, some staff from the actual process and, essentially, front line management from the process. They do not all have to be full time.

System Boundary

A key concern is where the system should start and end. Generally, activities that cannot be influenced are outside the system. But what is inside the system? A few thoughts:

- **Purpose**: If you use the word 'and' in your statement of purpose, perhaps you have two systems.
- **Shared resources**: If resources are shared (say medical consultants shared with other providers, or shared ERP systems) you will need to consider the influence of these resources. Can you assume they will agree? Would it help to involve them?
- **Customer involvement and 'co-production'**: Customers can be useful co-producers. We know the system should be end-to-end, but where is the end? Does the fire service start with a fire, or with prevention? Should prevention be considered another, separate system?
- **Supplier involvement and 'co-production'**: It would also be good to involve suppliers end-to-end, but do you have any influence over them, and how much impact does their involvement have on the system?
- **Loops within the system**: If you can establish some clear 'loops of responsibility', perhaps they should be considered stand-alone systems.
- **Key resources**: If key resources (managers? unions? support staff?) are omitted from the study, could they sabotage it, directly or indirectly? What is the risk of failure by omitting key resources?
- **Operations, HR and Marketing**: In most Lean service systems you will have to consider marketing and people. Marketing, because what are you going to do with the improved performance, and HR because what change is needed from the people in the system? So even if these two functions are not part of the system, there is a good chance that they should be involved in its redesign.

Step Two: Go though the 'Check' Stage

The six stages of 'The Vanguard Model for Check' are described in the first section of this book. They are very powerful. Working through the steps is important. It is also recommended that consideration be given to the CATWOE characteristics as discussed in the Systems section.

Why do you want to do this? First, because it clarifies system issues. Second, because it gives an insight into the proportions of 'value' and 'failure' demand. Ideally, failure demand should not exist, but it may be tying up large chunks of resource, driving away loyal customers, and preventing potential customers from being served. Third, because the step gives valuable insight into what the process is actually dealing with as opposed to what management thinks the process is dealing with.

Staff and managers from the process should both be involved in the 'Check' stage because involvement in the discovery of problems and issues is the most successful way of bringing about change. Both managers and staff often have fixed ideas about what 'the problems' are. Listening to customers' actual words helps to change minds. Staff and managers both see the problems, they design the solution, they get it going. Then it is sustained.

This step may seem like a waste of time when the team is most anxious to 'get in and start analysing or mapping'. Don't be deluded. Don't fall for 'We know our customers', or 'We know what the problems are'. The step is likely to be a time consuming one, so the team needs to be split up to cover a range of customers and situations. But it is time well spent.

Get the team to 'go to Gemba' (the place of action) and collect a sample of actual demands on the process. The start is the entry point for customers into the process. It may be the call centre, the front desk at a hotel or library, the A&E entry point, or the point at which orders are taken. This point may not always be in an office: it may be in a field emergency vehicle, at a check-in counter, or at home collection points. If possible, walk the first few steps with the customer. In a 'professional service' process this step may present some difficulty in terms of time or confidentiality. If so, ask the front line professional to make notes after each interview as to the nature of the request, but excluding personal detail.

A representative sample is required. This will require discussion. For example, the team may wish to cover types of customer, times of the day, service types, size of request, or urgency of request. What is not needed is an 'activity sample' (see later separate section) but simply an appreciation of the situation. As a rule of thumb, collect 200 observations or calls.

The team should record verbatim, as far as possible, what customers actually say. If requests for work are written, note them down. Use the actual words, but reduce the remarks to a sentence or a phrase or two.

Then the team should transfer the phrases to large (12.5 cm x 7.5 cm) post-its.

The Affinity Diagram is the next stage. First colour-code each post-it with a large green or red dot for Value Demand and Failure Demand respectively. Value Demand are 'first time' requests. Failure Demand are requests that should not happen if the process is working well.

Categorise the 'Top 10' demands. Seek logical groupings. For example, these may be product, service, age, complaint, location, time, or gender related. Collect similar post-its and group them into areas. This may involve more than one iteration.

Then group the post-its into two columns, Value Demand and Failure Demand, and as many rows as necessary. For example, the rows may be by contact type: walk-in, telephone, internet, post. There will invariably be one or more Paretos (dominant groupings). For example, 65% of demands arrive by phone, and 80% of failure demand arrives via the internet. Although not statistically valid, this will be very useful information. You may decide to collect up more information to give the conclusions more statistical validity, but for most processes the value will already have been gained.

The groupings will form a valuable insight into how the process should be mapped and which are the important issues.

Understand the System Capability (Variation and Delivery)

Capability is part of the Vanguard Check Stage. Here we elaborate further. Time and variation are vitally important factors in service. Lead time is very often the major differentiating factor, or the greatest source of dissatisfaction in service delivery. Think of the time taken to book a flight, to repair a car, or wait time to complete an application. But variation in time is also important. How confident are you that the parcel will arrive on time? Variation in wait time causes anxiety.

The ability of the system to meet current demands in time is important. Time-series data need to be collected on the end-to-end system performance. Note that 'end-to-end' should be from the external customer's viewpoint, not the organisation's viewpoint. At least use an external factual measure, not a subjective measure: the time from placing the order to actual receipt, not the time from booking the order into the scheduling system to the promised (or re-promised?) delivery date. The time series should cover at least a month, but the period will need to be discussed, particularly if seasonality is a factor.

- Select an appropriate end-to-end measure from the customer's viewpoint.
- Measure. Note that customer end-to-end times are very likely to cross departmental boundaries and will sometimes cross managerial or organisational boundaries.
- Draw a run diagram, covering a reasonable horizon.
- Establish the control limits for the chart. Use statistical process control software, or software such as MiniTab. If this is not available, calculate the mean and standard deviation and draw the upper control limit as mean plus three standard deviations.
- Examine for variation. See if the process is 'in control'. Are all points between the control limits, or between the upper control limit and 0? If they are, it is a good sign – the process can be improved without bothering about special circumstances. If there are points that plot beyond the control limits, it indicates that there are 'special causes' beyond normal variation. The cause of such situations needs to be identified if possible because they are unusual events that may de-stabilise the process. It is not always easy to go back and identify the reasons for some out-of-control plots, but do discuss them with the service team. Perhaps there are repair jobs that are shelved because an unusual spare part is not available, or the location is hard to get to, or the customer's credit rating is unacceptable. Whatever the reasons, you will need to think if these merit special attention.

See also the separate sections within the Tools section on Variation and Control Charts.

End-to-end delivery response time is often an important differentiator in supply chains and in service processes. Drawing out the run diagram will allow the team to make comparisons with competitors and to identify opportunities. For instance:

- How do healthcare end-to-end response times compare between hospitals?
- How do they compare against patient needs?
- What additional business would be generated by shorter response times?

- How do actual response times match with service level agreements?
- What percentage of completions fall within customer expected delivery times?

Look out for unsatisfactory actual end-to-end response time even though the currently measured response time is satisfactory. A classic example was doctors having an unofficial queue, but adding patients to their official queues only when the wait time was under-target.

If the end-to-end times are unsatisfactory, then one consideration has to be, which part of the end-to-end process should be tackled first? It is a judgment call as to whether system redesign will result in dramatic time reductions to bring the process within acceptable times, or whether the process needs to be 'chunked'. If the process needs to be 'chunked', where is the greatest potential for time saving? The Three Day Car Study showed that typical wait time for medium price cars in 2002 was 40 days, but actual manufacture and delivery times together were three or four days. The opportunity therefore lay in the order entry and scheduling system, not in manufacture.

Next consider CATWOE. A field maintenance service will be used to illustrate the CATWOE systems steps.

C: Clients or customers: There will be customers with and without maintenance agreements. There is also a service level agreement. But what are the customer expectations? Can they do various maintenance checks themselves? Are there urgent calls? Unnecessary calls? At what point should the end-to-end clock start running? How many calls are as a result of customer faults, rather than equipment faults?

Talking to customers reveals that they buy the items primarily for continuity of uptime/reliability.

A: Actors: Customer calls come into a call centre. All work is carried out by field maintenance teams sent from depots. But they use third parties for specialist work. Vehicles are supplied from a pool. Parts are obtained from suppliers. Sometimes there are part shortages – inventory control problems. Parts are ordered from a central system.

T: Transformation:

The high level picture is:

In greater detail:

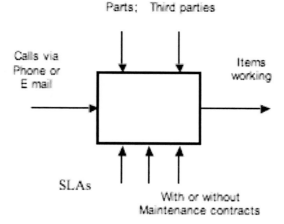

W:Weltanschauung: World view/culture/attitude: performance driven rather than customer problem driven. A little arrogant: 'We are the best'; 'Not much to learn from others'. The wider company is strongly sales-focused. Maintenance is seen as supplementary, not integrated with marketing.

O: Owners: The system is owned by the wider company.

E: Environment: The system boundary defines what is within the system and what is in the environment. This can be a crucial consideration. Is field maintenance seen as being necessary to support sales of the items? Sales and marketing work independently of field maintenance. The owners impose targets.

Step Three: Redefine the System and System Boundary

Now the team is in a better position to redefine the system or process boundary. What is to be included and what excluded is an important consideration. You will usually want a process to be 'end-to-end' – a complete 'cycle of service' – for example, the complete cycle from wanting a car to be serviced to the service being satisfactorily concluded. However, you may want to modify your earlier analysis if you find, for example, that the availability of spare parts is a major source of complaint. In the Custom type service category (see later) the team will want to consider what third parties to involve, if any. In the Interactive category there are sometimes several third parties who can 'spoil the party' – cleaners in a hospital or restaurants at an airport.

Step Four: Draw the High Level Map

This step would have started in Step 2 – check. Now it can be refined. The broad outline map of the process shows only the main steps or players. The purpose is to clarify the system that is being dealt with. The input and output should be shown in generic terms only – for instance, 'Customer Demand'. Show only the main stages and main interactions. This is not the actual mapping exercise, but it will form the framework for broad scale analysis and for detailed mapping. An example is shown for field maintenance.

A Level 1 map should not require the process to be walked or physically mapped. That comes later. The Level 1 map, unlike Level 2, may require some discussion but will be known to almost everyone. Managers should be able to write down the outline. To this outline map will be added the information from the 'Check' stage. This will generally not be known beforehand.

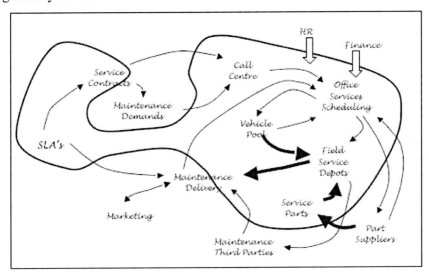

To the map shown above should be added:

- **Value and failure demand information**. In the example it was found that about 40% of calls were failure demand.
- **Rework loops**. In the example about 25% of calls were aborted due to incorrect parts, client not available, incorrect information e.g. model number. These were Pareto-analysed.
- **A run diagram or control chart** showing delivery performance over time. In the example the system was found to be generally 'in control', but end-to-end time was between one day and 25 days. The SLA was 48 hours.
- **Measures**. The various sections each have their own performance targets; call to fix time is not measured.

The high level map is a prime tool for management discussion. Often senior management will not wish to dive into the detail of the subsequent maps to be described, although they will want the broad conclusions from such mapping. The high level map is also a prime tool for concept re-design. Strip away the detail and get to the essence of the system. A high level map will often be drawn several times as more is learned about the current system and about future system possibilities.

Step Five: Examine the Current Measures

Having defined the purpose and the appropriate system boundary, it is important to examine the current measures of performance to see if they support or conflict with the purpose. An example from a call centre supporting a field service operation is shown.

What is not being measured can be as important as what is being measured. Is it end-to-end or overall performance from the customer's standpoint which is being measured?

Be particularly concerned with measures and especially any targets that are likely to drive deviant behaviour. Numerous examples from the British public service are given in the amusing, worrying, but very useful book *The Tiger That Isn't* by Blastland and Dinot, Profile Books, 2007.

Measure	Focus	Support the Purpose?	The Effect
Productivity (calls per hour)	Internal, efficiency based	No	Calls can be dropped or customers given inappropriate attention, resulting in failure demand
MTBF	Reflects the reliability of the machines supported	Yes / partly	Does not drive improvement, but may relate to preventable demand
Number of repeat calls	Attempts to measure the effectiveness of the field service	Maybe…	Games can be played by booking into another job number. May be the customer's fault
Calls waiting	The number of calls in the queue at any time	Partly	The number of abandoned calls is not known

Other Systems Level 1 Maps

Sometimes it is adequate simply to show the main activity groupings and their interactions. An example for a field service operation is shown.

From James Carr, MSc Dissertation, Cardiff Business School, 2007

The Creative Phase in Level 1 Mapping

With the high level map and the available 'check' and systems data – including a succinct statement of purpose – the team should consider whether the existing system is capable of meeting the purpose in the easiest, most simple way. Does the system need to be made more flexible in order to meet the variety of demands?

At this stage you will have a high-level view of the waste in the system, and the opportunities presented. Radical, bold, high-level systems thinking is required – not detail tinkering with the existing process. When you get into the detail during Level 2 analysis, you may find some good reasons why the redesign is not possible – but start out from the ideal, from what could be, and not from the negative 'why it can't be done' viewpoint.

Start out from a 'blank sheet of paper', from the ideal, and work backwards rather than forwards from the detailed current state. Give a vision of what might be.

In the example, why not:

- Allow customers to contact field service deliveries directly?
- Allow field service to fix the actual repair times at the customer site?
- Distribute vehicles among field service depots?
- Give field service direct responsibility for spare parts?

Sketch the ideal state. Discuss it with the system owners.

Now you are ready to get into the detail using Level 2 mapping and redesign.

Having obtained a view of the system, the team may decide to map the whole system at Level 2, or only a part. That is one of the bonus features of the three-level analysis – you only pursue that which is seen to be necessary or effective.

Level 2: Process Maps

The Service Mapping Typology

The range of possible service processes is huge. It is simply unrealistic to believe that there is one type of map that will cope with all service situations. Two common characteristics or axes will be used to distinguish the service mapping types.

Repeatability

This is to do with the repetitiveness of customers or transactions that go through the value stream. Repeatability refers to similarity by stage rather than by individual customer. It is from the organisation's viewpoint, not the customer's viewpoint. While every patient with a broken arm in a hospital may be different, and a patient may only have one broken arm in a lifetime, the stages that they go through in a hospital to get well are broadly similar. This does not necessarily apply end-to-end. A patient may be moved to a hospital in a variety of ways, and as an outpatient may have very different recovery paths, but in the hospital the process steps are very similar. Low repeatability, by contrast, again from the organisation's viewpoint, would occur infrequently: for example a consultant working on the new Wembley stadium.

While the broad stages may have high repeatability, the detail work done may be very dissimilar.

Low repeatability may also mean zero repeatability, or a task that that has never been done before.

Customer Involvement

Customer involvement refers to the frequency with which front line service providers come into contact with customers. By 'Customers' we generally mean external customers. Low intensity service providers may only meet the customer by means of a single briefing or a completed form. High customer contact involves frequent contacts and adjustments. On the whole, 'front office' operations are high intensity and 'back office' are low intensity.

Customer involvement does not refer to the length of the contact but to the frequency. Remember (see separate section) that a high degree of 'failure demand' to sort out a problem that should not have happened in the first place does not constitute high customer involvement.

The Mapping Typology

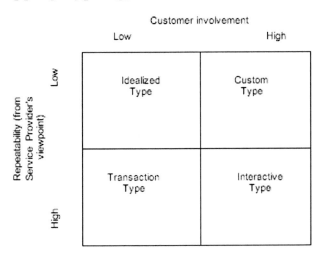

These two axes give a four-cell typology. But the cell boundaries are fuzzy. In fact, both axes are better represented as spectrums.

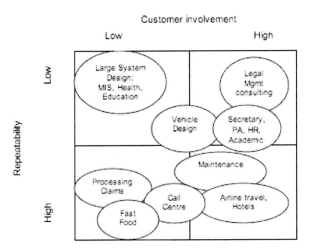

An end-to-end value stream may cover more than one cell.

It is important to remember that in service, as opposed to manufacturing, it is common for an individual to work part of the time in one type of process and part in another. This is because one person may work in more than one value stream. For example, a solicitor may do relatively repetitive work, such as conveyance, for part of the week, and then change to a court case or briefing a QC during another part of the week.

Idealised Type

The Idealised Type typically occurs in large system design situations. A service system is being designed or re-designed. It is normally high-level. There may well be a period of intense briefing with external customers while the project is being sorted out, but thereafter the next contact with external customers is towards the end of the process. For example, a security system, a distribution system, a course curriculum, a transport system, or an information system. Innovation is critical. Takt time has no meaning.

Custom Type

A classic Custom type occurs when an architect or consultant works with a client to solve a problem. The goal may be clear but exactly how to get there is not. Many PA or administrative tasks are of this type. Frequent adjustment is common, as, for example, when a travel agent works through an itinerary with the client. Many examples will be of the project management type, so project management theory and practice will be useful. This type has the following characteristics:

- Excellent understanding of customer need is important.
- There is open-ended scope for customers and work. A consulting engineer may seldom design a similar artefact although similar basic disciplines and tools may be used. A surgeon will have to examine each patient individually before deciding on a course of action.
- Innovation is a differentiator.
- The process can only be specified in broad outline. The framework to allow effective, creative work is the focus.
- Times can be estimated but there is great uncertainty. Takt time has little meaning.

Transactional Type

The Transactional type is the closest to manufacturing – the paper factory, some call centres. There is a low degree of customer contact – maybe none face-to-face, only by telephone, letter or internet. Insurance and banking 'back office' operations are classic areas. Production scheduling is often of this type. Someone in HR may work part-time in a creative value stream, and part-time in a transactional value stream. Takt time may well be meaningful, but needs to be treated with caution where there is a danger of generating poor quality work. In this type, decisions have to be made, but typically only within limited parameters such as Go/NoGo, the amount of money, or by referring to an enquiry system or flowchart.

A dental receptionist taking regular appointments may be of this type because many routine appointments (but not dental surgery) involve approximately the same steps. But visiting a dental surgery would be better mapped using Interactive maps.

Interactive Type

This type has the following characteristics:

- Frequent interactions with customers, often by several 'players' along the value stream. These 'players' may come from several departments or even several organisations.
- The customer builds satisfaction not through just one transaction or 'product' but through the accumulation of experiences or Moments of Truth, sometimes over an extended period.
- Front line delivery by service staff is a differentiator. There is a great deal of difference between an efficient but scowling check-in clerk and one who greets guests by name and with a sincere smile.

The four types of service will be used to position different types of tools for Lean service – particularly value stream mapping variants.

Once again, this is not to suggest that a service employee spends all his or her time in one segment. It is quite possible for an employee to work in two or three segments during a short period. An admin manager may work part of the day helping to set up a conference (Custom type), then do a spell of processing expense claims (Transactional administrative work), then talk with potential new hires (Interactive type).

Likewise, within a value stream the types may change. In a typical major hospital value stream involving an operation, there will certainly be a macro system design phase. Then, when the patient consults the doctor the process may be improved by Custom type mapping. Hospital administration and keeping track of the patient's paperwork may be improved by Transactional mapping. And the pre-op and post-op stages may be improved by Interactive mapping.

Working in Mixed Environments: Runners, Repeaters and Strangers and Time Management

Four service system types have been presented. In practice, many service workers do not work 100% of their time in one environment. This is a major difference between service and factory shop floor operations.

The proportion of time where the work is repeatable will seldom be zero. It may be that a manager's day is seldom the same but nevertheless there are weekly meetings, monthly reviews, and an annual budget cycle. Advantage should be taken of any repetition. In this case see the section on Transactional service management. Regularise where possible. This will be relevant for a small proportion of the time.

Regularity is a good Lean technique. It is line with levelling the work. Do a Runners, Repeaters and Strangers (RRS) analysis on office work. Runner work is done most of the time. Repeater work is done periodically – some (?) daily, some weekly, some monthly, some yearly. Stranger work is fairly unique or unpredictable. This work is primarily creative (which is not to say that work in other segments is not creative).

Splitting your activities into RRS categories is good time management and an effective management style in itself. Steven Covey recommends a 2 x 2 matrix for urgency and importance. It fits well with Lean thinking. Low urgency, low importance work should be avoided if possible. High urgency, high importance work always enjoys priority attention, so does not require much debate. The problem lies with high urgency, low importance work that tends to waste (or at least misapply) huge chunks of potentially good time. Such work must be deliberately managed to reduce waste. Examples are emails, meetings with agenda items of low relevance to some, and bureaucratic administrative procedures. Effective time management begins with recording and classifying. Is this 'mapping' or just good time management?

How to reduce the amount of low importance, high urgency work:

- First, examine the activities in terms of value demand and failure demand. As ever, try to eliminate failure demand activities or, better still, their root causes.
- Second, group the activities and try to do them in blocks of time, regularly but as infrequently as possible.

Use the following Lean Time Management Matrix:

	Runner Activity	Repeater Activity	Stranger Activity
Value Demand Activities	Use Transactional or Interactive principles.	- Use Creative principles. - Set aside time blocks. - Establish work time protocols. - Regularise visits, meetings. - Comms Board - Standard work & procedures	Group and move to time slots. Fit around the Repeater activities.
Failure Demand Activities	Priority elimination	Eliminate	Eliminate root causes.

The Repeater actions are further explained below. Keeping strictly to these procedures, and the associated measures, establishes the 'culture' of the organisation. 'It's the way we do things around here'.

- **Time Blocks**: Creative work requires longer periods of concentration, not broken up into smaller segments with frequent disturbances from email, telephone, people dropping in, and so forth. Research has shown that the human brain needs 'settle down' time for productive work.
- **Work Time Protocols** allow the blocks of time to be established and to work. For example, all may agree that no

emails will be answered in the morning. Except emergencies. Everyone knows this.

- **Standards**: These are the broad standards for Repeater activities. For example, all meetings will be concerned with ONE topic only, minutes will be written in a standard format, A3 sheets will be used for reports and signed off by all concerned, communication boards will be updated daily by specific individuals, a tidy desk policy will be in operation (although no taping up specific locations!), computer files will be organised (broadly) in a standard way, etc.
- **Regularise visits**. Many Lean managers (taking a leaf out of Toyota) have taken the notion of 'Gemba' to heart and decided that regular shop floor or office visits are essential. Do not try to fix appointments between 8 and 11, because that is Gemba time. The CEO of the Eden Project in Cornwall requires all managers to meet and greet 20 others before they start work.
- **Communications Board**: This is the essential tool for communication, problem solving, teamwork, and improvement. The daily or regular meeting is simply not an option. See the separate section on the use of this board. It is one of the three boards essential in a Creative environment.

Brown Paper Mapping Conventions

Brown Paper mapping is a method that can be used in all four categories of the Level 2 map. Some guidelines are presented.

Use a long roll of brown paper, set out along a wall.

Add post-it notes.
Colour-coding the post-it notes is a good idea. For example:
>Yellow: the main activities
>Green: data boxes
>Red: queues of paper or customers waiting
>Light blue: computer system and IT communications.

Add bold red dots to each post-it note to indicate if the activity is VA or NVA (or OVA or ONVA).

Some suggested icons are given on the Icon Sheet, but feel free to add or invent your own.

For some value streams, the person icon can be coloured to indicate similar people or similar team members.

Demand data is particularly important in service, so devote a special Demand Data Box to this topic. Show it at the top left side. The most important demands come from external customers. In the case of a sub-process, the demands may come from an internal source such as the number of expense claims sent in.

The data box should contain:

- a run diagram of typical total entry demand across a day or shift – whether value or failure demand
- an indication of value and failure demand using different colours
- if possible, indications of the upper and lower bounds of demand along the run diagram
- demand categories.

Work Shift Patterns should be shown in a Work Time Data Box on the top right hand side. Sometimes a run diagram (graph) showing numbers at work throughout the day will suffice.

Existing measures of performance should be listed in a bottom left hand side box. Measures are often the source of failure demand and rework.

The resources – principally human resources, but also any critical machines that need to be shared or that break down – should be shown in a box at the bottom right hand side of the sheet. List the names and their working hours if they differ. Note people who work in other value streams, and estimate how much time is available to the current value stream. Consider whether it is worthwhile writing down a critical skills matrix.

Consider early on whether you are going to use 'swim lanes'. The swim lanes idea is that each department or organisation has its own lane in which its activities are drawn. This can certainly emphasise handoffs and rework loops, but it may be better to use a separate Handoff Map (see separate section). Often it is not warranted. Sometimes lanes are reserved for other characteristics such as standards or quality – these can be added later.

Be particularly concerned with 'dirty data', the effect of which will escalate as it moves through a process. As a result, the elimination of 'dirty data' upstream is highly cost-effective. There are different types of data problems: data entry errors (caused by customer or employee), missing data, erroneous data, and clarity errors. Some of these overlap. Aim to eliminate or reduce these problems as close to the source as possible, because all subsequent stages may be affected. Start at the upstream end and estimate the extent of errors by sampling. If sampling is impractical (perhaps because the true state is not known), ask how much time is spent on correcting upstream errors or omissions. The data error rate should be written on the map. A most effective way of addressing such 'dirty data' is by 'failsafing' (or pokayoke) methods. See the later section on this.

Link the activities with lines drawn with flip chart pens.

Where there are decisions or branches, use a diamond.

Add appropriate actual documents along the bottom of the brown paper map.

If the level of activity is high enough, and it generally should be, the layout of a Brown Paper map could reflect the actual physical layout.

Service Mapping Symbols

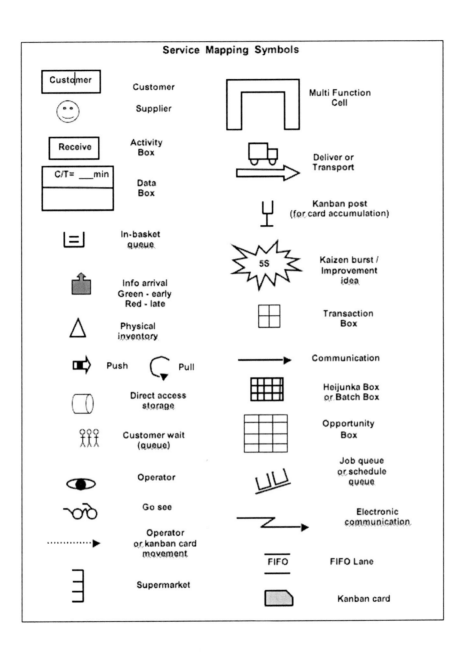

Customer / Supplier

Activity Box

Data Box

In-basket queue

Info arrival
Green - early
Red - late

Physical inventory

Push   Pull

Direct access storage

Customer wait (queue)

Operator

Go see

Operator or kanban card movement

Supermarket

Multi Function Cell

Deliver or Transport

Kanban post (for card accumulation)

Kaizen burst / Improvement idea

Transaction Box

Communication

Heijunka Box or Batch Box

Opportunity Box

Job queue or schedule queue

Electronic communication

FIFO Lane

Kanban card

Level 2: Transactional Mapping
(Low Customer Involvement; High Repeatability)

Typical situations:

- Repetitive office tasks in general
- Order processing
- Warehouse operations
- Some maintenance and repair tasks

General observations

This type of mapping is most like the 'Learning to See' (Rother and Shook) manufacturing mapping. It may also be known as MIFA (material and information flow analysis) mapping. Differences with standard 'Learning to See' maps include:

- Variety of tasks is often greater – tasks are more dissimilar than in typical manufacturing.
- Activity times are much more variable. Some are uncertain, as in maintenance.
- There are almost always more rework loops than in manufacturing – not because of worker incompetence but at the root, because of system design.
- Routings may vary to a greater extent than in manufacturing. This means that resource loadings are less predictable. A route may visit one person several times.
- Activities are more often by people rather than by machines, so capacity analysis needs special calculation – sometimes involving queuing theory considerations.
- Tasks may change volume much more frequently than in typical manufacturing. Volumes are quite likely to change during the course of a day.
- The supplier and customer may be the same person.
- Decision points or branching often need to be included.
- And, as is often the case in service, some work cannot be inventoried – at least not for long – although of course paper and customer queues are common.
- In short, have you ever seen an administrative process like 'Acme Stamping'? I haven't! Come to think of it – there aren't too many factories like Acme either!

This section discusses short cycle Transactional service, with activity times of, say, less than one hour. Longer activity times have some features in common with Custom environments and the reader's attention is drawn to that section.

Drawing the Current State Map

Two examples of a Current State map are shown – one for an administrative process and another for a maintenance process.

These illustrations are the formal maps that are redrawn after actual mapping to document the current state. During the mapping exercise, the map is made by the team using post-its assembled on a large sheet of brown paper. See the box on Brown Paper Mapping.

An Administrative Process

Features of note:

- The Customer Icons appear at the top of the page, one for each customer type or source of demand.
- The variation is given so that queue lengths and utilisation can be estimated – see the sections on variation and queuing in the Tools section.
- Often, transactional system activities are not worked on all day. There may be meetings or other streams to be worked on. So discuss and estimate how much time is taken up by this task each day or each week. Often the workload will not be uniform across the month. In this case, note the peak and average demand rate.
- Activity boxes run along the centre of the map.
- Data boxes appear below activities, including:

  - Number of people per stage
  - Unit processing time or rate per stage (minimum, maximum and typical)
  - Batching information
  - Error data. An estimate of the percentage of errors made. This is particularly important in earlier stages. You may also like to estimate the input error rate and the output error rate. That is, what percentage of (say) documents contains errors when the step is started, and what the percentage is after the step. The input error rate will accumulate as the document moves downstream, unless it is corrected.

- Failure Demand is indicated.
- In this case the actual number of customers calling in is unknown because the interactive voice response system (IVR) does not accept more than ten customers waiting at any time. The management measures of waiting time are an illusion.
- Tagging. To obtain activity and queue times it may be possible (if times are not excessive) to obtain estimates by 'tagging' either a sample of customers or a sample of documents. A customer may be physically tagged or monitored in the case of a walk-in process, or electronically tagged where an IT system is used. Where documents are flowing though the process, the tag can be a stapled note requesting each stage to fill in arrival and departure times of the document. Of course, it is not necessary to follow a customer or a document from end to end. Part flows can be monitored simultaneously and then collected up.
- At the entry point have a data box in which is written a note on the extent of 'dirty data' entering the process. 'Dirty data' may or may not result in rework.
- Queue symbols (either in basket or customer queue symbol) are shown between activity boxes. Minimum, maximum and typical queues are shown. In practice these times will often have to be estimated or obtained by questioning staff.
- Rework loops. Show these looping back to the appropriate stage. Show the range of rework activity loops – the minimum and maximum number of times a document or customer goes around the loop. These are very important.
- Decision diamonds are shown.
- Time line. Along the bottom of the map is the time line, using the standard Lean convention showing both total time and 'value add' or activity times. In most offices there are three types of time to consider. It is useful to estimate all three:

  - **The Process Time**: this is the actual work time at each stage.
  - **The Stage Time**: this may be the same time as the process time where there is one-piece flow, but this is unusual. It is more likely to be the time for a batch to go through a process – including queue time during the batch and sorting or collating time. Often a batch is worked on for a period of time, then there is a gap when other work is done or meetings take place.
  - **The Inter-Stage Time**: this is the time between stages that may include transport, postage, or, most

commonly, accumulation time, where for instance a batch is worked on once per day.

- **Total Time** is the sum of the average times. **Activity Time** is the sum of the activity times. Adding these up, using the typical times, will give an indication of the cumulative lead time – but only for right first time customers. It is very important to include an estimate of the time variation – minimum, most likely, and (say) 95% completion time. (Not 100% or maximum because there may be special causes.)
- **Shared resources**: whether these are people or machines, they need to be specially identified because they are barriers to flow. Shared resources need to be scheduled or prioritised, and hence smooth flow will not always be possible.

Loops as sub-systems

This step divides the value steam into sub-systems or loops. It will frequently take place after the Current State has been mapped, but for complex value streams it may be considered up front.

In the example, there may be two loops – before and after order picking.

In mapping terms, the sub-systems can be shown as 'loops'. Within each loop, a set of resources aims to achieve a particular purpose. They are a logical set. Loops or sub-systems can be used to break down a complete value stream. It is, however, important to note that constructing the end-to-end value stream is not the same as 'optimising' each sub-system. The parts must remain subservient to the whole. Loops may be focus for kaizen events if the complete value stream is too large to tackle. Loops may used to sequence the transformation to the future state.

Loops or sub-systems may also be a way of breaking down the mapping project itself. One sub-team to a loop.

The classic Lean way is to start downstream and work backwards. In a manufacturing-oriented process this makes sense because the customer is downstream. The single 'pacemaker' (see later) is usually well downstream, allowing upstream steps to be pulled. In a customer-intensive value stream, this is not the case. Prioritising the loops should be related to the impact on value or satisfaction.

Wastes and System Conditions

From the current state maps it is useful to draw up a table of the effects of the current system showing the 'System Conditions' which cause the waste or effect. A partial call centre example is shown. The analysis team should work through the table before attempting to draw a Future State.

Waste / Effect	System Conditions	Caused by
Cheating on targets and measures. Management is deluded.	Manager measures	Inappropriate measures and targets
Hanging up on callers; customer dissatisfaction	Monitoring of call lengths	Targets
Excessive customer wait time	Waiting queue not measured; system does not allow more than 10. Management deluded; customers dissatisfied	Technology of the call monitoring system
Duplication	Dual data entry; customer annoyance	System design
Handoffs	Departmentalisation, skill shortages	Capacity issues
Customer required to give policy number. Delay, annoyance	IT system record entry point	IT system design

Analysing the Map and Creating the Future State

The aim of the Future State exercise is
- to get work flowing more steadily, more quickly, more predictably, and more accurately. Note the word FLOW.
- to achieve the system purpose.

Achieving Flow

Flow is destroyed by interruptions. Interruptions are caused by rework, by lack of good data (or 'dirty data'), by batch and queue, by waiting for other data, and by lack of continuity of work caused in turn by breakdowns of equipment or stoppage of work due to telephone calls, emails, meetings and briefings. These fall into two categories: external to the process (meetings, socialising etc.), and internal to the process (rework, batch and queue etc.).

There are questions to ask on flow. These questions can be tackled in a kaizen event (or improvement event) over a few days. Kaizen events are not the subject of this book, but note that successful events require considerable preparation before the event, and a regular period of follow-up. Please refer to the references on kaizen including my *Lean Toolbox*.

- If you were designing the process from scratch, how would you do it to make achievement of purpose as quick and as hassle-free as possible?
- What are the causes of failure demand and rework loops? What would it take to eliminate these?
- Do the measures lead to unaligned behaviour? In other words, do the ways in which people try to meet their measures conflict with the purpose of the system? Example: monitoring call centre productivity may generate failure demand.
- Does each packet of information travel ahead of the work, or can it be made to travel ahead so that activities are adequately prepared and failure demand or rework is reduced? For example, is there a way in which a maintenance man can know what to expect before he gets there, so that he can bring the appropriate tools and spares?
- What is the best way to organise the work? In terms of Runners, Repeaters and Strangers? Can work be better grouped or blocked each day so that Runners can be done in a block (say) every two hours, Repeaters be done on regular days, and Stranger activities be arranged so they cause the least disruption?
- Where can work be flowed, one piece at a time?
- Is a work cell possible? In offices, as opposed to factories, cells are often difficult across processes that have more than one manager, and may even be difficult within an office because of people's reluctance to share their workspace. But the advantages can be huge for lead time reduction and for quality. Some incentive may have to be given, or the advantages demonstrated through simulation. If a 'full-blown' cell is not possible, think of various 'half-way houses', such as rearranging desks, taking down barriers, and improving visibility.

- If physical cells are not possible, consider workflow technology. But beware – do not automate waste.
- Can you have a one-stop process?
- Does all work have to travel along the same path? Is a fast track possible? For example, in mortgage applications do 'blue chip' customers have to go through the same route? Are all jobs of equal complexity?
- If not, can more simple jobs be dealt with by less experienced staff?
- Can you untangle the 'spaghetti' – either physical or informational?

Once the system conditions have been identified, the new design can proceed. Everyone needs to understand that the prime task is to do the work – including whatever it takes to eliminate repeat (failure) demands. The second task is to improve the system. There are no other tasks. In other words, a virtuous cycle needs to be established – eliminating failure reduces waste and frees up capacity, thereby enabling more failure categories to be systematically addressed. Start with the top ten categories and work down. Demands that are received but do not fall within the top ten need to be dealt with by a more experienced worker or manager. By definition, such demands will constitute a very small proportion of the total cases.

Don't have inappropriate measures (and especially targets) that stand in the way of doing this. Liberate the workforce to solve the customer's problems. This is a liberating experience.

A Maintenance Process (or 'Break Fix' Process)

Points of Note on the Future State Map:

- Note that the maps both have an associated layout diagram. This is very common in Transactional mapping. Refer to the section on layout and cell design in the Tools section.
- To develop the future state map, the participation of people from the area is required.
- The future state map must be consistent with the overall system concept developed in Level 1.
- Maps should also have time line performance data.
- In the current state, customer queuing was unknown. In the future state, queues are specifically monitored.

- Capacity is adjustable. If the queue length goes above a certain length – four in this case – an operator moves from Cell 2 to Cell 1. This may necessitate a physical move because of equipment.
- Cross training will be required.
- Failure demand has fallen because most issues are sorted out at the front end. This front-end-loading is good practice in many transactional situations.
- Push icons have been replaced by FIFO lanes. A push system is not necessarily first-in first-out, but a FIFO lane is. A FIFO lane should have a designated maximum length that would trigger a warning (light?) to indicate a non-normal situation.
- Kaizen bursts show necessary changes. An Action Plan for implementation must be developed from the map.
- The detail of the actual procedures for taking credit cards, what to do if stock is not available, the compilation of the pick schedule, etc., is detailed in Level 3 mapping. Such detail is not appropriate here, where the broad process is being established.
- There is a need to put in place an end-to-end measure. At least this is now possible.

Further questioning of Transactional Maps

The aim is to reduce time and waste. It is essentially a creative process. Preferably the people involved in the process should be used in its analysis and improvement. Bold thinking is a requirement, not piecemeal adjustment. The title of a classic 1993 article by Michael Hammer in *Harvard Business Review* gives the clue: 'Reengineering work: don't automate, obliterate!' That is the type of thinking that is required. The same *Harvard Business Review* article tells of how Ford used to have 400 accounts payable clerks compared with just seven people at Mazda. Although Business Process Reengineering has become somewhat discredited since the mid 1990s, due to its association with job cuts, don't throw out the baby with the bathwater. Many valuable insights remain.

The basic step is to examine the process chart and to split the activities into those which add immediate value for the customer and those which don't. Refer to the Seven Wastes for guidance. The concept is to achieve the added value benefit for the customer as soon as possible. Therefore try to make every value-adding step continuous with the last value adding step, without interruptions for waiting, queuing, or for procedures which may assist the company but do nothing for the customer. George Stalk of Boston Consulting Group refers to customer value sequence as the 'main sequence'.

Questions concerning the sequence of activities include the following. Note however, that these questions are really prompts for the team doing the work, not for the system designers working on high from remote process maps.

- Can the non-value adding steps be eliminated, simplified, or reduced?
- Can extra work be done early to prevent delay later on in the process?
- Can any activity that delays a value adding activity be simplified or rescheduled?
- Are there any activities, particularly non-value adding activities, which can be done in parallel with the sequence of value adding activities?
- Can activities that have to be passed from department to department (and back!) be reorganised into a team activity? Better still, can one person do it? What training and backup would be required?
- Where are the bottlenecks? Can the capacity of the bottleneck be expanded? Do bottleneck operations keep working, or are they delayed for minor reasons? To quote Eli Goldratt, 'An hour lost at a bottleneck is an hour lost for the whole system', and 'An hour lost at a non-bottleneck is merely a mirage'. Are bottleneck operations delayed by non-bottleneck operations, whether value adding or not?
- What preparations can be made before the main sequence of value adding steps is initiated to avoid delays? For example preparing the paperwork, getting machines ready.
- Can the necessary customer variety or requirements be added at a later stage? For example doing the basic 'vanilla' service but adding the 'flake chocolate' as late as possible.
- If jobs are done in batches, can the batches be split to move on to a second activity before the whole batch is complete at the first activity?
- Can staff flexibility be improved to allow several tasks to be done by one person, thus cutting handing-on delays?
- What is the decision-making arrangement? Can decision-making power be devolved to the point of use? Can the routine decisions be recognised so that they can be dealt with on the spot? Perhaps 'expert systems' can be used.

- Where is the best place, from a time point of view, to carry out each activity? Can the activity be carried out at the point of use or contact, or must it really be referred elsewhere?
- Do customers enjoy a 'one stop' process? If not, why not?
- If problems do develop, what will be the delays and how can these delays be minimised?
- What availability of information will make the value adding sequence smoother or more continuous? Is there more than one source of information, and if so can this be brought to one place? A common database perhaps? The long established MIS principle is to capture information only once, and let everyone use the same data.
- As a second priority, can the time taken for value adding activities be reduced?

Yet more useful thoughts from process reengineering come from the originator, Michael Hammer, who identified the essential characteristics of BPR as follows:

- Several jobs are combined into one: 'Is it essential to have a qualified accountant do that?' 'Does it really have to go to another person?'
- Workers make decisions: 'Why does that decision have to be referred to the boss?'
- The steps in the process are performed in a natural order: can process steps be overlapped? Is that non-customer benefiting task necessary?
- Processes have multiple versions: one simple route for the routine many, another for the complex few, rather than all going the same way.
- Work is performed where it makes most sense: on the spot if possible, rather than referring it back to a specialist.
- Checks and controls are reduced: inspect and fix defects immediately, cut out the waste of unnecessary checks.
- Reconciliation is minimised: build supplier partnerships with trust; a case manager provides a single point of contact; customers don't get shunted around.
- Hybrid centralised/decentralised operations are prevalent: make use of common information systems, but decentralise decision-making authority.

Managing Critical Resources

In the Transactional area, when creating the Lean operating system, there will frequently be resource-balancing issues with critical resources. Please refer to the section 'Managing Critical Resources' under the Custom Environment section.

See also the possible use of Cells and one-piece Flow in the Tools section.

Takt Time

Of the four service types used in this book, the manufacturing concept of takt time is most (only?) applicable in the Transactional segment. Even then it must be treated with caution lest it lead to unexpected behaviour. On the other hand, takt time can be very useful when applied in the right application with the right attitude. What is takt time? It is the time available for work divided by the amount of work in that period. So, it is expressed in time units, typically minutes in service, and is the customer-driven drumbeat rate of work – one every so many minutes. Work units may be orders that are picked, files or cases processed, maintenance tasks undertaken, calls received or made, or possibly even lines of code written. Of course, most of these will be highly variable and therefore caution is appropriate. Particularly in service, takt time must never be a 'stick' for productivity. Rather it must be seen as a tool to aid planning and to highlight issues.

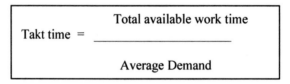

Note that it is available time in the formula, not the total time. Available time comes after deducting time for breaks – formal and informal – and for morning meetings, routine tasks such as clean up (5S?), and the like. Perhaps also short interruptions, for example answering the phone as a routine part of the day.

Very often in Transactional service it is appropriate to have more than one takt time during a day, so takt time can be segmented. In other words you can have (say) three takt times during the day – low takt during the first few hours to cope with the morning peak, midday takt to cope with lunch time demands, and high takt time in the afternoon.

Why may takt time be useful in Transactional service?

- As a way of calculating the required resources
- As a way of monitoring work with a view to improvement. But be careful, takt can be a disaster in service if it is used to monitor and control.

Takt time can be used to determine the necessary resources via the formula:

$$\text{Required people} = \frac{\text{Sum of activity times}}{0.8 \text{ of Takt time}}$$

So as takt time decreases, the number of resources required increases. And why the 0.8? First, 0.8 is an estimate, but it is there to allow for variability – this is further explained in the Tools section.

In service there is usually much higher variability than in manufacturing situations. Hence it is appropriate to use a lower percentage of the takt time when calculating the required resources. Calculating the number of people and improving the flow in a short cycle Transactional environment are often done using Yamazumi (or Work Balance) Board concepts. This is explained in more detail in the Tools section.

Standard Work

Like takt time, standard work in Transactional systems is often useful but needs to be treated with caution. In service, over-standardisation can lead to poor service, but under-standardisation can be equally problematical. Getting the right level of detail in standard work is a real skill. Do not try to standardise every task. And even tasks that have SOPs should only have standards relating to the vital few critical steps. Office people generally don't like working in a highly specified office factory where almost every keystroke is specified and every location is specified – 'over the top 5S'. Nor is this necessary. The big gains are often, as usual, in system or process design: for example, screen presentation and sequencing, avoidance of duplication, office layout, and form design.

Don't forget to go back to purpose and customer. Are those forms, copies, reports what the customer actually wants?

Standard work applies in other category types. See the separate section on this important topic.

A less intimidating, more participative type of standard work is the TPA idea of 'best of the best'. Thus if six office workers are doing the same job, ask them to compare their methods. One may be better at one activity, another at another activity. Ask them to share best practice. This may involve detailed observation or timing. This level of detail is Level 3.

List of Related Tools

- Total Productive Administration/OPE
- 5S
- Spaghetti and Layout Diagrams
- Activity sampling
- Cell design
- Muda Muri Equations
- Capacity
- Variation
- Quality tools
- Queuing
- TOC/DBR
- CONWIP
- Kanban
- Servicescape
- Measures
- TRIZ – free perfect now
- Service level inventory

Level 2: Interactive Mapping
(High Customer involvement, High Repeatability)

Typical situations

- in general, a customer 'cycle of service', or an end-to-end journey by a customer through a service provider
- visit to a restaurant
- airline check in and subsequent flight
- hospital visit or dental surgery visit
- car servicing
- university registration

Drawing the Current State Map

The current state map here builds on the 'Service Blueprint' originally developed by Shostack in the 1980s. It uses the 'swimlane' approach to show the role played by various parties in the service delivery process. The method developed here is a considerable expansion on earlier versions. See for example, Womack and Jones, 2005, and Zeithaml, Bitner and Gremler, 2006.

The central stream of an Interactive map is the 'cycle of service' – concentrating on the experiences of customers as they move through the process. This is an important distinction from 'Learning to See' value stream type maps where the customer is shown only at the beginning and end. Here it is all the customer's experiences, or Moments of Truth, that accumulate into the overall degree of satisfaction. A Moment of Truth is an occasion where a customer comes into contact with a service deliverer (person or object) and experiences a good, neutral or bad reaction. The Moment of Truth concept was originally proposed by Richard Norman of Harvard Business School, but it was made famous by Jan Carlsson of Scandanavian Airlines in his book and in his airline management.

Takt time has limited or no use in this type of map.

The Interactive map is used principally to enhance the experience of the customer. It is value adding. Of course it can be used to identify waste, but the prime purpose is to redesign the system for improved customer flow. If customer flow is achieved, waste in the form of failure demand, delays and defects will be reduced.

One question about Interactive maps – what customers do you select? No problem if there is only one customer type. But type depends on customer need. So an interactive map for a library visit, for example, may have to consider book users, web users, quiet readers, and audio-visual users. This is a judgment call. Consider the following:

- Group customer needs into a generic visit. All customers will not visit all stages, but the lessons to be learned from mapping will be retained.
- Decide on the dominant customer types. Map this as the main stream. Then add supplementary portions of other supporting maps. For example, most customers come in for routine car servicing, but some have special needs – minor or major repairs. These two can be added as supplementary maps.

Structure of the Interactive Map

The basic map has six horizontal swim lanes. From top to bottom they are typically:

- **The Tangibles**: This is the physical environment. Along this lane notes are written (or digital pictures are added) of signs, web screen appearance, physical layout and appearance. This is known as the 'Servicescape', a phrase used by Zeithaml and Bitner – see Layout in the Tools section. Tangibles have the effect of what Berry and Benapudi refer to as 'evidence-based management', so that customers 'clue in' to signals by things and people. Make sure that your facilities provide evidence of the story you want to portray.
- **Customer Moments of Truth**: This is the most important lane, following the customer's journey and experiences.
- **Communication Line**: This line is used to separate the customer from the organisation, but it is also used for communication links. Symbols, such as phones, will often appear.
- **Organisation or Service Provider Lane**: This shows the sequence of actions taken by the organisation to respond to customer requirements.
- **IT Lane**: This lane is reserved for activities and interactions with the IT system. Information should ideally travel ahead of the customer.

- **Measures**: Along this lane, note any measures that are used, for example call wait time.
- The boxes with four squares serve as checks for the Service Transaction Box elements (arrive, wait, serve, depart). See the Tools section for details.
- The twelve-box symbol at the bottom right is a reminder to look through the Opportunity Box. See the Tools section for detail.

See the example.

Steps in Mapping

- If possible start at the pre-map stage, and end at the follow-up stage. See note on 'The Wider System' below.
- Determine the entry arrival rate of customers. Often, draw a graph of arrival rate, customers per minute for example, against time. This is critical for good customer service analysis.
- It will often not be possible to follow the customer through a value stream as you might follow a product through a value stream, because the customer may not be physically present for some of the stages or because there are long gaps of inactivity on the part of the customer – as in car service or a hospital visit. But a typical customer's interactions can be followed.
- Some customer actions cannot be observed, but a simulated trial can be made. For example, ask someone to log into the website as a 'pseudo-customer' and look for the product or service. Or make an emergency call, or look up the company in the Yellow Pages. Get the pseudo-customer to go through the full process.
- Where possible, follow and observe actual customer experiences.
- Capture the broad activities, not the detail. 'Book the order', not 'Enter name and address'.
- Where activities follow in a sequence with little interruption, write these one below the other.
- Start a new column of activity where activities are separated by delays or queues.
- The sequence of activity may jump from customer to service provider and back. There may also be parallel paths, for example where a customer is enjoying a coffee or shopping at an airport while the aircraft is being loaded.
- Show the queues or delays by means of a suitable icon – in-basket, queue of people.
- Estimate or observe the activity times. Maximum, minimum and normal. It is particularly important to try to obtain service times because this will have a direct impact on queue time. See the separate section on Queuing.
- Where there are queues, note the queue 'discipline'. That is:

  - Single queue, multiple queues or multiple single queues
  - FIFO, or priority customers
  - If queuing takes place on the phone, note the type of messages that are given out.
  - Sometimes queues are joined by other customers from other streams – such as for airport security or for a hospital operating theatre. Here, note the queue size and

question the staff about maximum and minimum queues and delays.

- Note the number of resources employed by the service provider at each stage. Also note which department or organisation they belong to.
- If there is physical inventory, such as spare parts as opposed to electronic files or human queues, show these as inventory triangles. The existence of physical inventory that is inherent to the process, not peripheral to it, means that a whole raft of Lean related concepts may be possible. Integral inventory would be spares in a maintenance system, peripheral inventory would be paper or other consumables in an ordinary office. Integral inventory can make use of Lean concepts such as kanban, supermarkets, runner systems, partnership purchasing and vendor managed inventory. Peripheral inventory is often best managed by visual management methods, 5S, and re-order point methods. These are briefly discussed in separate sections.
- Note whether customers are treated in batches or one at a time.
- Finally, indicate the Customer Critical Path. This is the sequence of activities that a customer will have to wait for in order to complete the service end-to-end. Normally the path will start with the customer, go to the organisation, may well return to the customer and to the organisation a few times, and finally end with the customer.
- Show failure demand rework loops in another colour. Don't forget these – most Interactive value streams have failure demand.
- Add 'process owner loops'. This is often a better alternative to adding more swim lanes for each of the departments involved. Process owner loops can be drawn on transparent plastic to cover the map. Simply draw bold lines of different colours to surround activities in similar departments.

The Wider System

Sandra Vandermerwe suggests that the 'customer activity cycle' has three phases – pre, during, and post. While mapping is usually concerned with the 'during' phase, Vandermerwe suggests that a great deal of value adding opportunity exists by looking at the other two phases – closing the big loop.

The pre phase is before the experience begins, 'when the customer is deciding what to do to get the result'. In this phase there are opportunities to issue advice (on a mortgage loan), to collect information (about a forthcoming car service), to pre-book a slot (in a hospital), to give guidance (on a forthcoming holiday), to warn of delays (en route or when the customer arrives), to issue pre-reading for a course, and so on. Some of these may be revenue-earning activities, perhaps with partner organisations, others may attract or lock in customers. The pre phase should be seen as a major opportunity for creating customer delight, immediately or later. The customer path can be smoothed and delays avoided.

The post phase is after the experience, 'when the customer is maintaining the result or keeping it going – receiving, extending, upgrading and updating'. In this phase there are also opportunities to solicit feedback, to follow up on repeat purchases, to impress customers with excellent service if things go wrong (such as a Lexus recall that not only explained the need in detail but also gave gifts and checked over the vehicle), to join a 'fan club' or alumni group to maintain networking, to provide an upgrade or newer model on good terms, and so on. Again, some may be direct revenue-earning, others may attract future business, yet others may simply build reputation.

Analysing the Map

Several tools or concepts are available:

- The Kano model
- Standards
- Mistake Proofing (Pokayoke)
- Service Transaction Box if relevant
- Information Travel
- Value and Failure Demand
- Layout and Cells

Each one is described in a separate section. However, it is important that each concept is considered step by step, and not applied to the map as a whole. A systematic approach is key.

An illustration is shown for the first four steps

MoT	Kano Basics	Kano Perform	Kano Delighter	Standards	Fail Safe?	Trans-action Box ?
Park	Available	Suffic-ient space?	Designated parking	Car Size; spaces/ delegate ratio		Maybe
Register	Name tags available; signs; in attendance	Friendly; wait time	Online pre-registration	Max wait time	Photo? Sign in?	Yes
Get notes	Available	Quality & read-ability	Colour; extra documenta tion	Slides per page, font		No
Refresh-ment	Tea & coffee avail; water on tables	All day? Variety? Fresh? Sweets?	Danish pastries; fruit	On time at specific times	Signal if empty; checks	No

General points to consider:

- Always consider the purpose of the overall process. What is it there to do? And how can it be done more simply, with less customer hassle, and less error? The process must be consistent with the Level 1 analysis.
- How can information flow around the process? Does it travel with the object or customer or ahead or behind? If information does not travel ahead there are likely to be delays and problems when service providers discover that something is missing. Like a customer forgetting to bring in his passport. Like discovering that the repair cannot be done because a part is not available. Like finding a customer not at home when the delivery calls. So how can information be made to flow ahead? Can more relevant information be collected and transferred before the customer physically arrives?
- Do customers or information travel in batches? Is one at a time feasible?
- Is one-stop possible?
- Are parallel operations possible?
- Can expertise be put on the front line to reduce or eliminate failure demand? Failure demand is a John Seddon idea, explained in *Freedom from Command and Control*. This concept is further illustrated by the case study of the Portuguese

car dealer Simao, carried out by Cardiff Business School and explained in Womack and Jones' *Lean Solutions*. Here all necessary information is extracted from the customer before he arrives for his car service, thus ensuring a hassle-free non-repeat visit with all spares available. Queue time is minimised. This is also an illustration of information flowing ahead of the customer.

List of Related Tools

- Opportunity Box
- Service Transaction Box
- Cycle of Service
- Kano model
- Standards
- Failsafe/Pokayoke
- Layout and visual management

Further Reading

Valerie Zeithaml, Mary Jo Bitner and Dwayne Gremler, *Services Marketing*, 4th edition, McGraw Hill, 2006. Chapter 9 covers service blueprints.
Lynn Shostack, 'Designing Services that Deliver', *Harvard Business Review*, Jan/Feb 1984
Leonard Berry and Neeli Bendapudi, 'Clueing in Customers', *Harvard Business Review*, February 2003
Sandra Vandermerwe, *The Eleventh Commandment*, Wiley, 1996, Chapter 13
James Womack and Daniel Jones, *Lean Solutions*, Simon and Schuster, 2005, Chapter 4
John Bicheno, M R Gopalan, V S Mahesh, 'Extending the Effectiveness of Service Mapping', *Management Review*, Indian Institute of Management Bangalore, Vol 11, No 1, March 1999
John Bicheno, *The New Lean Toolbox*, PICSIE, 2004, and John Bicheno and Matthias Holweg, *The Lean Toolbox 4th Edition*, due for publication in 2008
Anthony Laraia, Patrica Moody and Robert Hall, *The Kaizen Blitz*, Wiley, 1999

Level 2: Custom Process Mapping
High Customer involvement, Low Repeatability

Typical situations

Custom environments include engineering and architectural design, advertising, media, computer programming and systems analysis. Project management activities.

Many office functions are of this type. They deal with an endless stream of mainly small projects, and some larger ones. A proportion of the jobs has some repeatability, and frequently involves high customer interaction – with both internal and external customers. Administrative secretaries, HR practitioners, professors, consultants, trainers are examples.

Takt time has little or no meaning. This is a high variety process and, as Seddon has said, the system must be designed to absorb variety. Therefore, standard work in the detail sense also has low applicability. Not so in the wider sense, however.

Mapping in Custom Environments

Academics to zoologists, with consultants, engineers, and solicitors in between, may think their work fits exclusively in this category. Most times, they would be wrong. Please read the sections on Runners, Repeaters and Strangers and on Level 1 Service Mapping, if you have not already done so. They are highly relevant to this type of process. The classic 'Learning to See' mapping tool is seldom appropriate in Custom environments such as illustration design, senior management, universities, creative arts, and cooking, but before rejecting mapping as an inappropriate tool in this type of environment, be aware that many creative environments have repetitive elements that can be mapped using conventional mapping tools, combined with what follows. Examples are engineering design, administration, management consulting, medical services, insurance claim visits, research in a laboratory, many hotel tasks, and many marketing activities.

Custom Environment Mapping is not 'mapping' as such. Rather it is establishing a supporting organisation, environment and principles that will allow the process to flow with low waste and low lead time.

In this type of environment, if good work has been done at the macro level mapping and analysis stage, the system will be well understood and what remains is detailed management and procedures.

Some general guidelines for Custom Environments:

Generally, three parallel displays (rather than 'maps') are required – one dealing with the **overall process** in broad terms, another with **resource analysis**, or how the creative resources (people) allocate their time, and the third a **'Communications Board'** to keep track of progress. These three make up an excellent interactive set.

The Overall Process Board: A diagram or map of the main process or project stages should be on display. This may be:

- The stages or gates in a new product introduction process
- The project stages in a civil engineering or architectural design project
- The stages in a consulting project

(All of these may be linked in with standard project management software.)

- The stages in a legal process
- The month-end financial reconciliation and reporting cycle
- A physician consulting patients with health concerns
- The annual policy deployment process

(These last four may also be regarded as Transactional. It is a judgment call.)

These are not maps in the analysis sense as used in other sections, but a display or precedence diagram of the main process steps.

A professional service organisation or function may have several parallel processes going at the same time, or they may be done as and when the need arises. Projects may vary considerably in scope or duration but may all still follow the same broad steps. For example, management consulting or market survey.

In all these cases it is usually only necessary to have one overall process map per type on display. Display the generic process to aid understanding.

For a large project, for example design engineering, where the project is the main or only focus of activity during an extended period, the actual precedence network may be shown.

Establish the main stages of the process. This will involve a high-level block diagram rather than detailed stages. The diagram should show key interdependencies – where a resource needs to wait for completion by another resource.

Please note that the Stages/Gates are not supposed to mean that a 'stage-gate' approach should be used in all cases. Stage/Gate represented a great advance over traditional new product development when it was introduced some twenty years ago. This approach uses formal gates through which the product or project must pass or be aborted. Gates may be set up, for instance, for technical, market, and financial viability. The approach was consistent with 'concurrent' engineering where several functions worked simultaneously on the project and came together at the gates. It may be suitable for larger projects, but it is certainly 'over the top' for many office and administrative Custom processes. Even in some new product development, the stage-gate approach is being superseded by the Toyota style 'Set-Based' approach. See later.

Draw in swim lanes to represent the different departments or sections which participate in the process. In these cases, the diagram will be similar to the Four Fields Map described in Level 3 – except that the level of detail will be far broader.

- Together with representatives of the various 'players', draw out the block diagram or precedence diagram. This is standard practice in many engineering projects.

- An important point is that the Overall Process Board should not be regarded as a one-off exercise to establish the stages. It should be regarded as a 'working board' on which ideas are posted and comments made. Checklists should be accumulated and built on in every Custom process, so the Overall Process Board should facilitate this process by having a column where 'Lessons Learned' can be added. It is expected that lessons learned will be added regularly. If they are not being added, this is an indication that management of this type of process is lagging.

Overall Process Board

Resource Analysis Board

Communications Board

Resource Analysis: These boards (typically whiteboards) are concerned with resource allocation – how key resources (people or teams) are spending their time. The idea of the board is to load level and flow the work. In that respect it is a form of Heijunka. The group manager will use the board for overall management, not chasing. He will be concerned with releasing work, moving some projects ahead and de-expediting others.

A possibility is that the equivalent of the Resource Analysis Board may be kept on the computers of everyone in the group, perhaps on Excel. This, of course, allows for updating and communicating the status by computer network. However, it is not so good for communication. So, even if the Resource Analysis Board is kept on computers, do keep a physical board as well.

The steps are:

• Identify the key resources or resource categories: perhaps engineers and technicians; barristers, solicitors, legal clerks; specialists and nurses; accountants and sub-accountants. Teams which normally work together are shown as one category, otherwise individuals are shown. 'Key resource' means a person or team who have core skills needed for completion of a task or project. Thus a print room, canteen, or mail delivery are not core skills even though they may be important.

- Set up two Resource Planning Boards: the first concerned with weekly activities, going out four to six weeks ahead, starting next week, and the second concerned with daily activities for this week. The week-by-week board is shown horizontally with activities going from left to right, and each row representing a key resource. The Weekly Board typically uses planning divisions of a week with activities shown in days. The Daily Board uses planning divisions of days where activity units are hours. The second board is similar to a Work Balance Board or Yamazumi Board turned on its side. A Yamazumi Board is a resource histogram showing the work elements that go into filling a manufacturing cycle (takt time). What is described here is on a much broader level of detail. Overload situations can be indicated.
- A task should be broken down into its smallest sensible element, particularly if it involves work done by a critical resource. See the section on Cells in the Tools section.
- Each week, regularly, the boards are updated by each resource (person or team). The resource simply indicates by drawing in blocks what activities they plan to work on (part) day by (part) day for the next week, and week by week for the following (?) four weeks. These are shown in the appropriate swim lane. Colour coding is used, for instance:
    - Blue for individual activities, not dependent on others
    - Green for teamworking activities, not dependent on others
    - Red for activities where commencement of the activity depends on another key resource, either internal or external to the group.
    - Yellow for unoccupied, spare capacity.
- This is ideally a voluntary, participative process, not a top down check. The purpose is smooth flow, problem solving, time management, not chasing.

A typical outline of the Resource Analysis Board is shown.

The Communications Board is the third element. This is described in a separate section in the Tools section of this book. The Communications Board has wide applicability outside the Custom service area.

The Communications Board is the 'glue' that holds the Process Board and Resource Analysis Board together. Use of the three boards together can be assisted by good time management and good Lean project management. See Lawrence Leach and Ronald Mascitelli respectively.

Together the three boards allow managers to address the critical concerns of capacity and time management.

Managing with Critical Resources

Critical resources are of course found in Transactional and Interactive environments but they are generic in Custom environments. In the first two they are generally easier to manage because they are more stable over time, whereas in Custom environments resource loadings change all the time. A key resource may also be a machine – in a hospital a bed, a CAT scanner, an operating theatre.

This section should be read together with the section on Cells in the Tools part of the book.

The management of the critical resources, and their smoothed flow of work, is the prime task of managers in Custom or project environments. This is often not sufficiently appreciated, and is probably a major reason for both client dissatisfaction and employee stress. In multi-project environments – a hospital, a design office, a legal practice – the management of critical resources is very challenging, but the point is that the manager needs at least a basic understanding of the problem.

In Lean manufacturing the supervisor, or preferably the team, balances the work using the Work Balance Board (also referred to as the Yamazumi Board). The same activity may be found in Transactional service environments, except that in manufacturing the team would balance to perhaps 90% of takt time whereas in Transactional service they would balance to perhaps to 80% of takt. In project or Custom environments a similar activity should take place, but with the following modifications:

- In this section the term 'resource' will be used. In office and service environments a resource is typically a person or a group with similar skills, rather than a machine. There may, however, be situations where the resource is a machine or vehicle, such as an operating theatre, ambulance, room, or print shop. In Ordnance Survey the resource is the plane used for map photography.
- Only the critical (or Drum) resources need to be balanced. Be aware, however, that loading of critical resources in custom environments tends to be erratic, and the critical resource can change over very short periods.
- Balancing is a regular activity because new projects arise all the time, and there is little repetition.
- Where there is sequence dependency of activities – as in a multi-resource project – a network or Gantt chart or precedence network should be drawn (even if sketched in outline only) to understand the dependencies and to estimate when critical resources will be called upon. In complex environments the use of a package such as Microsoft Project will certainly assist. Where there are no sequence dependencies the task is much simpler, with critical resources merely having to show on the chart what they will be working on and for how long. Non-sequence dependent activities may also include meetings and training. In many situations, of course, a critical resource will be involved in both sequence dependent and non-sequence dependent activities.
- Balancing is on a much broader time scale – perhaps days or even weeks, sometimes hours, certainly not minutes. So the balancing activity is against the days or hours available, not against a takt time, which generally has no meaning in Custom environments.
- When critical resources are loaded is determined both by the project network or Gantt charts and by non-sequence dependent activities. Both types should be moved earlier or later so that the load on critical resources is not exceeded. This is easier said

than done, given that some activities may be fixed in time and others are sequence dependent, so that adjusting a critical resource will have knock-on effects on other resources whose activities may need to be expedited or postponed. Most project management computer packages have a resource-levelling feature that can assist, but this, of course, requires that all activities are on the system.

- Nearly always the best method of load balancing is not to rely on a computer package (although a package may provide useful input), but to discuss the loading in a team setting with all critical and near critical resources present. The team could meet (say) once a month for broad guideline purposes, with the manager taking routine decisions between the meetings.
- The Lean 'pull' system (or CONWIP – constant work in progress – or Drum in Goldratt's Drum Buffer Rope system) should also work. That is, it should 'pull' work into the system depending on the utilisation of critical resources. Never launch new work until there is capacity available to do the work. The Drum Buffer Rope system says that work completed by the critical bottleneck allows new work to enter. If work is not completed, none enters. The Rope is the connection between the critical bottleneck and the entry point. The (time) Buffer protects the bottleneck from uncertainty.
- The critical activities should be loaded to perhaps 80% of full capacity, to allow for variation and uncertain task duration times. The 80% figure is an estimate and each individual service organisation will have to determine its own satisfactory figure.
- Time buffers (called 'feeding' buffers in Critical Chain project management) should be allowed where there are sequence dependencies that relate to critical resources – in other words where a critical resource may be held up by a non-critical activity.
- If work has to be completed by a particular time, Critical Chain instructs that a project time buffer be located at the end of the project but that no 'slack' or 'float' be allowed for anywhere else in the project except in front of sequence-dependent critical activities.
- The critical resource should not work on simultaneous projects – see Hal Mather's ship story in the Capacity Tool section. One at a time is good Lean practice, in any environment.
- Another valuable idea comes from Lean Construction or 'The Last Planner'. This is the idea that critical resource activities should be subject to a checklist of requirements which is gone

through before the activity is due to start. Checklists are not necessary for all activities, only critical activities. Checklists should include everything that might prevent the activity proceeding smoothly and in an error-free way. A critical resource checklist for an operating theatre (surgeon) would include all the instruments, supplies and availability of support staff. A critical resource checklist for a court appearance (solicitor) would include adequate briefing, clothing, coordination of all involved including witnesses, support staff availability, and travel arrangements to get there. This is very similar, of course, to the checklists that Toyota designers use. Last Planner checklists need to be built up by experience, as with any checklist, but the point is actually to keep, use and improve the checklist. The checklists become very valuable documents.

In so-called agile (or Lean) software development the concept is to break down the product into usable chunks ('chunking') and to try to ensure that the deliverables are completed in a continuous levelled stream. This is exactly like the TPS concepts of Heijunka and mixed model scheduling. It is also compatible with the ideas of kaizen. In agile software development the emphasis is on completing a working deliverable as soon as possible, and then going back and improving it – rather than going for the big, complete, perfect solution presented at the end. This is also similar to the Toyota 'set-based' new product development approach. So why not use these powerful concepts in Custom service or project environments – particularly the Interactive kind? It is surely advantageous for clients, who can then fine-tune the deliverable together with the service provider as they work through the project – whether it be a law suit, a new building, a university course or tutorial, or a new product advertising campaign.

A Note on Critical Chain Project Management

The phrase 'Critical Chain' originated with Eli Goldratt, who wrote a revolutionary book with the same title. Unlike critical path project management, the Critical Chain looks at both sequence dependencies and resource usage. The Critical Chain will normally not be the critical path. The Critical Chain is the longest path through the network after levelling the critical resources. Note the plural here. It is frequently the case that one resource is overloaded early on, another resource is overloaded later, and yet another later still.

Managing the project focuses on the critical resources. There will always be just a few of them or perhaps only one. These resources must be identified and utilised well:

- A time buffer (called a feeding buffer) after non-critical resources that lead into critical resources – so as to reduce the likelihood that the critical resource will be delayed.
- A project buffer at the end of a project. Then monitoring progress in two dimensions – the percentage of the critical chain complete versus the percentage of the time buffer that has been consumed.

Critical Chain project management aims to overcome two weaknesses in conventional project management:

- **Parkinson's Law**: activity expands to fill the time available
- **The Student Syndrome**: waiting until the last possible moment, when the due date is imminent, to begin an activity, so that any delay will then mean that the task will be late. Perhaps, as many students will attest, the start date is already too late to complete the task at the normal rate of work, so that overtime (or non-Lean lumpy) work will be required.

Readers who are in full-time project management and who may not be familiar with the following references are highly recommended to read:
Eli Goldratt, *Critical Chain*, North River Press, 1997 (a novel, like *The Goal*)
Lawrence Leach, *Lean Project Management*, Advance Inc., 2005

Toyota's 'Obeya' and Design Management

What is described above may be found, with suitable modification, in a small design group, a solicitor's office, a university academic or administrative department, or any office that undertakes a series of small projects.

The design of a major engineering artefact such as an aircraft, car, or major bridge will of course be far more complex. Nevertheless, it can be built up from modules set up on similar principles.

For example, at the overall product level, Toyota's design system is far more comprehensive, but it does use a chart room. The room is referred to as the 'Obeya' (big room). Around the walls are placed diagrams, flowcharts, plans, designs, resource allocation charts and the like –

everything that pertains to the progress of the design. Toyota, of course, is concerned with bringing new vehicles to market and this is top-level project engineering. The project manager or 'chief engineer', as he or she is called, has a small team but meets regularly with functional line managers in the Obeya.

Obeya is just one element of Toyota's Design Management system. The key elements of the process are summarised by Patricia Panchak as:

- Test first, then design – not design, then test.
- Customer interest is the engineers' job, not the sales and marketing team's.
- Capture the knowledge developed during the process.

Other elements include:

- A strong 'chief engineer' who has the task of translating customer requirements of values to the new design. He or she has responsibility for the success of the entire project but does not have authority over the line managers whose teams actually do the technical design work.
  - 'Set-Based' Concurrent Engineering whereby the design team tests several concepts for each sub-system, gradually narrowing the choice. The specifications slowly converge. This is in contrast to the stage/gate approach where the whole project may be abandoned at any stage, resulting in big waste. The Toyota way simply 'bookshelves' concepts that may be not feasible at the time, but may well be useful next time around.
  - The 'set-based' approach also involves delaying decisions as late as possible. A form of 'postponement', or variety as late as possible, as found for example with Dell and Benneton.
  - A system of coaching for new designers that involves them working in several departments and on the line, but then being mentored by a senior engineer.
  - A system of checklists that captures best practice.
  - A3s are used to standardise knowledge capture. Capturing the knowledge and lessons learned is important, but making it easy to access next time is just as important.
  - The functional teams are experts in their own technical area, and are supposed to pursue leading-edge developments. These 'bookshelved' developments may be brought out at a later stage.

A full description of the Toyota Design management process can be found in Morgan and Liker's *The Toyota Product Development System,* Productivity, 2006.

List of Related Tools

- Overall Professional Effectiveness
- Control Charts
- Information inventory
- Kaizen and Knowledge Management
- A3 problem solving
- Activity Sampling

Further Reading

Ronald Mascitelli, *The Lean Design Guidebook*, Technology Perspectives, 2004

Ronald Mascitelli, *The Lean Product Development Guidebook*, Technology Perspectives, 2007 (a really excellent review of many concepts relevant to Custom environments – not just product development)

Lawrence Leach, *Lean Project Management: Eight Principles for Success*, Advanced Projects, 2005

James Morgan and Jeffrey Liker, *The Toyota Product Development System*, Productivity Press, 2006

Peter Hines, Mark Francis and Pauline Found, 'Towards Lean Product Lifecycle Management: A Framework for New Product Development', *Journal of Manufacturing Technology Management*, Vol 17, No 7, 2006.

Patricia Panchak, 'Teledyne Benthos Adapts the Toyota Product Development System', *Target*, Third Issue, 2007

Herman Ballard, *The Last Planner System of Production Control*, PhD Thesis, University of Birmingham, 2000

Level 2: System Design Mapping
Low Customer involvement, Low Repeatability

Typical Situations

- Unstructured, typically 'messy' problems in 'human activity systems'
- Change management
- Design of a system such as an airport terminal, an investment in a new facility in China, or a university course
- Some Information Systems design, transport system design
- Organisational design
- Some Research and Development
- Writing a book, thesis or publication

In all of these there is low repeatability, but not necessarily low repetitiveness. Thus a scientist may seldom repeat an experiment or piece of analysis, but the sub-processes are likely to have repetitive stages. This is a less structured environment than the Custom type. Here we design the plant, in the Custom type we design the products that are made in the plant. Many of these situations overlap with project management, so material from the last section may also be relevant.

What is discussed here is the process design level. If, for example, you are designing a new facility in China, much further work will be needed at the micro design stage.

In this type of environment takt time is not applicable. It is also a fairly high variety process and, as Seddon has said, the system must be designed to absorb variety. Therefore, as with the Custom type, standard work in the detail sense also has low applicability. Not so, however, in the wider sense.

Drawing the 'Map'

Improving this type of process draws heavily on systems thinking, particularly that of John Seddon, Peter Checkland and Russell Ackoff, and on ideas from Goldratt's Theory of Constraints. As in other quadrants, the analysis begins with the macro (big picture) systems analysis.

An important idea here is 'back from the future'. In other words, design the ideal state and then move backwards to understand what barriers are in the way.

Checkland's soft systems methodology (SSM) was designed to tackle 'soft' problems, that is to say problem areas where quantification is not appropriate and the problem area is only loosely defined. Russell Ackoff refers to this as 'a mess', with the idea being to move from 'a mess' to 'an improved mess'. In fact this is consistent with the Toyota view that they do not try to design the perfect system first time, but rather implement an imperfect system and improve it over time.

The problem is often to find the problem. A manager may know that 'things are not what they should be' but finds it hard to pin down the problem due to a complex of interacting factors (in other words, a system).

SSM was developed by Peter Checkland and has been explained in several books. It has been used in many parts of industry, services and government. It is a tool for improvement rather than solution, since 'solutions' are seldom found in unstructured situations. It is referred to as 'soft systems' methodology, because 'hard' quantification is often not possible. However, 'soft' does not mean easy; the soft stuff is often the hard stuff.

The Rich Picture

SSM begins with the rather vague activity of building the rich picture. (Recall that Seddon calls this 'Check'.) The idea is to build up a rich understanding of this 'thing' we are about to analyse. This may take many forms: going to the Gemba and simply listening, market research, briefings by managers, inputs from customer focus groups, trends and projections from specialists and consultants, historic data, published information, and simply walking around. This part overlaps with the previously discussed high level analysis. Valuable insights can be obtained from

- **Value and failure demand**: This means listening, categorising, and quantifying.
- **Variation analysis**: This may involve drawing a run diagram or control chart (a) to identify 'special cause' events and see if the process is in control, and (b) to identify patterns of variation – trends, seasonality, cycles – and in the case of parallel processes

such as more than one training course, how much variation is within the process and how much between processes.

- **The RATER dimensions.** Which of these dimensions has the biggest gap?
- **Capacity and Constraint analysis.**

All of these are discussed further in the Tools section.

Reference Projections, Scenarios and Feedback Loops

The first two of these were suggested by Ackoff. Both represent a challenge to the status quo. Scenarios have been used by organisations such as Shell to look into risk and to challenge thinking. They are not a forecast but a description of a possible future state. Today many companies test future plans and policies against scenarios.

A reference projection is an extrapolation from the present, assuming that nothing will change in the wider environment. For example, market share is currently 30% and is growing at 5% per year. A reference projection would say that in ten years time, market share will be 80%. How likely is that? Probably something has to change. In that sense, this is similar to Goldratt's Theory of Constraints, which states that there is or will be at least one constraint – marketing, people, capital, skills, capacity, or whatever – in the way. Break or relieve the constraint and you will break through to a whole new plane. Reference projections are also a way of bringing 'an uncomfortable truth' home to managers, unions, and employees. For example, our costs are increasing faster than inflation. One reference projection for the British Health Service is that healthcare will absorb most of GDP by 2050.

Feedback loops are a powerful way to represent the dynamics of a problem. Such dynamics are hard to capture on a conventional map. See the Tools section.

Input-output diagrams

The first specific step is to draw one or more input-output diagrams. These diagrams show the 'transformations' with which the system is concerned. They are known as SIPOC diagrams in Six Sigma – Suppliers, Inputs, Process, Outputs, and Customers. For example, using people, machines, money, components to produce products. It is clearly possible to be much more specific, and the more specific the better. Begin by identifying the process that undertakes the transformation. Name it. Now add all the 'inputs' into the process and all the 'outputs' from the process. It is often useful to distinguish between the actual outputs and the desirable outputs. Also, distinguish between those inputs and outputs over which there is control and those over which there is no control. A useful question may be to ask who are the 'victims', 'beneficiaries' and customers. Drawing these diagrams forces you to think about just where the system begins and ends; this does not necessarily coincide with the organisational groupings. Input/output diagramming is really an attempt to clarify the process or system with which the team is dealing. Of course it is possible to think in terms of a hierarchy of input/output diagrams. There may be an overall transformation within which several interacting transformations are located. But often, at this stage, it is not necessary to think through the detail. As a rule of thumb, do not have more than four sub-input/output diagrams.

Purpose

The next step is to write down a statement. Checkland refers to this as the 'root definition', but here it will be called 'Purpose'. This is not the aim or objective but a description of what the system does or hopes to do <u>for the customer</u>. It may begin with the words, 'a system to ....'. Ackoff calls this 'the mission statement'. Ideally it should be a challenge to excite and inspire the players or employees.

Whatever it is called, Purpose should attempt to capture the essence and richness of the situation. The root definition may run to several sentences and include mention of the customers, the people (or 'actors') involved, the transformations (inputs to outputs) that it seeks to achieve, the 'world view' or philosophy of the system, the 'owners' of the system or the problem, and the environment in which the system operates. Checkland uses the mnemonic CATWOE to recall these features (see the section on System). The reasons for the existence and continuation of the system are usually incorporated.

Some prefer two versions of Purpose, one short and snappy and the other longer and more detailed. An example from health (Accident and Emergency): 'A patient quick-response system', or the longer version, 'A hospital system to receive and process patients in need of short-term care, in line with the patients' relative needs, with minimum delay and hassle'.

Conceptualisation

From the Purpose comes the system conceptualisation. Ackoff calls this 'Idealized Design'. Checkland's view is that this is put together by asking, 'What are the minimum necessary activities for this purpose?' How can this purpose be achieved as simply as possible? We are concerned with activities, so use a verb and a noun (e.g. 'transfer information'). These activities should be the minimum necessary. It is very important to note that these activities are derived directly from the Purpose or root definition and not from the actual situation. Conceptualisation is an opportunity for creative synthesis, for 'what might be', not a description of 'what is' at the moment. The reality of the real situation must be kept apart. The only guidance is from the Purpose itself.

But on a more down to earth level, Conceptualisation simply means developing the concept as if there were no restrictions of resources or organisational politics. Just pretend that the current organisation or system burned down today, and you have to start all over again. However, 'no restrictions' does not mean sci-fi way-out futuristic design. It is design with today's implementable, available technologies.

Although it is 'blue sky' thinking, it is also useful to think 'Blue Ocean'. This concept comes from a book of that title by Chan Kim and Renée Mauborgne, who challenge you to think about a strategy that would enable you to be placed so that you would not have any competitors. Quite a few have tried this, a recent one at the time of writing being Tesco's Fresh and Easy grocery chain in the USA.

Many formats can be used to present the ideal conceptualisation. Service blueprints and value stream maps, as discussed in this book, are certainly possibilities. The conceptualisation should show the interactions between the parts. Usually a diagram is drawn with the activities written inside activity boxes or 'balloons', and the interconnections between balloons are shown by means of arrows. Different types of arrow may be used to denote information, materials, customers, and other flows. A boundary may be drawn around all the balloons to indicate what is inside and what is outside the system. Then the flows into and out of the system are drawn – people, money, materials, customers, satisfaction, etc. It is useful to show where these flows come from and where they go to. Also identify on the diagram what the major external influences are. The measures of performance used by activities or by parts of the system may be included.

To summarise, the conceptualisation is a creative synthesis showing the activities, boundaries, interconnections, flows, and influences. An important idea is that the concept is holistic; it does not seek out specific improvements to sub-systems before the full concept is complete.

Comparison and Recommendation

Conceptualisation is an abstract exercise. Now comes a systematic comparison with the actual situation. The team 'returns to the real world' and begins to list what changes are feasible and practical. What activities are shown in the concept and what are found in practice? Do the information flows correspond? Are the organisational groupings correct?

In the 'real world' structures commonly evolve which result in product or information flows that double back on themselves or responsibility for a task being split between several sections. The conceptualisation can be broken down into sub-systems that work together more closely than with other sub-systems. Because the conceptualisation has proceeded from the root definition it should overcome the problem of artificial boundaries that may exist within any real organisation. For quality management this is often very important: for instance, should purchasing be part of manufacturing? Should design work closer with marketing? These queries should benefit from the analysis, insights, creativity, and holistic nature of the previous stages, leading to a list of suggestions for change.

The strength of this methodology, as against a pure creativity exercise, is the disciplined structure that the analysis brings. The ideas generated are not random, but are seen in context with other requirements and constraints.

A Methodology for Developing the Future State

The methodology integrates the experience of conventional Lean value stream mapping with years of experience from the 'Soft Systems' approach developed by Peter Checkland. The steps are:

1 Understand the nature of the administrative or service system – primarily to do with the frequency of customer interactions and the degree to which the transactions are essentially routine or essentially creative. Repetitiveness is another useful dimension.
2 Select the appropriate type of mapping tool, or combination of mapping tools.

3   Develop the current state map – 'what is'.
4   Build the rich picture of the system.
5   Develop the 'what might be' conceptual design of the product service bundle or 'ideal state'.
6   Decide on the appropriate focus of people and process.
7   Compare 'what is' with 'what might be'.
8   Develop the list of feasible, desirable changes.
9   Develop the Action Plan.

'What Might Be'

Once the particular value stream has been identified, the customer must be the starting point. Not only today's customers but also tomorrow's. Both the needs ('holes not drills') and the do-not-wants are required. This gives a 2 x 2 matrix – although it may well be useful to segment customers by, for example, spending category. A useful segmentation is to think of customers you want and customers you do not want. Begin by listing – through brainstorm, focus group, market research, direct observation, or all of these – the fundamental customer needs. The Kano model of Basics, Performance factors, and Delighters is useful here. Try to focus on ultimate needs to avoid short-term myopia: needs are sustainable, but wants may reflect current technology or current solutions. Then think about tomorrow's customers: will they be different in terms, for example, of age, spending power, education, expectations, free time and so forth? Then once again list the needs and do-not-wants of tomorrow's customers.

The Kano model, Brainstorming, and the Focus group are useful tools.

An understanding of customers requires an understanding of the product service bundle. Note the words 'product service bundle'. Every administrative task or service is a bundle of product and service. They are products in the sense that they transform an input into an output – or, as in the previous section, they fulfil a need. But they will have service elements insofar as there will be customer Moments of Truth. An airline aims to deliver passengers safely on time but the customer experience can be very different. Two insurance companies can both meet claims within the same time period, but with varying degrees of customer satisfaction through, for example, ease of use, friendliness and lack of hassle. Another way of looking at it is to use the Zeithaml *et al* RATER dimensions: The 'R' – reliability – is mainly the product; the 'ATER' – assurance, tangibles, empathy, responsiveness – is mainly the service. The product service bundle can be summarised by 'the "what" and the "how"'. The 'what' is the product: you buy a broadband service, but how is it installed and supported?

Develop the product service bundle concept in a workshop with the use of two colours of post-it sticker, one colour showing the product and the other the service. This is the ideal state. This stage should be done without considering practical constraints, but nevertheless avoiding science fiction by considering only what is possible today or in the very near future.

Prioritising

The next stage is to prioritise the process-people mix. Begin by positioning or debating the position of the value stream on an adaptation of Peter Wickens' 'Ascendant Organization' matrix. Peter Wickens is the former HR director of Nissan UK.

- The process axis should reflect the current state of processes in relation to the ideal state. Indicative (though not foolproof) measures would be 'hard' measures such as on-time performance, defect rates, rework, failure demand percentage, lead time in comparison with competitors. It should also include the skills of the workforce, rather than the effective use of those skills – you may have a highly skilled but demotivated workforce.
- The people axis should reflect the current state of employees (or 'actors') who are delivering the product service bundle, state of morale, willingness to adapt and change, commitment, friendliness, 'culture' (a dangerous word!).

It is NOT correct to equate process with 'product' and people with 'service'.

Of course the ideal is the 'ascendant' quadrant with high focus on both people and process. Wickens says that this is seldom the case, and many organisations are either 'anarchic' – focused on people but with poor process capability, or 'alienated' – the reverse. Virtually all publications on mapping ignore the people aspect. This may just about do in some manufacturing organisations but certainly will not fly in administrative and service organisations, particularly those with high customer interaction.

Several hints as to the extent of people focus can be found from the following questions:

- Are measures focused on customer requirements or on managers' requirements?
- Is there trust or fear?
- Is there pride in work?
- Is a clear vision known to everyone – not just senior management?
- Are problems welcomed?
- Are managers seen regularly at the Gemba?
- Is feedback sought from customers?
- Does feedback reach those who can make a difference, or is it ignored?

Positioning the process on the Ascendant Matrix just described should indicate where to begin the change process – with people or with process. Remember Deming and Ohno. Deming's '94/6' rule implied that 94% of problems lie with the process – the responsibility of management – and only 6% with the people. Ohno said that Toyota gets brilliant results from brilliant processes and 'average' people, rather than average results from brilliant people with poor processes. There is considerable evidence that it is easier to change the processes first and then the people, rather than the other way round. Change happens when people see that the new processes actually work and have the commitment of management behind them. On the other hand, there have been remarkable service transformations which have focused in the first instance on people aspects. Examples are Scotrail (differentiating itself from British Rail), and Air Seychelles and SAS airlines, both of which focused on Moments of Truth improvements through their people.

Wickens says, '…with all the talk of eliminating waste and increasing labour productivity, the one element that is left out of the equation is the impact of ever-reducing waste and ever-increasing labour productivity on the people who are subjected to it! Most companies dress it up by talking about "working smarter, not harder" but the reality is that as waste is eliminated…and people move towards spending greater time adding value, the pressure on them can, in fact, increase even though each individual activity may be less strenuous' (Peter Wickens, *Energise Your Enterprise*, Macmillan, 1999, p 60).

The important message is that a good Lean service or administration future state needs to consider both process and people. People aspects – including the attitudes and behaviours of management and the measurement system – need to be compatible with the process.

Comparison and Developing The Action Plan

The Action Plan comes out of a comparison between the 'what is' current state map, and the insights from the 'what might be' exercise, including the discussion of the product-people focus. The Action Plan should include people assigned to specific milestones. The planning horizon would normally be six months.

Further Reading

Russell Ackoff, Jason Magidson and Herbert Addison, *Idealized Design*, Wharton School Publishing, 2006
Peter Checkland, *Systems Thinking, Systems Practice*, Wiley, Chichester, 1981
Brian Wilson, *Systems: Concepts, Methodologies, and Applications*, Wiley, Chichester, 1986
Peter Checkland and Jim Scholes, *Soft Systems Methodology in Action*, Wiley, Chichester, 1990
Peter Checkland and Sue Holwell, *Information, Systems, and Information Systems*, Wiley, Chichester, 1997

Level 3: Detailed Mapping

Level 3 mapping is particularly appropriate for Transaction mapping, is sometimes used in Interactive mapping, but is unusual in Custom or System Design areas.

It would be unusual to use Level 3 mapping detail for an end-to-end process. This is what old-style industrial engineers attempted to do. Much of that activity would be waste, because in the earlier Levels it is likely that whole swathes have been modified or scrapped.

Three methods will be described here: the application of the '3P' method in service, the Six Sigma mapping method, and Four Fields Mapping.

The '3P' Method for Service

The Toyota 3P – or Production Preparation Process – is a methodology for exploring different ways in which a product should be built. It is a manufacturability review, following the design – or more correctly done in parallel with the design. There seems to be no good reason why a 3P should not apply in service design, following a Level 2 consideration.

3P is considered vital because the decisions made at this detailed level may affect waste and flow for years to come. Having done a great job in Level 2, don't now throw much of it away.

A 3P uses a multifunction team. An important idea is to consider a range of ways in which the product might be made or the service delivered. Toyota, probably for provocation, likes to consider at least seven ways to make a product. A 3P is usually conducted as a mini kaizen event – possibly over a one or two day period. Many of the detailed options the team comes up with will need further investigation – but note that this is done subject to the designs that have been decided in Level 2. It should not be a ponderous process: multidiscipline is preferable, including the presence of front line service delivery staff, perhaps aided by experts in particular fields. The idea is to work through a range of possibilities. In many cases, this will also include a visit to the Gemba and an evaluation process to consider any tradeoffs between, say, cost, quality, speed, and customer satisfaction. Also, of course, there is the important point that the chosen alternatives should be compatible with one another.

So your team has come up with a good service delivery concept in Level 2, taking out much unnecessary waste and failure demand. Nevertheless, within your future state concept there remain many possibilities. Consider a few:

- **Queues**: A single queue leading to multiple servers, or multiple queues, or priority queues for certain customers? If a queue builds up, what action, if any, should be taken? If it decreases, what action should be taken?
- **Signs**: What signs should be erected, their appearance, their wording? Bear in mind that too many signs can confuse.
- **Equipment selection**: What equipment (hardware) should be used – computers, internet, displays, but also desks, chairs, lighting and so on? Should present equipment be used? New is not necessarily better.
- **Software**: Although the choice of computer software may be beyond the scope of the team, at least the displays, ease of use, capabilities, and requirements for both staff and customers should be covered.
- **Automation**: What should be automated, if anything? Should automatic voice answering be used?
- **Signals**: What signals are appropriate for staff and for customers? For example, should customers be informed about long waits? Should the wait be estimated? How should system conditions be signalled – lights, digital displays, computer flags? Should signals of poor performance be automatically escalated?
- **Records**: How should they be kept – or should they be kept at all?
- **Front desk presentation and appearance**.
- **Health and safety issues**.
- **General decoration**: Even if an interior designer is used, (s)he should be involved in the event.

For each one of these, don't rush in and accept the first option that comes to mind. Time taken here is very well spent.

The power of 3P is that multidiscipline views are brought to bear. The outcome is 'their' design, not one imposed from on high.

Six Sigma Detailed Mapping

There are a number of variations in the way Six Sigma organisations perform the detailed mapping tool.

The sequence below shows a six-step approach which builds the map into a detailed state which can be revealing and useful when analysing the variables that affect the output.

1 Identify process steps within the project boundaries.
2 Identify Output variables and add them above the appropriate operation.
3 Identify Input variables and add them below the appropriate operation.
4 Partition variables into C,N,X categories.
5 Add customer specifications.
6 Highlight value adding activities.

The C,N,X approach is a useful method employed for partitioning Input variables. If there are variables that require holding constant in order to achieve the desired output or reduce variation, these are labelled 'C'. You would often expect these to have a Standard Operating Procedure (SOP) or 'Something On Paper'. They may also be guided by standard steps given by a computer screen. Those variables that are not currently controllable (often because the resource provision is outside the system boundary) are labelled 'N'. Finally, those variables that can be changed to various settings are labelled 'X' for experimental purposes. Not all processes have Xs but there may be a desirable experiment to run with Cs in the future.

The map below shows the process steps necessary to make a cup of tea.

What seems a fairly straightforward task which many of us carry out without a second thought can be built up into a useful map for understanding the process, its inputs, outputs and current controls. If the six-step process is completed on this example, then the process owner would see immediate improvement opportunities to reduce variation through the introduction of standards (with adherence audits) and to failsafe (pokayoke) all designs.

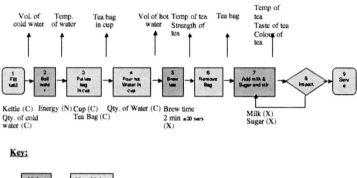

Vol. of cold water   Temp. of water   Tea bag in cup   Vol of hot water   Temp of tea Strength of tea   Tea bag   Temp of tea Taste of tea Colour of tea

Kettle (C)   Energy (N) Cup (C)   Qty. of Water (C)   Brew time
Qty. of cold   Tea Bag (C)   2 min ±30 secs
water (C)   (X)

Milk (X)
Sugar (X)

Key:

| Value Added | Non-Value Added |

Four Fields Mapping

Four Fields mapping is a swimlane map with some features similar to the Service Blueprint discussed under Level 2 Interactive mapping. However, a Four Fields map is far more detailed and is generally used internally for administrative processes rather than for following a customer, as is the Service Blueprint.

The four fields (or columns) are:

- **The functions, departments, participants**: Each of these is shown under its own swimlane and the activities to be performed within each swimlane are indicated. Classic IT or computer programming symbols, such as activity box, document, decision point, data storage, etc. are used.
- **Time**: The time for the activity is written next to the activity. Variation is not usually given, but this would be an improvement. Delay times are also included.
- **Resource**: The times taken by critical resources are written in this column. If there is more than one critical resource, more columns can be added.
- **Standards and criteria**: If there is a standard this is recorded. Otherwise, the criteria used for making the decision are given.

It is also common to record the stage of the process in the far left column.

Note the last two columns could be replaced by:

- Measures that relate to that particular stage or activity
- Customer satisfaction with the stage – either by showing a rating out of five or with a happy or sad face icon.

An example for booking in an order into a distribution

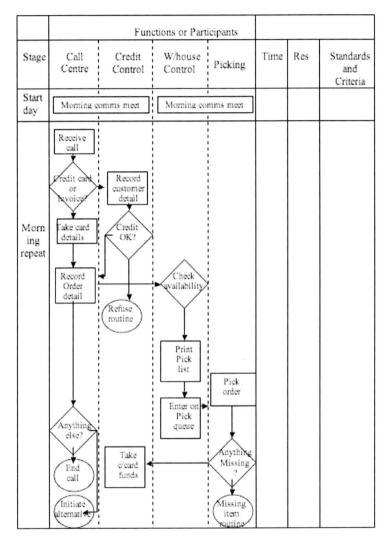

Note:
- The time is divided into stages, which are not necessarily continuous.
- There may be repeating sequences.
- The lozenge at the start of the day to indicate cross functional activities.

Four Fields mapping can be used at a higher level, for example to give detail about a design process interacting with different departments, holding meetings, interfacing with data bases, etc.

The value in a Four Fields map is that it is inter-functional. So the functions should all participate in drawing the map. Wasteful activities are picked up by the team, and opportunities identified.

In practice, Four Fields mapping is done using the above format but with post-it stickers. It therefore resembles Brown Paper mapping described under Level 1.

Further Reading

John Bicheno and Philip Catherwood, *Six Sigma and The Quality Toolbox*, PICSIE Books, 2005, for more in Six Sigma, including many tools
Ronald Mascitelli, *The Lean Product Development Guidebook*, Technology Perspectives, 2007

Reference

Peter Hines, 'Four Fields Mapping', MSc Lean Operations Notes, Cardiff Business School, 2004

Part 3: Tools for Lean Service

5S

5S housekeeping is probably the most popular tool in Lean service. There is good news and bad news. The good news: it is easy to do, usually has a positive impact on quality and productivity, and sends out a powerful message that Lean 'has arrived' and is for everyone. The bad news: 5S can be a diversion from real priorities, can be seen as merely tidying up, and can give Lean a bad name though over-zealousness.

The real objectives of a 5S program should be:

- To reduce waste, particularly time spent searching and time lost due to poor layout.
- To reduce variation.
- To improve productivity.

5S programs work well in situations where the need to achieve these three objectives is well known and 5S is seen as the way to do it.

Don't do 5S as an independent activity. It will not be sustained. Do 5S because everyone recognises that to meet the purpose of the system, to meet customer demands effectively, a change in the way work is laid out is required.

But 5S is also a mindset thing, changing attitudes from 'I work in an unorganised, messy office' to 'I work in a really well-organised office where everyone knows where everything is and any out of place or missing item is noticed immediately'.

The classic 5Ss are:

SORT

Throw out what is not used or needed. The first step is to decide, with the team from the area, the sorting criteria. For example, the team may decide that items to be kept at the workplace are

- items that are used every week
- items that are needed for important quick customer response
- items for health and safety,

whereas the less frequently used can be located firstly in cupboards, and secondly in the storeroom.

Then the team needs to classify exactly according to the sort criteria. Touch every item systematically. If it is to be kept at the workplace, is the quantity correct? If never used, or in doubt, then red tag or throw out. A 'red tag' is a label with the date; if no one accesses the item within a specified period it should be thrown out, recycled or auctioned. An auction is a meeting with the whole team who decide together on red tagged items – what to throw out, what quantity to be kept at various locations, and the locations. The sort stage should be done regularly, say once every six months, but as a regular activity not as a re-launch of 5S. You know a 5S programme is not working when it is really a frequently repeating sequence of 2S or 3S activities.

Be careful of over-zealousness and over-the-top. Permit some personal items to be kept at the workplace within reason. Also permit personal discretion and some location choice. Readers may recall the case, rightly reported with some ridicule in *The Times* of December 2006, concerning a taped-up location for a banana on a desktop. If that is your manager's idea of what Lean is about, resign immediately!

Some offices have been known to use Feng Shui to get the 'vibes' right. Is this also OTT?

SIMPLIFY
(or Set in Order or Straighten)

Locate what remains in the best place. A place for everything, using shadow boards, inventory footprints, trolleys or items the right height, and colour-matching equipment to areas – or simply good sensible locations. Like a kitchen where the family knows the location of cutlery and plates and doesn't have to be told. Are drawers and doors really needed? The best location is the obvious one, such that it is silly to put it anywhere else. And everything in its place. Something not in place and not in use indicates a problem. The standard is 'The Dental Surgery'. Why? Because everyone can relate to that standard of excellence, and knows the consequences of failure.

Locate items by frequency to minimise stretching and bending. Repeat this stage whenever products or parts change. Use a Spaghetti Diagram for analysis. Ergonomic principles should play a role here, and an ergonomic audit may help. There are many excellent, inexpensive books on office ergonomics – there is no excuse not to use them.

All this may sound like a waste of time, but, to quote an NHS booklet, it 'releases time to care'. Spend time up front organising the workplace, and benefit from the time and errors saved thereafter. The same booklet makes the point that it all begins with the team leader, by personal demonstration.

SCAN
(Sweep or Shine or Scrub)

Keep up the good work. This includes physical tidy up, on an ongoing basis, and 'visual scanning' whereby team members are always on the lookout for anything out of place, and try to correct it immediately. Some companies adopt a 'five minute routine', where people work out a five minute cleanup routine for each day of the week so that by the weekend everything has been covered the required number of times. Designate exactly who is responsible for what and what the standard is. This stage will require suitable cleaning equipment to be suitably located and renewed. There could be a sign-off chart for routine cleaning, such as computer screens and notice boards, that cleaners might otherwise miss.

'Cleaning is Checking,' means that these are integrated. You don't just clean up, you check for any abnormality and its root causes. The garage analogy is to clean up first: this enables oil leakage to be identified. Continue to clean up any leakage that occurs. But then ask why leakage is occurring, and decide what should be done for prevention. You don't check oil, water, tyres, and tyre pressure on your car every time you drive, but you do check them when you clean your car. Same principle.

Scan may also include calibrating, keeping track, observing, monitoring, looking out for wastes, lubricating, dusting, computer monitor cleaning, and routine servicing.

It would be good to engender

- the 'Mary Poppins' effect – making clean-up fun, or
- the 'Tom Sawyer' effect – demonstrating to others that they are really missing out by not tidying up!

STANDARDISE
(or Stabilise or Secure)

Only now is it possible to adopt standard procedures. This is the real bottom line for 5S. See the sections on Failsafing and Standard Work. But 5S standards also need to be maintained. So develop standards for the first three Ss.

Standardising also includes measuring, recording, training, and improving, and may include work balancing.

SUSTAIN
(or Self Discipline)

Everyone participates in 5S on an ongoing basis. Sustaining is about participation and improvement, about making the other 5S activities a habit. Carry out regular audits on housekeeping. Some award a floating trophy for achievement. Others erect a board in the entrance hall with current 5S scores. Yet others have a weekly draw out of a hat and then all first line managers descend on the chosen area to have a close look.

Some companies add a sixth S: **SAFETY**. Although it is good to emphasise safety, a good 5S program should stress it as an aspect of each of the five stages. It may confuse to list safety separately. Safety procedures and standards should also be developed, maintained and audited as part of the programme. The removal of unsafe conditions should certainly be integral to 5S.

An alternative for 5S is CANDO – Cleanup, Arrange, Neatness, Discipline, and Ongoing improvement.

Some companies adopt regular walkabout audits and competitions. See the section on The Communications Board. The first line supervisor audits daily, the area manager weekly at random times, the section manager monthly, and so on.

5S as Root Cause

5S lies at the root of many issues in service. All staff need to be sensitised to this fact, and to be encouraged to make improvements as soon as possible – not to have to wait for some kaizen event. For example:

- when a nurse arrives at a patient, or a repairman arrives at a site, and discovers that there is something missing – it is a 5S issue
- when a document cannot be found – it is a 5S issue
- when a surgeon encounters an unfamiliar layout in an operating theatre – it is a 5S issue
- when customers have to ask for the location of an item in a supermarket or shop – it is a 5S (or visual management) issue
- when lecturers can't find working flipchart pens – it is a 5S issue
- when a stationery store runs out of paper – it is a 5S issue
- on and on....

In all these cases it is no good just to correct the error. The situation must be highlighted and a simple non-bureaucratic procedure put in place to solve the problem permanently.

5S Sustainability

Many companies now claim that they are doing 5S but are in fact doing 2S sporadically. Having no 5S sustainability is a waste, and the programme requires increasing effort to re-energise. The real productivity and quality benefits of 5S are in the later Ss, particularly standardisation, not the relatively easy-to-do first two.

Hirano suggests a host of 5S activities, carried out at various frequencies: Among others:

- A 5S month, once a year (?), to re-energise efforts
- 5S days, one to four per month including evaluations
- 5S seminars by outside experts – with lots of photos
- 5S visits to leading outside companies
- 5S patrols, following a set route
- 5S model workplaces (this has become popular in NHS hospitals)
- 5S competitions
- 5S award ceremonies
- 5S exhibits
- 5 minute 5S each day.

Doing all this sounds like overkill, but putting a few in place has proved helpful in sustaining 5S.

Extending the 5S Concept

The 5S concept can be applied more widely, especially in service. Four areas are given in the table. There are probably many more applications.

	Inventory	Suppliers	Computer Systems	Costing Systems
Sort	Throw out all dead and excessive stock.	Select the best two suppliers in each category. Scrap the rest.	Delete all dead files and applications.	Do you need all those costs and variances? Prune them!
Simplify	Arrange in the best positions.	Cut all wasteful, duplicate transactions.	Arrange files in logical folders, hierarchies.	Cut transactions. Review report frequency. Incorporate overhead directly.
Scan	Regularly review dated stock and ABC category changes.	Improve supplier performance by supplier association & kaizen.	Clear out inactive files regularly.	Audit the use made of costing reports and transaction size & frequency.
Stabilise	Footprint, standard locations	A runner system, payments	Systems, formats	Adopt reporting standards.
Sustain	Audit ABC, frequency of use.	Audit performance.	Audit perform & response.	Review and reduce.

Further Reading

Productivity Press Development Team, *5S for Operators*, Productivity, 2002
Hiroyuki Hirano, *5 Pillars of the Visual Workplace*, Productivity, 1995
Karen Kingston, *Clear Your Clutter with Feng Shui*, Piatkus, 2002
Nick Downham and NHS Institute for Innovation and Improvement, *Releasing Time to Care: The Productive Ward*, NHS, 2007

Total Productive Administration, OEE, and OPE

In this section we consider how the principles of Total Productive Maintenance (TPM) can be applied in the office, in other service environments, and to the service worker rather than to the machine. But, as I warned in the Introduction, be very careful about simply adapting manufacturing tools to service.

TPM is a long-established area, very often closely integrated with Lean manufacturing. It aims, through anticipatory activities, to ensure that machines are available when needed. TPM has a number of 'pillars':

- **'Autonomous maintenance'** – where operators take over considerable responsibility for routine maintenance and monitoring;
- **Planned maintenance** – like taking your car in for routine service, thereby aiming to prolong life and reliability;
- **Equipment improvement** – aiming to improve the operating characteristics such as quality capability, access, and problem detection (hence the expression 'a machine is at its worst when new');
- **Early management of new equipment** – correct installation, training, procedures.

TPM recognises that the maintenance task goes well beyond the maintenance department, to involve all – hence 'total'.

A particular focus of TPM is Overall Equipment Effectiveness or OEE. OEE is the multiplication of
- Availability x
- Performance x
- Quality

These are related to the 'Six Big Losses'. Availability is subdivided into two forms of 'loss': breakdowns or equipment failure, and changeover and adjustment. Performance 'loss' is due to minor stoppages (usually defined as an unplanned stop of ten minutes or less), and reduced speed. Quality 'loss' is due to defects arising from process errors and from rework and scrap.

Thus an availability of 90%, a performance of 80%, and a quality rate of 95%, would equate to an OEE of .9 x .8 x .95 = 68%

A point about OEE is that it highlights the area where attention is most needed. Having prioritised the areas for attention, root cause analysis can be applied to reduce or eliminate those losses.

Now use these principles with service professionals such as doctors, engineers, lawyers, accountants. This is called Overall Professional Effectiveness (OPE). These people also suffer losses, but often don't realise how much effective time is being lost and where it is being lost.

OPE Categories and the Six Big Service Losses

OPE Element	Six Big Service Losses	Examples
Availability	Failure and breakdown; in general time away from value adding activities	Internet not working; computer failure; major interruptions greater than 15 minutes
	Start-up losses and waiting; inter-task transfer time	Customers, patients, work instructions that don't turn up on time; waiting for colleagues; delayed start at beginning of day; stopping early at end of day; waiting for other people or information; waiting for machines; looking for misplaced documents or computer files
Performance	Interruptions	Any unplanned interruption during the day; non-work phone calls, colleague chit-chat, relaxation breaks, going for a coffee
	Skill losses; inefficient method or wrong person doing the task	Any work that could or should not be done at all, or that would be better done by others (less or more skilled)
Quality (and Failure Demand)	Process errors; dealing with complaints	Failure demand in general, Any form of rework; data entry errors
	Customer errors	Customer (both internal and external) errors causing rework or delays

Note that

- The categories are not 'faults' or 'people problems'. OPE should not be about blame. OPE (like OEE) should take the view that the vast majority of problems lie with the process, not with the person. It is only management that can fix the process. This is simply applied Deming philosophy.
- OPE is about recording and detecting problems in order that the situation can be improved.
- It is not about spying or checking up.
- The categories may not suit all service occupations. As with OEE, an OPE exercise must begin by defining suitable categories and gaining consensus.
- Trends are important rather than actual numbers.
- Follow up is required. OPE needs to be incorporated into a root cause improvement approach, possibly requiring fishbone analysis, process redesign, work redesign, and standards.
- As with OEE, the OPE is only recorded during the effective hours. Non-effective hours will therefore have to be agreed. Non-effective hours certainly include lunch and coffee breaks, but may also include, by agreement, group meeting times, training time, and a block of time for informal office networking etc.

OPE data is the basis for much further investigation.

Recording the Data

The recording of losses needs careful thought. Times need to be recorded across the day. To check, the sum of the time working plus the sum of the six categories of times should equal 100% of the working time. Note that working time is not break time, or meeting time. These times should be subtracted from the official length of the work day. Recording will certainly fail if it is seen as an imposition or worse, so a convenient and easy way must be found. Experience shows that recording will only work if a positive outcome is seen as the result, and people believe that so doing will improve both their own effectiveness and that of the organisation. Possibilities include:

- **Voluntary self-recording**, activity by activity as work proceeds.
- **Estimation**: At the end of every hour, or half day, or day the professional estimates the time spent on each category. One organisation uses timers that beep every hour as a reminder.

- **Sampling and Rotation**: Everyone does not need to participate. A representative sample or done on rotation are possibilities
- **Tagging**: For paper intensive operations, add a traveller on which times are recorded. This requires further analysis or estimation.
- **Observation**: Get a secretary to record several people in the area, a nurse to record doctors and colleagues. And so on. All part-time activities, of course.
- Some professionals, for example consulting engineers and solicitors already record their time usage for client billing purposes. Only a small adjustment is needed to record OPE.
- **Activity sampling**: This technique is discussed in another section of the book. It is also effective for OPE – with the agreement of those being sampled, of course.

Using OPE Data: Comparative Analysis

Three people with similar OPE figures may have very different causes of lost effectiveness. Consider three professionals, each working a net eight hours and with a planned time of fifteen minutes per client.
- A is delayed for two hours waiting for a client, she is interrupted for 63 minutes, and no-one needs to re-see her for clarification.
- B experiences no delays but has frequent interruptions totalling 2.5 hours and needs to re-see two clients.
- C is delayed for half an hour, has no interruptions, but needs to re-see one third of all clients.

	Availability	Performance	Quality	OPE
A	6/8=.75	297/360	1.00	62%
B	1.00	5.5/8	((5.5x4)-2)/22	62%
C	7.5/8=.937	1.00	.666	62%

So all three have approximately the same overall effectiveness, but the reasons are very different. This may then enable 'best of the best' analysis.

Best of the Best Analysis

'Best of the best' analysis is a useful initial technique in OPE that can be used wherever similar tasks are taking place – a sort of internal benchmarking. In the case just discussed the 'best of the best' is 100%. B is best on availability, C is best on performance, A is best on quality. Now, are there things that each person is doing which result in these high performance figures in their respective categories? What can they learn from one another? The power of this analysis is that the best methods are already in existence within the organisation – no consultants or process analysis are required. Just communicate the best practices, and embed them.

Five Whys, Six Serving Men, Fishbone Analysis, and Run Diagrams

Once you know the contribution of each OPE element to the overall OPE, you will be able to prioritise and focus attention on the critical losses. Conventional root cause analysis using the fishbone diagram (with the 'M's' of men/people, machine, method, measures, materials, mother nature/environment), together with asking 'Why?' several times over, may be a powerful way to identify possible countermeasures. This is also known as Concern, Cause, Countermeasure analysis. Gather the people from the area, draw out the standard fishbone and brainstorm possible causes. You can also use Kipling's 'Six Honest Serving Men': 'I knew six honest serving men, they taught me all I knew; their names are What and Why and When, and Where and How and Who'. This is also known (more boringly) as Five Ws and an H analysis.

- What is its purpose?
- Why is it necessary?
- When should it be done?
- Where should it be done?
- How should it be done?
- Who should do it?
-

You may find that a process map is unnecessary.

Another dimension is time. Here the run diagram comes into its own. The diagram is simply a graph showing the three elements of OPE against time – perhaps over a month. From experience, you know that availability, performance, and quality in service typically vary more over a month than they do in manufacturing. (See the figure.) Quality performance is stable but low. Availability seems to peak around the middle of the month. Performance drops off early in the month then recovers. Why is this? Look for the drivers that are influencing this behaviour.

Extending OPE: Group and Value Stream

Peter Willmott, doyen of UK TPM consultants, recommends thinking about OEE on three levels, floor-to-floor, door-to-door, and value chain. Here we use the same concept, modified for Service.

Person OPE: This is OPE at the individual level, as discussed above.

Group OPE: This is the OPE of a group working on similar tasks. Don't average the results of individuals, but take the group as a whole. What is the group availability? The number up and running gives availability. Interruption time for the group can be estimated, as can the time spent working at an inappropriate skill level for the group as a whole. What is overall quality rate? Here snapshots may be more appropriate – like taking activity samples rather than recording the full times.

Value Stream OPE: This is the end-to-end performance of all sections and groups delivering the service or product. A good idea is to take value stream OPE from the customer's perspective. Availability refers to the system uptime or the percentage of time that clients can get the service they require. Performance refers to the percentage of the total remaining time (after availability losses) that the value stream is performing to the appropriate skill level. For example, the percentage of time that the doctors' group spends doctoring, researchers spend researching, engineers spend engineering. Quality measures how much time is lost due to interruptions and the overall wasted time or failure demand percentage for the group as a whole.

Extending OPE: The Full Service Delivery

In many service delivery systems there are typically three elements necessary to deliver full service: the person, the machine, and the system. These three elements apply, for example, in hospitals, banks, hotels, universities, airlines, and restaurants, as well as in logistics support services and maintenance.

Taxi Service	Availability	Performance	Quality
The Driver	Available when needed; fit for work; reliability; 'tangibles' (appearance) % time available; absenteeism record	Knows where to go – the best route; friendly?; assurance? **Actual time taken as against estimated time given by GPS**	Driving and traffic errors; knows how to talk to customers; can overcome customer problems; empathy; responsiveness Errors made per 100 trips; or customer satisfaction rating
The Taxi Cab (Conventional OEE)	Available as needed; no breakdowns Cab availability	No adjustments needed; fit for the traffic conditions Rating on roadworthiness; mechanical state	Cab is clean; standard checks after each ride Rating on cab cleanliness and appearance
The Information System (may include computer system, GPS for driver, credit card machine, radio.)	Available as needed % uptime	Response time adequate Response time against standard	Good information given; no misdirections given to the cab driver. Number of errors (e.g. address, directions)

In the example above we take a taxi service. The taxi driver needs to be skilled, the taxicab needs to be available, reliable and clean, and the cab company system needs to be able to direct the right cab to the right address at the right time. So each of these has OEE or OPE elements. The RATER dimensions have also been added. A possible measure of performance for each of the nine aspects is included, although the measures would have to be decided for each specific case.

OPE and related concepts therefore provide a comprehensive framework for improvement.

Prevention and Monitoring in TPA

Peter Willmott uses a human health analogy for TPM: an apple for daily prevention activities ('an apple a day keeps the doctor away'); a thermometer for monitoring body temperature; and a needle for injecting vaccine to prevent disease over the longer term. These also can be adapted for TPA. Take the taxi service example again.

Taxi Service	'Apple'	'Thermometer'	'Needle'
The Driver	Keeping up with changes in the road network; keeping fit	Alertness, health check up, absenteeism	Advanced driving certificate? Taxi Drivers competence test
The Cab	Daily checks of cleanliness and roadworthiness	Inspection check on the condition of the cab – mechanical, appearance, comfort	Regular cab maintenance service, annual roadworthiness
The Information System	Housekeeping w.r.t. files, virus checks, checks that GPS etc is working	System response time, uptime, accuracy of information held	Using the latest operating system, latest GPS maps

Note that the 'apple' and the 'thermometer' are related through what is termed 'Cleaning is Checking' in TPM. In other words when the cab is cleaned, perhaps once per day, various routine checks are also carried out.

The apple, thermometer and needle analogy used with person, machine and system has wide applicability in any field service operation, in warehousing and distribution, in services such as hotels and airline services, as well as in many office-based services.

The routines (activities and checks) are best developed by a representative team from the front and back offices. The procedures need to be written up, and then ideally shown on a visual management board. For example, a magnetic board with counters that are placed each day when the activity is done, as well as a 'problems and issues' whiteboard where 'deviations' are noted, then responsibilities for their resolution. See the section on Communications Board.

Reference

Peter Willmott, 'Notes on TPM and Notes on TPA', MSc in Lean Operations, Cardiff Business School, 2007

Inventory (and Information Inventory) in Service

In service there are two categories of inventory: information and physical. Both have been significantly affected by the internet, which has opened up whole new areas that can improve customer service and remove waste. Moreover, the economics of both types of inventory have changed significantly. Do not think only in terms of physical inventories – think instead of any work that can anticipate customer demand.

Anticipation and Service Inventory

There is a belief that service cannot be stored or inventoried. This is true for 'pure service' at the end of the product service spectrum. But remember that all administration, office, service work is best seen as lying somewhere along the product service spectrum. Customer-facing encounters cannot be stored, but some preparatory administration, documentation, procedures, and preparation can be done ahead of the encounter to smooth the customer flow and limit delays. So in administration and service, 'inventory' may not mean physical items but anticipatory information or activity.

There are precedents for this in traditional Lean, in at least four overlapping areas:

- **Changeover reduction** (Single Minute Exchange of Die or SMED) principles try to do as much preparation as possible before the actual changeover. This is not physical inventory but, like inventory, it makes prior preparation for the service delivery.
- **The Postponement Principle**, or variety as late as possible, attempts to keep options open as long as possible, thereby gaining efficiency from repetitiveness but also delivering unique customer packages. The classic example is in fact a service supply chain example – Benetton's 'Jerseys in Grey', where jerseys are manufactured but not dyed. Shops hold minimal inventory of each colour, but are linked by EPOS systems to allow jerseys to be dyed to order.
- **The 'variety funnel'** is a traditional Lean map that traces the stages at which variety expands. For example, a common car platform may expand into five body types, then into 25 engine-body types, hundreds of body-colour options, and millions of body-engine-interior combinations. The idea is to reduce unnecessary variety and also to squeeze the funnel so variety is retailed as late as possible.

Similarly, the stages at which variety occurs in an administrative or service process can be mapped. In an insurance value stream the initial stages may be the same, but may then branch for different types of claim, or customer, or urgency. The question is how many channels are appropriate at each stage? Delaying the point at which the funnel expands helps to smooth the flow of work.

- **'Mass customisation'**, a phrase made popular by Joseph Pine, is where you try to get the advantages of volume (or 'mass') but one-at-a-time. An example is Dell's use of modularity in computer manufacture but also in service spares, enabling the Dell model of direct build-to-order to operate. Other examples of mass customisation include variations of postponement discussed above: for instance, packaging and labelling as late as possible, and the increasing use of print-on-demand technology and make-your-own maps as offered by Ordnance Survey.

Other examples of anticipation inventory include:

- Anticipating a hotel or hospital check-in. Some hotels (like Ritz Carlton) prepare documentation in advance of arrivals from established visitors so that literally only one signature is required. Duplication of data entry is avoided. Moreover, this can be extended to include prior preparation of the guest room, for example type of bed and pillow, shampoo, and refreshments.
- Southwest Airlines has remained profitable through many innovations, one being to minimise turnaround times. This is the use of straightforward manufacturing changeover (SMED) principles.
- An unnoticed revolution is the provision of PowerPoint slides to course attendees, which reduces the need to take detailed notes. This in turn reduces time and improves quality. Today many students hear lectures on an iPod.
- The use of pre-prepared meals at restaurants, even up-market restaurants, is long-established. The issue is at what stage it is appropriate to hold the postponement buffer. Customer expectation of lead time is the important variable, but others are taste and cost or risk.
- The 'Self' concept is also powerful. Allow customers to take over much of the task before the encounter in their own time at their convenience. Examples include pre-check-in at an airport computer terminal before proceeding to 'Fast Bag Drop' as at BA. BA also allows customers to print out their boarding pass at home. A European hotel chain allows at-home registration and automated key pick-up which minimises waiting and staff.

- Supermarkets can anticipate customer requirements more accurately by using loyalty cards, in order to be able to stock up the shelves at specific stores to cater for the specific local demand mix.
- Anticipating car service arrivals. The Portuguese car dealer Simao attempts to collect as much relevant information as possible over the phone before the customer arrives for the car service. This organisation was studied by Cardiff's Lean Enterprise Research Centre and reported in Womack and Jones' *Lean Solutions*. Simao ensures that not only are check-in delays minimised but also that the correct service parts are available as far as possible. This in turn helps to reduce physical inventories.
- Hospital theatre operations can adopt SMED principles by preparing as much as possible beforehand. The *Sunday Times* reported in 2006 on a UK hospital where operating theatres are run in pairs, the one being prepared while the other is dealing with a patient. Surgeons circulate between the two theatres with minimal delay.
- On some international trains, passports and documentation is checked en route. Why not on planes? Or even in the departure lounge?

Time reduction is the critical reason for anticipatory 'inventories', but quality is also likely to improve, through less rush, greater standardisation, and more automation. Time reduction and quality improvement in turn mean that cost is likely to fall.

Inventory Classifications

A standard way of classifying inventory is via ABC analysis. A items are expensive, B items intermediate, and C items low cost. This can be modified by importance. For instance, a low cost item in a hospital may nevertheless be life critical and therefore upgraded to A class. The same applies to difficult-to-procure items. A items need careful attention; C items you are not so concerned about – you may just decide to have sufficient so that you don't run out.

Another dimension is the frequency of use of the items. Use the 'Runners, Repeaters and Strangers' (RRS) classification. This book has a separate section on RSS when used in service mapping. Here a Runner item is used frequently, perhaps every day, whereas a Stranger is only used occasionally.

We now have a way of classifying service inventories as shown in the figure:

	A items	B items	C items
Runners	Worth specific design – tight kanban or pooling; kept on location	Kanban	Stock kept at location; kanban?
Repeaters	Small stock kept at location; others centrally; kanban	Keep centrally, loose kanban	Small stock kept at location; most kept centrally
Strangers	Kept centrally	VMI?	Centralised; VMI?

The table is just an example, but it illustrates some possibilities.

Kanban is a 'pull' replenishment system: when a container is emptied a card on the container is sent to signal replenishment. Tight kanban means that there is close control.

Decentralised means that replenishment decisions should be left with local areas. Purchasing economies are probably offset by wasteful bureaucracy.

VMI is vendor-managed inventory: a supplier comes in regularly, sees what has been used, and tops up the quantity.

Colour Coding, the Square Root Function and other tricks for Service Inventory

Colour coding is simple and useful. Just paint the items that are supposed to be in the same location the same colour. Out-of-place items are immediately visible.

The Square Root function is a rule that says that with normal variation in demand, the amount of inventory needed centrally is the square root of the sum of the squares of the items that are needed if kept at decentralised locations. For example if 4 and 3 items are required to meet a certain service level at two locations, then the square root of

16+9 or 5 is needed at one location. Approximate. Think about this when considering how many ambulances, fire engines, policemen, emergency supplies, or distribution centre inventory are needed. However, against this must be set the decrease in response time. This may be an answer to the common practice in service and manufacturing of 'squirreling away' needed items – but of course trust is necessary (a systems approach!).

Standardisation is (may be?) a great way to reduce inventory. Can all field service units, aeroplanes, wards be similarly equipped? Probably not, but what can be standardised? See the separate section on Standardisation.

RFID (radio frequency identification) is becoming more feasible – less expensive and more reliable – for A and perhaps B items. It can help to track the location of important items. Also for security. A bit of a high-tech solution that may signal a command and control mentality.

Information Inventory

Personal computers and the internet are allowing service providers to re-think the push-pull point, also known as the postponement or decision point. This is the point along the value chain downstream of which service provision must wait for customer pull. As you move towards the high interaction end of the spectrum, providers such as professional services have traditionally not been able to anticipate customer requirements, and so long lead times have been an inherent feature.

Anticipation information 'inventories' are now much easier. Consider:

- Automated check-in for an airline, either at the airport or, in the case of BA, by printing out your boarding pass at home. No queuing.
- Hotels that keep data on frequent visitors, including sometimes credit card details, and pre-print the registration card. Sign in and collect your key. No delays.
- Online travel booking that keeps customer details.
- Insurance companies that keep property details online before a customer has made the initial contact (according to Chopra and Lariviere).
- Law firms that anticipate applications for company registration or accounting firms that deal with tax completion. Both of these

are done by segmenting the classes of applicant to smooth the delivery process.

- Online credit rating that can be carried out immediately while a loan application is being made.
- Decision support software, used by doctors and financial advisors, for example, to give quicker better service – or to be used directly by customers.
- Ipod and PowerPoint downloads for lecture courses. This potentially changes the whole ethos of a university, and perhaps some schools.
- Print-on-demand technology for books.
- In general, standard letters and forms can be produced, but this carries the risk of inappropriateness, like standard menus from a call centre. Customers can pre-print and submit application forms.

All of these are possible because the cost of holding information inventory is very low, and has massive economies of scale – unlike physical inventories. Fast updating is also possible. Like some physical inventories, information inventory can become outdated. But in all these cases, the real opportunity is not cost reduction but convenience to the customer.

'Information inventory' can, of course, be an aid to improved flow and to reducing peak demands – both of which are important to Lean service.

A trade-off can be made between, on the one hand, opportunities for growth through improved customer experience and reduced cost – including reduced peaks and staffing – and on the other hand, the cost of setting up the systems.

The question as to where the push-pull point should be located is, as Chopra and Lariviere suggest, an important decision that applies to an ever wider business audience.

So the fourth Lean principle, about the desirability of 'pull', is not quite the same for manufacturing as it is for service. In manufacturing it is almost always good to move the 'postponement' point as far downstream as possible. In service it is more complex and increasingly relevant.

Physical and Information Inventory Interface

The internet has also fundamentally changed physical inventories.

- As Christopher Anderson has pointed out in *The Long Tail*, the economics of some types of inventory, particularly downloadable types, have changed dramatically. In an audio store, CDs must compete for shelf space and cost money to hold. So an audio store can only afford to keep high-selling items. But on the internet, the cost of stocking an album is near zero. Even very low sellers generate profit. Hence the long tail, and less relevance to Pareto analysis. But more than this: the potential world of suppliers is also vastly increased. So, a visit to a record store in 2007 reveals that most audio CDs, except the top sellers, have gone. DVDs have replaced them. But will DVDs go the same way?
- To a lesser extent, the same applies to physical, (mainly) non-perishable items, distributed through warehouses rather than shops. Here the limitation is delivery: when will delivery companies learn that many people work during the day? Some companies are moving to overcome this – such as the use of dry-cleaner pick-up bins with an access key for out-of-hours collection. Could this be a trend that develops into each street having one cubic metre deposit boxes, accessed by pin codes that are given out by the deliverer?
- Loyalty cards, such as at Tesco UK, enable companies to track individual purchase decisions and preferences. As a result, Tesco tailors the blend of own brand 'value' items and 'finest' items to specific stores.

Physical Service Inventories

This book does not deal with physical inventory theory. This section comments on independent inventory demand, where there is no interdependency on an end item having a bill of materials (or 'recipe'). Independent demand inventory is, of course, a major concern for some service organisations such as shops and repair centres.

The inventory service level is related to cost in a non-linear way as shown in the figure. The figure also shows a typical current state. You can calculate the current state from routine aggregate inventory control theory, provided that you have reasonable knowledge of demand patterns for each stock-keeping unit (SKU).

Moving from the current state to any one of the alternative future states involves BOTH a decrease in cost AND an increase in service level. There are several alternatives, as shown: from retaining the current service level but reducing cost, to reducing cost but retaining the current service level, to improving both.

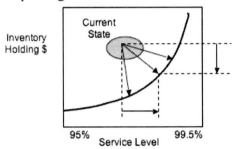

Service levels should be fixed for A (high value), B (medium value), and C (low value) items.

But what about forecasts? Conventional inventory demand control includes trend, seasonality, cycles, and random noise uncertainty levels. In service, a few more categories are necessary:

- **Trend**: positive or negative
- **Seasonality**: yearly period or specific holidays
- **New**: new product launch
- **Erratic**: up and down cycles caused by, for example, promotional activities
- **Lumpy**: caused by special but predictable events (e.g. sporting)
- **Slow moving**: occasional demand
- **Dying**
- **Obsolete**: dead – no movement.

Each one of these needs separate consideration. In moving from the current state to an improved state, some categories (e.g. obsolete) may be cut, others (e.g. erratic) increased.

Dependent inventory demand (such as with a bill of materials) is usually found within manufacturing. But not exclusively. A 'bill of material' may be 'attached' to some service offerings:

- A cancer patient
- A hotel guest, booked into bed and breakfast
- An airline passenger.

In each case a standard list of requirements is made. There is uncertainty, of course, but as with manufacturing, the netting process (comparing what there is with what is needed) continuously makes corrections.

Distribution Inventory: A Lesson from Tesco

Tesco is the 'Toyota' of food retailers – although food is increasingly only a part of the offering at its supermarkets. Tesco has carried out the usual Pareto analysis of SKU usage, but it has gone further than most. Traditionally in grocery stores there has been a distinction between the ways in which fresh foods and ambient items are managed. But why? Tesco has adopted a method that they call 'Flowthrough'. This involves:

- **Little/no stock of fast moving, predictable lines**. Top usage items, perhaps the top 2% of SKUs that account for a much higher percentage of unit sales, are replenished several times per day by vehicles that go on a 'milkround' with mixed model loads. This gives enormous competitive advantage: inventories are kept low, allowing a greater range to be kept on shelves but also minimising stockholding costs.
- **Ordering slow moving lines on a 'pick by line' basis**. This is the pull system in operation. Instead of delivering low moving items in traditional larger quantities, Tesco has worked hard to reduce the economic order size. This of course involves cooperation with suppliers as to packaging and also a re-think right along the distribution chain.
- **Matching product characteristics to the picking method**. Another break in traditional thinking is to push the actual pick point further upstream.

Tesco thinking on distribution was significantly influenced by a study which showed that a very high proportion of distribution costs occurred in the final 50m of the journey to the shelf. This is where considerable unloading, moving, unwrapping, shelf stacking, arrangement and pricing occur. Much of this is necessary non-value added activity. So Tesco is moving to a 'one touch' method for higher volume items. Here the manufacturer pre-packs product directly onto trolleys which are simply wheeled into their final place on the supermarket floor. No unpacking, double handling, shelf stacking. They look good, too.

The SKU Pareto is the vital tool that enables distribution decision-making. The SKU Pareto is simply cumulative demand against ranked products, enabling those few 'A' products that account for a high percentage of total demand to be identified. At the other end of the curve, the many 'C' products accounting for relatively small demand are also identified. This analysis can be done both by item number and by turnover along the cumulative demand axis. This is conventional, but Tesco takes it further.

Tesco thinks in terms of a cube with frequency along one axis (daily to weekly distribution), stocking point along the second axis (regionally to nationally), and distribution method along the third axis (flow to traditional stocking). Every SKU is found an appropriate location within this cube. There are sometimes other factors, such as temperature-sensitive or hanging or boxed products, that require special distribution considerations. Typically, the highest moving A category ambient items are locally distributed with the highest volume SKUs flowed, intermediate moving B items are regionally distributed, and low moving C items are nationally distributed using pallets for higher volume and mini-loads for the lowest volume. Demand changes, of course, so the locations within the cube change too. An adaptive, learning system is thus required. So there is no one channel for all – a lesson that Coca Cola learned about its distribution channels to different types of customer many years ago.

Demand Amplification

Lean supply chain thinkers know the dangers of demand amplification: excessively large warehouses, inventory pipeline costs, and risk of obsolescence or past sell-by date. Tesco has worked hard to reduce the effects of amplification by:

- Recognising the threat of amplification, and giving it management priority
- Reducing the number of levels in their supply chain
- Reducing the number of decision points (where another player in the chain decides on the quantity to order)
- Encouraging the trend towards smaller, more frequent batch quantities.

Further Reading

Sunil Chopra and Martin A. Lariviere, 'Managing Service Inventories to Improve Performance', *MIT Sloan Management Review*, Fall 2005, pp 57-63
Chris Anderson, *The Long Tail*, Random House Business Books, 2006
Barry Evans, 'Obsessed with the Customer: The Success of Tesco's Lean Operations', *Proc. Innovations in Lean Thinking – Annual Conference*, Lean Enterprise Research Centre, July 2007.
Further details on the Cost – Service Level Trade Off curve may be obtained from Mobius Consulting, www.mobiusconsulting.co.uk
Conventional service inventory management is discussed in Richard Metters *et al, Successful Service Operations Management*, Thompson, 2003

A Framework for Lean Service Quality

Drawing on the ideas of Hinckley, improvement in service quality
should be approached in each of three ways.

- The first approach is through a reduction in **complexity** in service
  process design.
- The second approach is through a reduction in **variation**.
- The third approach is though the prevention and reduction of
  errors and mistakes. The prevention, detection and elimination
  of errors and mistakes forms part of Jidoka, one of the pillars of
  the Lean temple.

For each of these three approaches (complexity, variation and mistakes),
there are six possible sources of problems: man/people, machine,
material, methods, measures and 'mother nature'. This gives a 3x6
table. In this section, tools relevant to each approach will be discussed.

	The Service Product	The Service Process
Complexity	Focusing on customer purpose, Kano model, Value Analysis and FAST	Layout ('servicescape'), 5S, Mapping, Value Analysis and FAST
Variation	Six Sigma, DFSS	Six Sigma, visibility, SPC, TPA, 7 Quality Tools, 5S, SOPs, Guidance notes
Mistakes and Errors	Pokayoke (mistake proofing)	Pokayoke, 5S, SOPs, visibility

Complexity

'Complexity' refers to both product and process, both from the
customer's viewpoint and from the service provider's viewpoint.

- From the customer's viewpoint, service product complexity
  refers to the ease of use of the service, and the ability to
  understand the service product. For example: how easy is it for
  a customer to understand the benefits and dangers of a pension
  plan? Service process complexity refers to the number of steps

required to obtain the service, or the number of handoffs that the customer must pass through.

- From the provider's viewpoint, service product complexity relates to the training that is required to deliver the service satisfactorily. Service process complexity refers to the number of operations, the number of handoffs, and the difficulty of each operation.

Relevant tools are described briefly below. Notice their overlapping, or synergistic nature.

- **Purpose analysis**: To clarify what the system is there to do, and what it is not there to do, is a huge aid to simplification. Does this sound obvious? Perhaps – but many service systems are in practice there to meet some imposed target or some manager's measures. The purpose must be an end-to-end purpose. Sub-systems often have their own local goals which are in conflict with the end-to-end purpose.

- **The Kano model**: Clarify the basics that must be done, the performance factors, and possible delighters. This helps to establish priorities. See the section on the Kano model.

- **Value Analysis** is a long-established series of methodologies that aims to deliver system functionality in the most beneficial way. This can follow from Purpose and Kano. Value in value analysis terms is function/cost. Function Analysis System Technique (FAST) is a team-based methodology that breaks down a product or service, such as making tea, into its basic functions, and then seeks to improve them through innovation by, among others, asking the Five Hows, and Five Whys.
  - FAST can be used with service products by breaking down the product into its elements, defining the purpose of each element (using verb plus noun, like 'provide security'), then using creativity tools to look at alternative ways in which the function could be provided better at the same cost, or the same at lower cost.
  - For service processes, FAST uses a map – a VSM or service blueprint is a good starting point – but expressed in verb plus noun terms, beginning at the left hand side with the purpose and expanding on the Hows. How-Why questions are applied along the map, typically in an expanding tree structure, to show alternatives, until suitable alternatives emerge. Creative thinking is required to

- **Layout, 5S and Mapping** are all discussed at length in this book.

- **Design for Six Sigma (DFSS)**: DFSS uses a defined set of steps called IDDOV (Identify, Define, Develop, Optimise, Verify) similar to the DMAIC steps in Six Sigma. It also uses a similar project organisation with Champions, Master Black Belts, Black Belts, and Green Belts.

  The Identify and Define stages aim to clarify the customer and his or her needs. Typical tools are the Kano model and Quality Function Deployment.
  The Develop stage involves brainstorming and identification of alternatives, and their evaluation. Techniques include TRIZ, Pugh analysis (Concept Screening), and FMEA (failure modes and effect analysis).
  The Optimise stage is not as robust in service design as it is in product design, which typically uses the Taguchi methodology for design optimisation. In service design the concentration is on prevention of defects and maximisation of customer benefit, rather than on detection and reduction of defects.
  Finally, the verify stage involves looking at the capability of the service process, by looking at required skill levels. Notice that, as with Six Sigma, a lot of attention is given at the front end. It is appropriate to take care at early stages to define the customer, the purpose, the environment, and the usage.

  Many of these tools are described in Bicheno and Catherwood, *Six Sigma and the Quality Toolbox,* and other publications on Six Sigma.

Variation

A principal approach for the reduction of variation is Six Sigma. But foundation tools for the limitation of variation include TPM, 5S, standard work and changeover reduction.

Before starting out on a sophisticated Six Sigma programme, a Lean company should ensure that they have made reasonable progress with 5S, visibility and standard work and, in many environments, with TPM, before starting out on a sophisticated Six Sigma programme. Not to do so is akin to sending in the medical specialists before the public health engineer. The medics will have point impact, but it is unlikely to be sustained. The public health engineer working to achieve clean water and removing pollution from sewage is likely to have much greater and more lasting impact. Then the medics take over to do their valuable work. This is not to say that a 5S program needs to be fully implemented: it is a question of picking off the 'low hanging fruit'.

Statistical Process Control (SPC) is a good technique for variation monitoring and control, provided that its limitations are recognised. SPC is concerned with monitoring the process, not the product or the people. If the process is good, and capable, then the products or services produced by the process will also be good.

Mistakes and Pokayoke

The toolbox for the control of mistakes, 5S, standard operating procedures, pokayoke, or mistake-proofing. 5S and standard work are discussed in separate sections. Here we discuss mistake-proofing. Mistakes are a 'big deal' in service: Stephen Spear quotes a figure of 98,000 deaths a year in US hospitals due to errors.

For that reason, mistakes are given special attention in this book.

Mistake-proofing (Pokayoke)

The late Shigeo Shingo did not invent mistake-proofing ('pokayoke' in Japanese, literally mistake proofing), or failsafe, but he developed and classified the concept, particularly in manufacturing. Mistake-proofing in services has developed more recently. The classic work is Shingo's book *Zero Quality Control: Source Inspection and the Pokayoke System*. More lately C Martin Hinckley has made a significant new contribution through his work *Make No Mistake!*

A mistake-proofing device is a simple, often inexpensive, device that literally prevents defects from being made. The characteristics of a mistake-proofing device are that it undertakes 100% automatic inspection (a true pokayoke would not rely on human memory or action), and either stops or gives warning when a defect is discovered. One example is a cell entry in an Excel spreadsheet that has been set up to take only specific data such as a number or a date. Amazon will not allow you to complete an order online before all data have been completed, and some of them checked. Note that a pokayoke is not a control device like a thermostat or toilet control valve that takes action every time, but rather a device that senses abnormalities and takes action only when an abnormality is identified.

Shingo talked about 'little' pokayoke and 'big' pokayoke cycles. 'Little' is where the mistake is stopped. 'Big' investigates why it arose in the first place. Both of these are necessary. But from a system viewpoint there is an even bigger cycle, and that is to look at the whole system and ask if the entire process or system can be failsafed – or, as Ackoff says, if the problem can be 'dissolved' from an end-to-end perspective. Remove the root cause from the system. Design it out.

Shingo distinguishes between 'mistakes' (which are inevitable) and 'defects' (which result when a mistake reaches a customer). The aim of pokayoke is to design devices that prevent mistakes becoming defects. Shingo also saw quality control as a hierarchy of effectiveness from 'judgment inspection', where inspectors inspect, to 'informative inspection', where information is used to control the process as in SPC, to 'source inspection', which aims at checking operating conditions 'before the fact'. Good pokayokes fall into this last category.

According to Shingo there are three types of mistake-proofing device: 'contact', 'fixed value', and 'motion step'. This means that there are six categories, as shown in the figure with service examples.

	Control	Warning
Contact	Parking height bars; bar coding on patients, and wrist bands on babies	Staff mirrors; shop entrance light beam; Disney queue warning signs, allergy warnings.
Fixed Value	French fry scoop; pre-dosed medication; valid ranges in Excel spreadsheet.	Kit carts with indentations; shadowboards; ink warning on printer; hamburger age flag;
Motion Step	Airline lavatory doors; 'Pick to light' warehouse picking system	Spellcheckers; beepers on ATM's; tax form completion checks; manager visit display board

This Table was developed from an original by Case and Stewart, 1995.

The **contact type** makes contact with every product or has a physical shape that inhibits mistakes. An example is a fixed diameter hole through which all products must fall; an oversize product does not fall through and a defect is registered. The **fixed value method** is a design that makes it clear when a part is missing or not used. An example is an 'egg tray' used for the supply of parts. The **motion step type** automatically ensures that the correct numbers of steps have been taken. For example, an operator is required to step on a pressure-sensitive pad during every assembly cycle, or a medicine bottle has a press-down-and-turn feature for safety. Other examples are a checklist, or correct sequence for switches that do not work unless the order is correct. McDonald's is famous for its large number of failsafe devices – from timers, to flags, to French fry scoops. A **warning type** may be an outline diagram of a patient's body showing which bits need which type of attention – this may prevent cutting off the wrong arm or applying ointment to a cut instead of a burn where the patient has both!

Shingo further developed failsafe classification by saying that there are five areas that have potential for mistake-proofing: the operator (Me), the Material, the Machine, the Method, and the Information (4 Ms plus I). An alternative is the process control model comprising input, process, output, feedback, and result. All are candidates for mistake-proofing.

Shingo says that pokayoke should be thought of as having both a short action cycle, where immediate shut down or warning is given, and a long action cycle, where the reasons for the defect occurring in the first place are investigated. John Grout makes the useful point that one drawback of pokayoke devices is that potentially valuable information about process variance may be lost, thereby inhibiting improvement.

Hinckley has developed an excellent approach to mistake-proofing. He has a classification scheme consisting of five categories of mistakes – defective material, defective information, misadjustment, omission, and selection errors. The last four have several sub-categories. For each category, typical mistake-proofing solutions have been developed. Thus, having identified the type of mistake, you can look through the set of possible solutions and adapt or select the most suitable one.

Pokayoke with Near Misses

If you were a patient in a hospital, what would you prefer: (a) being in a ward where many mistakes are reported, or (b) being in a ward where no mistakes are reported? Think about it. Is (b) because they are so good, or is it because they are so fearful or fed up with reporting problems about which no-one does anything?

Preventing mistakes also means anticipating mistakes. Near-miss analysis is a vital part of this. Aviation authorities have a well-ordered near-miss investigation sequence. There is a lot to learn from this. Bates, quoted by Spear, says that for every death due to medication error there were ten injuries and 100 instances where harm was averted. In health and safety there has been long-standing recognition of unsafe acts and unsafe conditions. Near-misses need to be routinely recorded and analysed in a 'no fears' environment:

- In hospitals, we assumed that the critical procedure had already been done but luckily found out that it had not, or we had to delay the operation when we discovered that the medication had passed its 'use-by' date.
- In restaurants, we nearly cooked sirloin rather than fillet, or nearly allowed nuts to get into the dessert.
- In consultancies, we nearly sent out the wrong report version, or disclosed confidential information.
- In a bank, we nearly allowed confidential credit card information to go out with the regular garbage.
- In maintenance, we just happened to have the right spare available, otherwise a repeat trip would have been necessary.

A near-miss is also spotting a situation where a customer could have complained but did not. Remember the rule of thumb that only 10% of customers actually complain.

Making complaining easier is a part of this. But begin from Deming's 94/6 rule that 94% of problems are due to the process, only 6% due to the people. So, what is it in the process that has led to the problem? Again, Ackoff's maxim that trying to dissolve problems is better than trying to solve them is relevant.

So a near-miss procedure needs to be easy to record, non-threatening, no-blame and either addressed immediately or as part of a routine process – perhaps around the daily Communications Board meeting or the weekly review. It may need to be built into an established, visible Concern, Cause, Countermeasure (3C) procedure. Please do not rely only on Standard Operating Procedures – a SOP simply cannot anticipate all situations. Setting up a near-miss procedure is the responsibility of management. Otherwise near-misses will simply go on for years, until a near-miss becomes a hit with possibly severe results.

Admitting to Mistakes

Admitting mistakes to customers has been shown to be a very effective thing to do, to retain customer loyalty (Goodman). It turns out that customers are often more loyal if a company admits its mistakes and apologises than if no problem has arisen in the first place!

And allowing for customer mistakes and company mistakes by allowing a 'no quibble' returns policy is also good both for inning customers and for retaining them. This famous policy was adopted by Marks and Spencer, and is now widely copied.

Pokayoke with Cycle of Service

Pokayoke is one of the standard considerations used with 'Interactive' mapping. See the section on Interactive Mapping. Here the customer's Moments of Truth are followed through stage by stage, and each stage is checked to see if the step can be mistake-proofed. But 'cycle of service' should, of course, begin with the 'pre' stage, follow through with the 'during' stages, and conclude with the 'post' or follow up stages. Godfrey *et al*, working in healthcare, have suggested useful ideas that can be linked into Interactive mapping but also extended to wider service.

Much of the following overlaps with 5S and visual management activity. Gwen Galsworth, talking about four levels of visual management, gives the analogy of a railway road crossing: passive (a warning sign), assertive (a flashing warning), aggressive (a physical barrier or lifting gate), and assured (a bridge separating road from rail).

Pre-Stage: Elimination: This is where the possibilities for accidents and errors are eliminated even before the routine work begins. Examples:
- Remove sharp objects, locate shadow boards and identify standard locations as part of a 5S activity. For example, a shadow board located near the point of use (perhaps on a trolley in a hospital) not only makes it apparent when an implement is missing but prevents the wrong implement being used by having to fetch it from another location.
- Eliminate handoffs to create a one-stop service.
- Eliminate the need for multiple data entry.
- Eliminate unsatisfactory human work conditions through ergonomics, leading to errors and injury.

- Eliminate sources of noise and reasons for eye protection. Many video and record shops have far higher levels of noise than are found in many factories requiring ear protection.

Pre-Stage: Replacement: Replacing human actions by automated actions for safety and error reasons. Examples: automatic smoke or gas detection, automatic air extraction, safety belt warnings, warning lights on office equipment, message waiting on answer phones.

During Stage: Facilitation: Make the work easier to carry out and less error prone. Examples: valid ranges in a spreadsheet, checklists, colour coding, traffic light data presentation rather than numbers, ergonomics in general, provision of ear and sign protection.

During Stage: Detection: Examples: kit carts, non-completion of required fields in data entry, workplace audit boards showing that various levels of management have visited the area, monthly reporting boards.

Post Stage: Mitigation*:* Reduce the effects of an error. Examples: cross checking, double-checking, asking air passengers to check for items left behind or hotel guests to check for their room key. Several lecturers on service management courses tell the story of the hotel concierge chasing after them because they hadn't been reminded to check their room before departure. Have flipcharts for recording types of problem so that they can be addressed by future kaizen activity.

In a more general context, many of these actions can be seen as 'Fitting the Task to the Human' rather than the other way around. This has long been a quest in ergonomics. The attention of the reader is drawn to the many good books on ergonomics, such as that given in Further Reading, which discuss issues such as workstation design (chairs and table heights), lighting, vision, noise, vibration, fatigue, lifting, and even stress and eating habits at or before work.

Pokayoke and Customer Mistakes

Customers also make mistakes – and may then blame the product or service! Stephen Tax quotes the World Health Organization which has identified the failure of patients to take prescribed medications correctly as a major problem. Customers should be thought of as 'co-producers', according to Tax. Vanguard Consulting, working with the UK police, has shown that a very high proportion of '999' calls are not emergencies as defined by the authorities, such as assault or heart attack, but are in fact events that can be given much lower priority.

Customer mistake-proofing can be a matter of attitude on the part of the service provider. Start with the assumption that customers want to succeed and are not lazy, rather than simply blaming them for being stupid or lacking motivation, or even benefiting from their 'mistakes' (such as taking out gym membership only to give it up after a short while). Customer punishment is the often-adopted explicit or implicit solution. This is like Theory X and Theory Y. So what can the organisation do to help the customer to retain the gym membership, to use the useful features on a phone, to attend on time, to stick to the diet, to avoid the lost receipt, or to pay on time? Tax *et al* point out that this can be a source of real competitive advantage.

Customer failures may not be apparent in a superficial mapping study. But customer failures should be apparent if you conscientiously adopt the 'check' stage advocated by John Seddon and described in the high level mapping Tool section. 'Check' looks out for Failure Demand by noting the actual words used by customers when they call in or make demands on the system.

A suggested methodology is:

- Listen to customers' actual words during routine Moments of Truth, when demands come into the system. Sampling is usually necessary. This is by far the most powerful source of data because the comments are unsolicited. Separate failure demand from value demand. For definitions of value and failure demand see the separate section.
- Question existing customers about their experience in using the product or service. Questionnaires are useful, but their interpretation and use is different from the usual. Often questionnaires are used for evaluation or market survey purposes. Here they are used to help to identify causes of failure.
- Question lost customers. Why did they leave?
- Collect complaints – not only formal written complaints, but also verbal complaints which need to be collected by front line staff in a blame-free, 'no-fears' problem-solving environment. Do not use complaints only to look at internal processes, but also use them to look at why the customer failed to do what was expected by the organisation.

- Observe customers using or attempting to use the product or service. Xerox copy centres used to do this. Quicken software was developed by 'over the shoulder' methods. This may include following a new patient in a hospital, a new customer in a bank, and monitoring keystrokes.
- Monitor what John Seddon calls 'dirty data' – incorrectly filled-in forms and the like.
- From all these sources, group the failures into categories, using the Affinity Diagram, where post-its are grouped together. Be particularly aware of customer 'failures' or complaints.
- Then, seek the root causes of customer failure. Why did the customer make the mistake, why did he get lost, why did she use the service incorrectly? Use the Five Whys and the fishbone diagram. Do a self-test: put yourself in the shoes of a customer or ask a member of your staff not concerned with the process to use it.
- Solutions come in many forms: 5S, simplification, training, and technical. On creative thinking in general see books by Roger von Oech. For more technical solutions refer to Martin Hinckley and, of course, TRIZ.

Peter Willmott, doyen of UK practitioners on Total Productive Maintenance, gives more than 20 checks that everyone can carry out on their car with no technical skill but using only their 'god-given senses'. Pointing out these checks to new car purchasers would certainly end many mistakes as well as prolong the life of the car and perhaps the life of the user. Why not extend this practice to many types of product and service?

To summarise: the greatest problem with mistakes is recognising the problem in the first place. This must be followed by the right attitude to its solution: that the customer's problem is in fact your problem.

Further Reading

Shigeo Shingo, *Zero Quality Control: Source Inspection and the Pokayoke System*, Productivity Press, 1986
C Martin Hinckley, *Make No Mistake*, Productivity Press, Portland, 2001
Richard Chase and Douglas Stewart, *Mistake-Proofing: Designing Errors Out*, Productivity, 1995
An impressive, award winning, web site with numerous examples and pictures is at:
http://csob.berry.edu/faculty/jgrout/pokayoke.shtml
A Blanton Godfrey *et al*, *Healthcare Focused Error Proofing*, North Carolina State University, 2005
Stephen Spear, 'Fixing Healthcare from the Inside, Today', *Harvard Business Review*, September 2005, pp 78-91
Stephen Tax, Mark Colgate, David Bowen, 'How to Prevent Your Customers from Failing', *MIT Sloan Management Review*, Spring 2006
K Kroemer and E Grandjean, *Fitting the Task to the Human: A Textbook of Occupational Ergonomics*, (5th+ edition), Taylor and Francis, 2000
Gwendolyn Galsworth, *Visual Management*, Productivity

Kaizen and Knowledge Management

Kaizen is the Japanese name for continuous improvement. As such it is central to Lean operations, whether in manufacturing or service. The word stems from Kai (to change or take apart) and Zen (to make better). It brings together several of the tools and techniques described in this book and a few more.

Although FW Taylor is a hero to many industrial engineers, the writer included, he did separate the thinkers from the doers. This is exactly opposed to the spirit of Kaizen. In many Western companies the FW Taylor view persists. Consider that most new innovations come from R&D, and that salaries of top managers are huge multiples of those of front line staff. In Kaizen, everyone is a knowledge worker. It is about bottom-up innovation. But more than this: it is about the 'Knowledge Creating Company' where 'tacit' knowledge is tapped. Tacit knowledge is 'know-how', 'the way we do things around here', based on years of practical experience, much of it not written down. This is opposed to 'explicit' knowledge that is written down in codified formulas, procedures and principles. So there are two 'worlds': front line staff and operators exchange 'tacit to tacit' knowledge and some explicit knowledge, while engineers, managers and academics exchange 'explicit to explicit' knowledge. One strength of kaizen is that it sets out to bridge the gap by moving knowledge from 'tacit' to 'explicit', thereby exposing whole rafts of ideas and enabling them to be explicitly incorporated. And 'explicit' knowledge can become 'tacit' by force of habit. Is this why Toyota doesn't send its people on MBA programmes?

According to Imai, author of the original book on Kaizen, it comprises several elements. Kaizen is both a philosophy and a set of tools.

The Philosophy of Kaizen: Quality begins with the customer. But customers' views are continually changing and standards are rising, so continuous improvement is required. Kaizen is dedicated to continuous improvement, in small increments, at all levels, forever. Everyone has a role, from top management to shop floor employees.

Imai believes that without active attention, the gains made will simply deteriorate (like the engineers' concept of entropy). But Imai goes further. Unlike Juran, who emphasises 'holding the gains', Kaizen involves building on the gains by continuing experimentation and innovation.

According to Imai there are several guiding principles. These include:

- **Questioning the rules**: standards are necessary but work rules are there to be broken and must be broken with time.
- **Developing resourcefulness**: it is a management priority to develop the resourcefulness and participation of everyone.
- **Trying to get to the Root Cause**: try not to solve problems superficially.
- **Eliminating the whole task**: question whether a task is necessary.
- **Reducing or changing activities**: be aware of opportunities to combine tasks.

Essential features include:

- **Kaizen is continuous**: this indicates both the embedded nature of the practice and also its place in a never-ending journey towards quality and efficiency.
- **It is usually incremental in nature**, in contrast to major management-initiated reorganisations or technological innovation (for example, the installation of new technology or machinery).
- **It is participative**: it entails the involvement and intelligence of the work force, generating intrinsic psychological and quality of work life benefits for employees.
- **Its solutions are 'low-cost, no-cost'**: not about installing equipment or systems, but about improving present systems.
- **It taps into the 'tacit' knowledge of all staff**, surfacing this knowledge to make it explicit.

The Kaizen Flag

The Kaizen Flag is a famous diagram developed by Imai and widely copied and adapted. The flag portrays the three types of activity with which everyone in a Kaizen organisation should be involved. These are 'Innovation, 'Kaizen', and 'Standardisation' against organisation level. An adapted version is discussed below.

In the original, senior management spends more time on 'innovation' to do with tomorrow's products and processes, less time on 'kaizen' to do with improving today's products and processes, but also a small proportion of time on 'standardisation', that is following the established best way of doing tasks. In top management's case this would be policy deployment and budgeting. A standard method is the current best and safest known way to do a task, until a better way is found through kaizen.

Middle managers spend less time than top managers on innovation, about the same time on kaizen and more time on standardisation. Operators spend a small, but significant, proportion of time on innovation, more time on kaizen, and most time on standardisation.

Kate Mackle, former head of the British Kaizen Institute and now Principal in the consultancy Thinkflow, explains that innovation is concerned with preventing waste from entering tomorrow's processes, kaizen is concerned with getting waste out of today's processes, and standardisation is concerned with keeping waste out.

The version of the flag presented below is based on Imai's original, but takes into account both experience and the ideas of the decision process developed by Ilbury and Sunter.

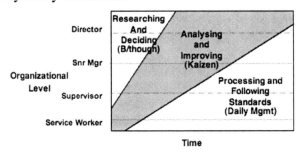

Here 'processing' is following the current standard best and safest known way.

Kaizen and Experimentation

In manufacturing there is the famous Lean 'water and rocks analogy'. The water, or inventory, covers the rocks, or problems. So you deliberately experiment by reducing the water level (take out inventory) to expose the rocks (problems). Not just any problem, but the most pressing problem. Reducing the inventory is supposed to be a 'win-win' strategy: either nothing happens, in which case you run tighter, or you hit the prominent problem, which is good because it is exposed. This is one form of point kaizen. It is also PDSA – plan, do, study, act.

In service, you should also deliberately experiment. The nice thing is that the scope for experimentation in service is vast and the evaluation much faster than in manufacturing. How so? Because there are numerous parallel activities in service: hotel rooms, flights, bank or shop branches, insurance claims, on and on. Why not, therefore, set up trials with, say, room make-up in a quarter of hotel rooms, trial menus at particular locations, or claim procedures for 10% of claims? Then get your customers to help to evaluate?

This kind of experimentation could be part of the Level 2 or Level 3 redesign process. You will need to collect ideas for the trials from employees or customers, or ideas coming out of the mapping process. This concept is by no means new. Google allows new ideas to be posted on their intranet and voted on by employees. IDEO undertakes controlled experimentation: many small failures but a few great successes. Harrah's Entertainment experimentation in Casinos is described in a case study. Harrah was able to conduct experiments, each involving a control group and an experimental group of customers who were given different incentive packages, with the location of slot machines, and with different staff training programmes.

Experimentation, of course, is not enough. The better ways need to be spread and incorporated.

Further Reading

Maasaki Imai, *Kaizen: The Key to Japan's Competitive Success*, McGraw Hill, New York, 1986
Maasaki Imai, *Gemba Kaizen*, McGraw Hill, New York, 1997
Ikujiro Nanaka, 'The Knowledge Creating Company', *Harvard Business Review*, 1991, reprinted in *HBR* July-August 2007
Jeffrey Pfeffer and Robert Sutton, *Hard Facts, Dangerous Half Truths and Total Nonsense*, Harvard Business School Press, 2006
Rajiv Lal, *Harrah's Entertainment Inc.*, Case 9-502-011, Harvard Business School / ECCH

Kaizen Events
or Improvement Events

Kaizen events are useful if not essential supplements to ongoing individual-based improvement activities. They can incorporate all the types of mapping described in this publication, and implement many of the improvements over a very short period of time.

At the outset we should say that kaizen events have developed from manufacturing where the focus is on the internal process – it is inward looking. This is still the thinking in many service organisations. But there is another opportunity: the customer-focused kaizen event. Here the focus shifts to solving (or dissolving!) the customer's problems or improving the customer's effectiveness. This means putting yourself in the shoes of the customer. It means redefining the system boundary to include the customer. Of course many processes, like the Custom type and the Interactive type, have strong customer involvement all the way through so it is only natural to include them.

Be careful. <u>It is very tempting to rush into a kaizen event</u>. It may even produce good results and make everyone feel good. But what happens if the process is the wrong process? Then the event is simply rearranging deckchairs on the Titanic. So it is essential to do an overall systems evaluation first. What is the purpose of the system? Will the event contribute to the best overall solution from the customer's point of view? Only then….

Given that the right theme has been identified, a company and its customers could be benefiting within a week from a leap in productivity in one area of its plant or office. Events are about 'going for it', about a preference for doing it now and reasonably rather than later but perhaps never, even though it could be done better; they are about learning by doing, by trial and error. They are also about involvement in office and service processes by office and service people. They are about real empowerment to 'just do it' without asking for permission to make every little change. A well planned and followed through event has a good chance of sustaining its improvements over an extended period. Poorly planned and executed events, however, have frequently slipped back to the original state – and given such events a poor name in some organisations.

Today, 'Kaizen Blitz' (the name used by the US Association for Manufacturing Excellence) is well proven in both service and manufacturing companies. In the UK, Industry Forum (IF) has adopted kaizen events as a standard approach originally for automotive suppliers (referred to as the Master Class process). The IF methodology has spread to aerospace, the metals industry, and construction, among others. Some consulting groups such as TBM and Simpler have developed their own versions.

The IF methodology was aimed at rolling out the kaizen event process. Each event would also have the aim of training more facilitators to be able to run more events and introducing the concept to supervisors and others from areas intended as targets in the future.

An appropriate quote to introduce kaizen events is:

> 'Whether you believe you can,
> or whether you believe you can't,
> you're absolutely right.'
> (Henry Ford)

Today we recognise that successful kaizen events require a great deal of preparation and follow up to be successful. The IF methodology, for instance, consists of:

- A one-day pre-diagnostic to select the area, discuss expectations, and review measures and the measurement systems that are in place.
- An initial preparation period during which measures and basic quality and demand data are collected. This is the scoping stage.
- After about two weeks, a three-day Diagnostic event takes place. The aim here is to establish and clarify what is to be the aim of the event itself. The team is chosen. Mapping is typical here, as is basic education on the Seven Wastes and the Seven Tools of Quality. The chosen team makes a presentation to management and everyone concerned on what they aim to do during the event. Objectives are agreed, and all necessary authorisations made. During the event, you do not want to have to seek permission to make changes. Assurances must be established on possible reduction in manning levels. Sometimes a Lean game is played by the team and perhaps by the operators from the area.
- A further period of preparation takes place over the next few weeks. The measures are firmed up. Final preparation takes place. This may include, for instance, building ahead of schedule to ensure continuity of service during the event, and warning support staff such as maintenance and electricians to be

on hand for the event. Any foreseen resources such as tools, tables, boards, racks, and post-its must be acquired.

- A check day takes place during this period for any final arrangements.
- The event itself is a five-day workshop. The idea is to go round the PDCA cycle a few times, ending with some tested, standardised changes. The workshop is facilitated by an IF engineer. Measures are taken each day. On the last day a presentation is made. Follow up actions are given to specific people.
- After the five-day workshop, three one-day follow up sessions are held at monthly intervals. These are to ensure that changes which could not be put in place during the workshop are in fact implemented. Examples are moving a machine embedded in concrete or targeting a quality issue that was not 'cracked' during the workshop.
- Finally, the IF engineer stays in contact with the organisation for an extended period to check sustainability.

A kaizen event can target different aspects. Layout and 5S often come first. Safety may be chosen in an environment with difficult union issues. Later, follow-up events can address lead time and manning.

Below is a proven methodology.

Generally:

- The workshop itself is the easy part. The harder and longer parts are the preparation and follow-up.
- The participation of managers, supervisors and team leaders is essential. The participation of customers is highly desirable, if not essential, certainly in the Interactive and often in the Custom types of process.
- Do not rely excessively on kaizen events – they are only a small part of wider Lean implementation.
- Events should be co-ordinated through a wider Lean implementation program. Although non-bottleneck kaizens are acceptable from the point of view of motivation, the first priority should be on bottleneck or problem areas that will make an impact on cost, quality and delivery.
- All participants should have a clear understanding of how the particular event will contribute to the overall Lean vision and objectives.
- A good facilitator is essential.

- Early successes are contagious.
- Visual management (e.g. a 'war room' for maps) is needed.
- Recognition is vital.
- Involve a few 'outsiders' – people outside the area but not necessarily from outside the company.
- A standardised approach should be developed on a site.
- Write up the event on an A3 and display it on the wall for a standardised period of perhaps 18 months.
- Follow up is crucial. Loose ends must be closed off within a few weeks at most.

The Kaizen Event Process

Some weeks ahead of the event:

- Select the area – probably from mapping and end-to-end value stream or from an accumulation of problems. Certainly take the overall 'systems view' of the process, including the customer, to avoid working on a process that should not be there in the first place.
- In service events, give specific consideration to whether the system boundary or problem area should be extended to include customer systems.
- In all service cases it is important to see the process from the customer's perspective. This aspect must be covered before the event begins.
- Select an appropriate time for the event. This is more important in an office than a factory because variation is usually larger.
- The group needs to be warned about the event, and participants from the group sought.
- Measures: decide on relevant measures for the area, and take the measures.
- Team selection: one or more facilitators, front line managers from the area, the event owner, participants from the area, subject matter experts, people from the next most likely area for an event, outsiders. Around twelve is a good number – bigger for bigger areas, smaller for smaller areas.
- Give consideration to 'tagging' in office areas where there are longer cycle activity durations. Tagging could involve placing 'travellers' on documents, or it could be done electronically - requesting people to enter arrival times and departure times on the traveller. Of course, this needs to be explained to the group.
- Draw up an 'Event Charter'. This sets out

- the focus or principle concern of the event
- the aims of the event – what it is hoped will be achieved
- current issues in the area to be addressed during the event
- the event boundary
- demand data: how much work the office or area handles per day, and how this varies across the day, week, month
- the dates of the event and duration
- who the participants are to be – including the facilitator
- what extra rooms will be used
- catering arrangements
- health and safety considerations (if electrical points or heavy items may be moved)
- any approvals that may be needed should be signed off
- the extent to which work will continue in the area (if at all) during the event. If not, what to do.
- any training that may be required.

The event itself (typical)

- **Day 1**: Introductions, aims and scope, background. Why the event is important, event methodology, basic Lean training including mapping, waste awareness, tools such as the fishbone diagram, and, if relevant, practice on observation timing.
- **Day 2**: Go to the area and observe, map the routings, time durations, discuss the process with the people. Possibly with the customers in some types of service process. Many offices have longer cycle operations so it may not be possible to observe or time all activities, so tagging (see above) or sample events may be used. If possible observe several cycles. Begin to generate ideas.
- **Day 3**: Generate ideas, discuss round the maps, formulate plans to implement. Start the implementation.
- **Day 4**: The main day for implementation. Try out and adjust. Discuss with office workers and other shifts. Begin to prepare flipcharts for the presentation on Day 5. Check or estimate the measures.
- **Day 5**: A final check and adjust. Document the new process. List follow-up items. Prepare an A3 summary sheet. Finish flipcharts for presentation. Present to area managers and senior directors. Agree next steps. Enjoy the free buffet.

After the event it is necessary to

- Close off any outstanding points. On the last day of the event the persons responsible for doing or coordinating these mopping-up mini-projects must be identified. The event champion or a line manager MUST follow these up. In at least one service organisation, kaizen events lost credibility due to the ever-increasing list of outstanding topics that were never closed down.
- Have a review session every (say) month for a period of (say) six months. These may be very short meetings. But they are there to look at the continuing performance of the area, and, very importantly, to record lessons learned. In other words they are 'after action reviews'.

Some lessons learned about kaizen events over recent years

- The workshop itself is the easy part. The harder and longer part is the preparation and follow-up. An approximate time split is 40% preparation, 30% workshop, and 30% follow-up.
- The participation of managers in events is essential. Without this they will be lukewarm or even critical. Management participation also helps to overcome the problem of seeking authorisation.
- The participation of the supervisor or team leader from the area is essential.
- Moreover, the supervisor should attend one or two events in other areas before it is the turn of his or her area. Think how you would feel if a team descended on your area for a week and produced a 40% productivity improvement. Not too good – you may be motivated to show that what has been done was not all that good in retrospect. Ideally, when it is the turn of the supervisor to have a kaizen event in his area, he will already be the most enthusiastic participant, having experienced it elsewhere.
- Kaizen events should be co-ordinated through a Lean Promotion Office (or similar) in relation to a wider Lean implementation programme, via value stream mapping.
- All participants should have a clear understanding how the particular event contributes to the overall Lean vision or objectives.

- A good facilitator is invaluable. The ability to spot waste and opportunity builds slowly. Take the opportunity to transfer some of these skills.
- Blitz events work better in supportive companies. See the quotation from Henry Ford above. Do not set expectations too high. Under-promise and over-deliver.
- Sustainability remains the big issue.

Finally, we have identified a number of good and not so good practices:

Good:

- Have a systems view of the context into which the study area fits.
- Evidence of senior management leadership and direction setting, staff access to management, and recognition of successes.
- Link the event to some benefit to the employees – such as space saving used for a coffee area, or improved furniture.
- Have a short follow up review session every month for a few months.
- Customer and stakeholder focus.
- Employee involvement.
- Training and development and use of the Investors in People Standard.
- High energy and participation from everyone involved.
- When management is engaged, road blocks are removed quickly.
- When everyone involved in events is prepared to 'roll up their sleeves' – this has a strong impact on the people on the office floor.
- External help is invaluable in events until they become well established.
- Have events across the board at all stages end-to-end: customer facing, clerical, administrative, operations, distribution, maintenance.
- Awareness in Lean generates pull for training in some areas of the organisation.
- Learn from failures. Some events will fail – have a careful look back and seek answers.
- Measurement and feedback on the measures is important.

Cautions:

- Target kaizen events on key business metrics, not just in areas willing to participate.
- Build on what has been learned and leverage to other areas without it necessitating another kaizen event.
- Develop internal competencies – don't depend on external consultants/trainers
- Ensure all actions chosen for completion during kaizen event are directly related to achieving the charter.

Not so good:

- Lack of identification of critical success factors.
- Lack of understanding of the concepts of quality and continuous improvement by some managers and employees.
- Insufficient integration of continuous improvement activities.
- Existence of a 'blame culture' when mistakes occur which may inhibit innovation.
- Benefits not showing on financial radar, benefits not reaching the bottom line.
- Poor follow through – failure to close out on actions.
- Lack of visibility for non-participants. Use visual displays/ storyboards on the floor during and after the event – keep everyone informed of progress.
- Reliance on 'quick fixes' and fire fighting.

Further Reading

Nicola Bateman, *Sustainability: A Guide to Process Improvement*, Lean Enterprise Research Centre, Cardiff University and Industry Forum, 2001. *See LERC website.*

Sid Joynson and Andrew Forrester, *Sid's Heroes: 30% Improvement in Productivity in 2 Days*, BBC, London, 1996

Anthony C Laraia, Patricia Moody, and Robert Hall, *The Kaizen Blitz: Accelerating Breakthroughs in Productivity and Performance,* John Wiley and Sons, New York, 1999

Siobhan Geary, *Kaizen Blitz*, MSc dissertation, LERC, Cardiff, 2006

The best magazine/journal on 'kaizen blitz' is *Target: The Periodical of the Association for Manufacturing Excellence.* More recently the magazine has begun to include office and administration examples.

Acknowledgements

Thanks to Andy Brophy of Hewlett Packard.

Thanks also to Bjarne Olsen of SAS who really brought home the importance of involving the customer.

Standard Work and Standard Operating Procedures in Service

Standard work is somewhat controversial in service. This should not be the case. It is a question of degree. Nobody questions the need for correct procedures in the case of a heart attack. And there are certainly better, standard, ways of conducting meetings, of communicating with the workforce. In service it is said that 'punctuality is the courtesy of kings and the stern duty of business people'. Punctuality is standard.

Moreover, especially in service, standards are actually a force for empowerment, for liberation, for creativity, rather than being restrictive. This has been described by Adler as 'The Toyota Paradox'. The military uses 'rules of engagement' to direct the modern soldier in fluid situations where 'thinking on your feet' is vital to success. The soldier knows that if he stays within the broad framework he will have the full weight of his government, or indeed the UN, behind him. He may shoot to kill if fired upon. He must treat prisoners within certain parameters. These are standards. Similarly, the maxim used by the Ritz Carlton Hotel group, 'We are ladies and gentlemen serving ladies and gentlemen,' is a superb short statement of standard.

Why is it then that standards are controversial in service? Because they can be misapplied by unwitting, unthinking management. A 'standard' that requires a call centre worker to handle a call within three minutes, or not to take 'no' for an answer first time around, or not to use initiative to solve customer problems, is misapplication. Ohno, the great Toyota champion of standards, would have been appalled.

John Seddon believes that 'standardisation stops the system from absorbing variety'. This is a serious and valid consideration. Certainly OVER-standardisation prevents a system from adapting to the infinite variety of customer requests. This is what is so wrong with many menu-driven answer machines and with standard forms sent out in all cases. It just adds to failure demand. So, be warned. But then 'don't throw the baby out with the bath water'.

The best and most sustainable standard is a standard that is so good, so obvious, that doing the task any other way is seen as just plain silly. This may have to be demonstrated. But that is the end state, the vision to strive for.

Any standard that generates failure demand – causing the customer to do it all again, but this time with less good will – should be scrapped. So should a standard which becomes confused with a target and generates silly behaviour, such as an ambulance driving around the car park so that the patient will not join a measured queue. Another poor use of a standard is where it becomes confused with an accounting or costing standard – especially with absorption costing, where failure to meet the budgeted rate of work leads to under-recovery of overhead and hence pressures to over-produce to 'recover' the overhead. This is plain nonsense in the context of Lean. Similarly, requiring office workers to tape standard locations for pens and folders on their desks. On the other hand, procedures in an accident and emergency room need to be much more carefully specified. Not top-down imposed, but discussed, reviewed and updated by the people doing the job for the people doing the job. In some cases, such as medicine, help in establishing the standard may be required from an expert.

So, a balance needs to be sought. There is a double Pareto. First, not all processes in service need a standard procedure. Perhaps only the 'Top 10' recurring processes in an area require one. Second, within those processes, only a few critical steps need to have standard requirements – typically to ensure quality and reduce failure demand. (By contrast, how on earth can a service worker work with 50 or more standard procedures? Much less learn them?)

Three useful quotations set the scene:

'To standardise a method is to choose out of many methods the best one, and use it. What is the best way to do a thing? It is the sum of all the good ways we have discovered up to the present. It therefore becomes the standard. Today's standardisation is the necessary foundation on which tomorrow's improvement will be based. If you think of "standardisation as the best we know today, but which is to be improved tomorrow" - you get somewhere. But if you think of standards as confining, then progress stops.'

(Henry Ford, *Today and Tomorrow*, 1926)

'In a Western company, the standard operation is the property of management or the engineering department. In a Japanese company it is the property of the people doing the job. They prepare it, work to it, and are responsible for improving it. Contrary to Taylor's teaching, the Japanese combine thinking and doing, and thus achieve a high level of involvement and commitment.'

(Peter Wickens, former HR Director, Nissan UK)

'A proper (standard) procedure cannot be written from a desk. It must be tried and revised many times in the production plant. Furthermore, it must be a procedure that anybody can understand on sight.

For production people to be able to write a standard work sheet that others can understand, they must be convinced of its importance.'

(Taiichi Ohno)

From the first quotation we learn that a standard is not static, but improves over time. From the second we learn that a standard is not imposed from on high. From the third we learn that standards are inherently practical. A good standard comes out of a bottom-up questioning culture, ever seeking a better, simpler, safer way to do a task – not a top-down imposed way of working. If you have no standard you cannot improve, by definition. So standards are part of PDCA.

Standards should not be there to 'catch you out', but to enable. This is like a tennis or golf lesson. You don't hide your weaknesses from the coach, you bring them out because you want to improve. That is the essential spirit that needs to be fostered.

Standard and Davies explain that there are three key aspects of standard work which need to be understood. Standard work is not static, and when a better way is found the procedure is updated.

1   Standard work supports stability and reduces variation because the work is performed the same way each time. Moreover variations (defects, deviations, discrepancies) are easily recognised.
2   Standard work is essential for continuous improvement – moving from one standard to a better standard without slipping back.

Note that 'standards' does not mean the rigid, workstudy imposed, job specification that is associated with classic mass production. Such standards have no place in the world of Lean, and especially in service. For such 'jobs' industrial sabotage and absenteeism are to be expected. Beware, however, of the human relations based reaction against 'work standards', which are often confused with workstudy. Allowing standards that are too loose on critical aspects may lead to no standards, which in turn leads to decreased safety and productivity.

In service a standard may be a written Standard Operating Procedure (SOP). But it may also be a checklist, or an understanding about methods with your colleagues. The second type may be the most enduring. But it should not be left to chance. Get the groups to discuss their standards formally, at standard intervals. Group norms then kick in. In any case, it is not necessary to cover all the steps. Only the main or critical steps need development.

So, in service, a standard might just be a checklist of the essential steps or data that must be covered. The rest is left open.

Also, beware of thinking that standards have no place in non-repetitive work such as maintenance, service, design, or senior management. Good, flexible maintenance and service work are built by combining various small standard work elements. Good design comes out of creativity combined with standard methods and materials, adhering to standard procedures and gateways. At Disney Florida, for example, visitors to Universal Studios walk through section by section. Within each section, the section time is divided into blocks and in each block certain loosely-scripted material must be covered by the artist. Do visitors notice this? No, they enjoy the professional but personalised delivery.

Management standards should exist for meetings, communications, budgets, and many other activities. Strike the right balance of detail.

Spear and Bowen in a classic article discuss the apparent paradox of TPS that activities, communications and flows at Toyota are at once rigidly scripted yet enormously flexible and adaptable. They conclude that it is the specification of standards and communications that gives the system the ability to make huge numbers of controlled changes using the scientific method. Without standards and the scientific method, change would amount to little more than trial and error.

Peter Wickens, former HR Director of Nissan UK, explains that for an 'ascendant organisation' there must be both concern for the people and control of the processes. Without concern for people you have an 'alienated organisation'; without concern for the processes you have 'anarchy'. This is a good way of thinking about standards in service. Both dimensions are needed.

Despite what some people think about Frederick Taylor, there remains 'one best way', with available technology, to do any task, which will minimise time and effort and maximise safety, quality and productivity. To some this may sound like boring repetition, but the 'new' standards are about participation in developing the best and safest way, mastery of several jobs, and the ability to adapt to changes in the short term.

Below is another way of looking at service standards.

	Value Demand	Failure Demand
Special cause variation	Problem solving standards	Eliminate these sporadic problems; standards not applicable
Common cause variation	Appropriate standards or checklists covering critical points	Eliminate 'chronic' common case problems; could have standards for service recovery failure.

Deming, proposing the PDCA cycle, saw improvement moving from standard to standard. Juran emphasised the importance of 'holding the gains' by establishing standards following a process improvement, rather than allowing them to drift back to the old ways. Recently the concept of the 'Learning Organisation' has become fashionable, including 'knowledge harvesting' from everyone in the organisation. How is this to be achieved? By documenting experience, in other words by establishing standards from which others may learn. Supervisors should have prime responsibility for maintaining and improving standard work.

Too many service operations-based organisations delude themselves on standards. It is tempting simply to impose work standards by getting industrial engineers or workstudy people to do the work and to post standards at workstations, or, which is worse, to keep them in a file. Then, of course, there is no buy-in, no foundation for continuous improvement, and worst of all a great likelihood of large process variance. So the quick way turns out to be the least effective way and often a total waste. Traditional 'Taylorism' is suitable only in the sweat shop. It is far better to work through the few critical stages, get the workers to know why these stages are important, but leave the rest alone.

One good bottom-up way of establishing standards is to get service workers to discuss their methods of doing a task among themselves. Differences emerge. But then let them discuss and develop the 'current best known way', or 'best of the best'. The same thing applies on 5S activities: the fact that everyone may not use the same files, tools, computer systems, filing, layouts, greetings, room cleaning sequence, and so on, indicates that there is possible room for improvement. Not by imposition – that soon falls apart – but by open discussion.

And in new product development, design, and product launch, do what Toyota does and accumulate checklists of things to look out for. The checklists become the accumulated knowledge of the company. Knowledge management. If you don't do this simple thing, you are doomed always to 'learn the hard way' and to 'start from scratch'. What a waste!

Leader-level standard work is very powerful. Establish a routine that requires different tasks, audits, or visits to be done at regular intervals. Perhaps at director level once per quarter, manager level once per month, team leader level every day. Team members are expected to do a problem review every morning. That is the standard.

How do you build 'culture'? Through broad standards. By regularity. It becomes 'the way we do things around here'. We hold a problem review meeting every day. We discuss better ways to do tasks. We hold after-action review meetings. We build checklists. We try never to let a customer go home dissatisfied. Culture emerges out of the standard practices. But standard practices, like many things in Lean, are not left to chance: the 'what' and the 'why' (and the 'will do') come down from the top, but the 'hows' are developed locally, sometimes with expert help. If you are a manager, be aware that standards begin at the top but are carried out at all levels. The day you walk past an unacceptable practice and don't enquire (NB do not impose) is the day that quality and culture begins to slip back. And the day that the manager ignores the standard because he is 'above all that' is the day that the organisation has set out on 'the road to perdition'.

Further Reading

Robert W Hall, 'Standard Work: Holding the Gains', *Target,* 4th Quarter, 1998, pp 13-19

Taiichi Ohno, *Toyota Production System*, Productivity Press, 1988

Charles Standard and Dale Davis, *Running Today's Factory*, Hanser Gardner, 1999

Spear and Bowen, 'Decoding the DNA of the Toyota Production System', *Harvard Business Review*, Sept/Oct 1999

Control Charts for Service
and 'Fooled by Randomness'

Control charts are an important tool in service

- to distinguish between common cause and special cause variation
- to understand the extent of the natural variation
- to know when a process is 'out of control'.

Here we will consider the use of control charts in service but will not get into a technical discussion on setting up a control chart. For this the reader is referred to one of the many books in the area such as Bicheno and Catherwood, and to Statistical Process Control (SPC) software such as MiniTab.

Deming was fond of saying that many managers do not understand variation and therefore often draw wrong conclusions about performance. In Deming's famous Red Bead exercise a group of six people take turns to scoop out beads from a box containing red and white beads, using a paddle. The paddle contains 50 spaces for beads. Red beads represent defects. Of course there is no way of controlling the number of red beads – it is a matter of natural variation. But the number of red beads is interpreted by the manager as representing good or bad performance. The 'good' are praised, the 'bad' fired. You realise the farce of the situation. But of course in the real world salesmen, managers, stockbrokers, and many others do get rewarded and punished when the performance is due merely to chance – good or bad 'luck'.

(For a devastating critique of this kind of behaviour see Taleb's book *Fooled by Randomness*, and Alfie Kohn's *Punished by Rewards*.)

This is just one instance where a control chart would be useful. Calculate the upper and lower control limits within which 99.7% of natural variation occurs. The upper and lower control limits are set at the average plus and minus three standard deviations respectively. Only if a point falls outside these limits is a 'special cause' signalled. The process may then be 'out of control'. Otherwise it is 'common cause' variation, and 'in control'. This is much like an engine temperature gauge on an old car. The temperature does vary on hot and cold days and on going up a long hill, but as long as it stays within the green zone (the limits) there is no cause for concern. If, however, it goes into the red zone you stop and investigate: perhaps the fan belt has broken or you have a radiator leak. It is a 'special cause'.

Control charts are called statistical process control charts, not statistical product control charts, because the intention is to control the process, not the products or services that come out of the process. If the process is in control and capable, then the products that come out of the system will be fine.

Why is this relevant in Lean service? First, if you ignore variation you may fall into the red bead trap. It's like drowning in a river of an average depth of one metre. Second, because you don't want to go chasing after common cause variation. Third, you would like to know how much variation is due to common causes. Fourth, you would like to investigate only those specific special causes. So, for instance, if you have a service level agreement (SLA) to meet a maintenance time target, first understand whether the process is 'in control'. The point is, if the variation is such that the process is 'out of control', it doesn't matter whether the SLA target is being met – it is inherently unpredictable and unstable. The special causes must first be investigated. On the other hand, if the process in control, then you can begin to shift or redesign the whole process, confident in the knowledge that there are no unseen 'bombshells' at work. Note that a process may be 'in control' but still not meeting the SLA. And further, in drawing the control limits, you can get a feel for how variable the process is and ask if this is acceptable. Two processes may have the same average performance, but be very different in terms of customer satisfaction.

Beware: a SLA may have no relevance to a customer, but may be there simply because a manager has decided it is a good idea.

Note also that control limits are not specification limits. Control limits relate to the natural variation of the process, while specification limits are what the managers or customers would regard as being the bounds of acceptability. In the case of an SLA, the SLA would be the upper specification limit and the lower limit would be zero. A process is out of control when readings go beyond the control limits, not the specification limits.

Many control charts, especially in product-based systems, are sampling charts – in other words samples are taken every so often to monitor the process. But you can also have a control chart which is essentially a run diagram monitoring every occurrence.

Consider the following chart from Vanguard Consulting concerning the time to meet claims.

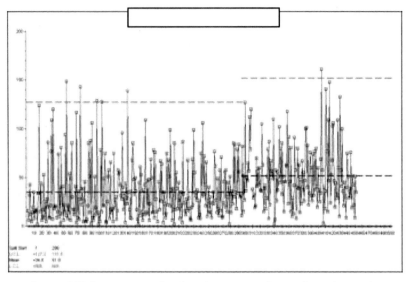

Note that a shift has occurred. Also there are a few points above the upper control limit, indicating that there were a few special events that warrant looking into.

A further use of control charts is to monitor the process and to detect shifts. For instance, a call centre uses a control chart to monitor the length of calls. Samples are taken a number of times each day. Then a new product is introduced. Soon afterwards the call length monitoring system indicates that call length is increasing – it has gone beyond the previous control limit. Is this due to inadequate instructions issued with the new product? Is it because the new product is more complex? Or what? The point is that the shift might have been missed if the call lengths were not being recorded on the call centre control charts. Note here that the control chart is used for problem detection and NOT for 'checking up' on the performance of the staff. Everyone needs to understand this.

There are various 'out of control' signals other than a point plotted beyond the control limits. For instance, seven successive points plotted above the average indicates an out-of-control condition.

Attribute Charts

The charts just discussed are 'variables' charts, meaning that the observations can take on any value. By contrast 'attributes' charts have only two states, good or bad, pass or fail. So, for example, customers either complain or don't complain. They are therefore a little less powerful than attributes but they are still very valuable, especially in service. There are two types: **proportion** (p-chart) or **number** (c-chart). Both share the same general formulas for upper and lower control limits, namely average plus and minus three standard deviations.

An easy-to-remember value for the standard deviation of a number – say the number of complaints in an airport where the number of possible points of complaint is indeterminate (so proportion has no meaning) – is that the standard deviation is the square root of the average. So if there were 49 complaints on average per week before the improvement programme and 35 on average afterwards, can we say that an improvement has taken place? Answer: the lower control limit is $49 - 3$ standard deviations of the average $= 49 - 3*7 = 28$. So on the evidence of one week we cannot say that a real improvement has taken place – it may just be random variation. Of course, if complaints persisted at around 35 we could conclude after three weeks that a real change has taken place.

Zone of Tolerance

Statistical Process Control thinking has been extended into the service area by, among others, Zeithaml, Bitner and Gremler, Berry, and Johnston and Clark. All recognise that service is a variable entity – it is never absolutely consistent. And customers perceive service delivery differently. All these authors refer to a 'zone of tolerance' roughly equivalent to the distance between the upper and lower specification limits (not the control limits) on an SPC control chart. The difference here is that beyond the control limit on one side indicates satisfaction and on the other side indicates dissatisfaction.

Johnston and Clark refer to a customer satisfaction 'zone of tolerance' located between 'zones of delight' and 'dissatisfaction'. Zeithaml *et al*'s 'zone of tolerance' falls between zones of desired service and adequate service – meaning that there is a grey zone between the minimum acceptable level of service and the 'zone of delight'. These conceptual models are useful in thinking about the bounds of service quality.

The 'zone of tolerance' model can be used with performance measurement or mapping. Just like traditional SPC, samples of perhaps five random customers are taken through time for

- waiting in a queue at a supermarket

- response time for maintenance work
- levels of satisfaction at a hotel, on perhaps a 1-10 scale.

First, however, if we are to use 'zone of tolerance' in a quantitative sense we need to establish

- the upper and lower specification limits – perhaps by questioning managers or customers
- the upper and lower control limits – derived from previous performance records.

The figure shows that the process is 'in control': the average of the samples falls between the control limits, and all samples except one fall within the 'zone of tolerance'. The point outside the 'zone of tolerance' indicates that there may be some dissatisfaction among customers – in this case wait time is being plotted so above the specification limit is inadequate service. So here there are no special events at work, but the process is nevertheless not capable of always delivering adequate service.

Strictly speaking, if a variable such as wait times is being monitored with samples, a range chart should also be shown. The range chart shows the difference between the highest and lowest values in each sample. A range chart is necessary because two samples may have the same average but different ranges.

Both sets of authors make the point that the zone can shift depending on the importance of the factor and on prior experience. Thus the zone is wider for first-time buyers but narrows for service recovery situations. The size of the band may also be affected by the level of interest and commitment.

Johnston and Clark use the 'zone of tolerance' concept much like an SPC control chart, maintaining that various 'transactions' or Moments of Truth can be plotted in the chart. A succession of points plotted in the 'dissatisfied' zone leads to the equivalent of out-of-control conditions (a dissatisfied customer) but several points above the zone result in 'delight'. Some behaviour may be compensatory: a poor experience may be compensated by several satisfactory experiences. A poor experience may also shift the 'specification limits' upwards, making the customer even more demanding, but a great experience may lower the zone, thus making it easier to achieve further delight.

Zeithaml and Bitner have done interesting work identifying the factors that shift the specification limits (although they don't refer to them). The upper limit of the zone (leading to desired service) is influenced by implicit and explicit service promises, by word of mouth and by past experience. The lower limit is influenced by

- 'service intensifiers', where, for example, an anniversary dinner might imply reduced tolerance
- service alternatives: where there are fewer options there is more tolerance
- the degree of influence that a customer has on the service provider
- factors that are perceived to be out of the service provider's control
- the predicted service.

So control charts can be useful on both a practical and a conceptual level. They can be linked into mapping – under the 'check' stage, into measures, and into loyalty considerations.

Further Reading

Valerie Zeithaml, Mary Jo Bitner and Dwayne Gremler, *Services Marketing*, 4th edition, McGraw Hill, Boston, 2006, Chapter 4
Leonard Berry, *Marketing Services: Competing through Quality*, Free Press, New York, 1991
Robert Johnston and Graham Clark, *Service Operations Management*, FT/Prentice Hall, Harlow, 2001, Chapter 4
John Bicheno and Philip Catherwood, *Six Sigma and The Quality Toolbox*, PICSIE Books, 2005
Nassim Taleb, *Fooled by Randomness*, Random House, 2004
Alfie Kohn, *Punished by Rewards*, Houghton Mifflin, 1999

The Opportunity Box and Transaction Box

The Opportunity Box is a conceptual tool to help with prioritisation of improvement activities, especially in relation to Interactive mapping. The intention is that it is applied at critical Moments of Truth – those that have high 'leverage'. The Opportunity Box idea can also be used in relation to loyalty considerations.

The basis is that there are different categories of customer, from favourably disposed to highly critical. How much effort should be put into converting customers into a more favourable category?

Here we will call the categories:

- **Apostles**: these customers are enthusiastic and loyal. They spread the 'good news' by word of mouth. They believe in the service provider. Their confidence is hard to shake. They often give helpful feedback because they have the welfare of the supplier at heart.
- **Hostages**: users of the service but with little loyalty. They only use the service because they have to. Perhaps they have a contract or they live near to the service provider – but when the contract changes or a new facility opens there is a good chance they will defect.
- **Apathetics**: couldn't care less. The service is regarded as satisfactory. They don't have great loyalty, but often are repeat customers through force of habit. They don't complain, nor do they praise. They just use the service.
- **Terrorists**: the habitual complainers. They actively use word of mouth to talk down the service. They may write letters to the company, the press, or to a blog. The worst kind are those who bring very little business to the service provider but cause big costs because of the time needed to deal with their incessant complaints.

There are several classifications available. See Johnston and Clark for many more categories. Keiningham *et al* propose three categories: desired customers, break-even customers, and costly customers.

Against this is the effort that is currently expended at the Moment of Truth – either minor, mid or major. 'Effort' could include changing the policies or procedures, reducing defects, making the service more convenient, or simply being more friendly.

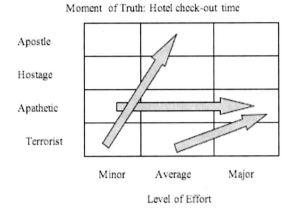

Moment of Truth: Hotel check-out time

The methodology is:

- Identify an apostle, hostage, apathetic or terrorist. The first and last types identify themselves, but market survey may be used.
- Ask that person for the stage in the service provision that they have found particularly good, particularly annoying, or, in the case of hostages and apathetics ask them simply to identify an important stage in their dealing with the service provider.
- Ask what needs to be done to improve that stage or Moment of Truth. What would it take at that stage to make the individual think differently about the service provider?
- Then assess what the present level of effort is and how much effort it would take to make the customer think differently.
- There are now two points in the opportunity box.

Putting extra effort into improving the apathetic is not going to pay off. Certainly a little extra effort into some 'terrorists' could pay big dividends. But putting in greater effort into the other group of 'terrorists' needs careful consideration. Perhaps it would be better to bribe them to leave.

Service Transaction Box: Four Elements of (almost) every Service Transaction

In service, it is the front line staff who have the greatest impact on customers and the greatest potential to delight or disgust. This happens many times every day.

Almost every service activity, but particularly front line, has four elements: arrive, wait, serve, depart – even if an element lasts for only a few seconds. These four elements warrant special attention at each activity because they may be important Moments of Truth, capable of ruining a complete value stream experience.

Hence the mapping symbol that acts as a reminder to check out each of the four elements.

Arrive:

- What are the first impressions?
- What is the state of 5S?
- What led the customer to the transaction?
- How easy was it to access?
- How clear are the signs?
- Was the arrival noted or acknowledged?
- Is there a help line for non-satisfactory arrivals?
- Was the site open as advertised?
- --
- --

Wait

- How long is the perceived wait?
- How long is the actual wait?
- What was the expected wait and was this matched?
- Is the wait seen as fair?
- Is there information on the expected wait time?
- Are the servers seen to be busy or distracted or disinterested?
- Is an undue wait explained?
- Was the wait abandoned? (Why?)
- --
- --

Serve

- Were the opening words appropriate?
- Was the customer expected?
- Was service courteous?
- Did the server listen?
- Was the transaction dealt with correctly and accurately?
- Is the information correct?
- Were the customer's needs or expectations met?
- Was the customer greeted in a friendly manner?
- Was the customer greeted by name?
- Was the level of formality appropriate?

- Was the transaction dealt with efficiently?
- Was the server distracted during the transaction?
- Was the server dressed appropriately?
- Did the server give a sense of assurance?
- --
- --

Depart

- Was the transaction closed appropriately?
- Did the customer give feedback?
- Was the customer asked for feedback?
- Did the customer wish to give feedback?
- Could the customer give feedback?
- Did the customer depart with expectations met?
- --
- --

(This list was developed with the aid of MSc Lean Service students, 2007.)

A3 Problem Solving and Reports

The A3 method has grown hugely in popularity among Lean organisations in recent years, and with good reason.

A3 refers to the standard sheet of paper: two A4 portrait sheets, side by side. The story is that it was the largest size of paper that could be conveniently faxed.

A3 is:
- A standardised problem-solving methodology incorporating the PDCA cycle.
- A standard report format. Rather than a multi-page report that may come in various formats depending on the whim of the writer, A3 forces the writer to be concise. Recall the quote from George Bernard Shaw: 'I am sorry to send you this long letter – I did not have time to write a short one'. For the reader, another advantage is that he or she knows exactly where to look for the salient points. So, 'Don't give me a report, give me an A3'.
- A standard documentation and easy-filing method.

A3 is actually a family of report formats, used for planning, budgeting, communication, and problem solving. Here we consider only the generic problem-solving type.

The general format of A3 is current state analysis on the left hand side and future state and implementation plan on the right hand side. There is often space along the bottom for 'sign off', for people who have seen or agreed to the analysis.

The standard layout is shown in the figure below.

You can see that the left hand side is Check and Plan, and the right hand side is Do, Act and again Check.

In the following section the various headings in the figure will be explained. Note that writing on the A3 should be clearly readable, not microscopic: about the same size font as this book or bigger.

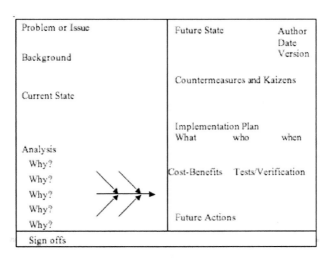

Top right corner: The author or team, the date and the version number.

The Problem or Issue: A statement of the problem. One sentence.

Background: How did the problem arise? This is often a clue to the solution. Also, set the situation in the context of the wider value stream. A short statement of history. Two sentences maximum.

Current State: Can take various forms. A process map, possibly with kaizen bursts. A cartoon. A sketch of a product part. A data table. Try to make the current state lively and interesting. Invent icons. Draw happy and sad customers.

Analysis: A standard approach is to use either the Five Whys methodology or a fishbone diagram. When using Five Whys there may be several answers to each Why. So prioritise by circling the most likely answers. Similarly on a fishbone diagram, circle the likely causes. Sometimes a run diagram is useful. In fact, any of the classic Seven Tools of Quality can be used. These should be addressed to the first two of the classic 3C approach: Concern, Cause, Countermeasure. Countermeasure is dealt with on the right hand side.

Future State: same comments as for the current state.

Countermeasures and Kaizens: These should be short sentences. It is good to have short and long term (permanent) solutions in mind. The kaizens may be short, focused actions – 'point kaizens'. Include verb plus noun to indicate the actions. 'Erect sign to direct customers'. In technical problems, a small sketch could be added.

Implementation Plan: Simply a list of actions, together with by whom and by when. A more complex case may include a simple network diagram to indicate the sequence.

Cost Benefits: Not a great ROI or discounted cash flow analysis, but a simple outlay of actual cash and expected money benefits in the immediate period ahead. State it as: £1000 within 12 months. Not all improvements generate cash, so include the other benefits: quality of worklife, happier customers.

Tests and verification: After the countermeasures have been implemented, the new solution should be expected to produce various results. State these, so they can be verified later. They should be related to the cost benefits.

Follow up: Wider issues might have been raised. A sentence or two would be appropriate.

Sign off: Along the bottom various line managers concerned with the issue should see and sign off the A3. They could, of course, annotate and discuss with the team.

An A3 can be used at different levels. It is used:
- For routine problem solving – point kaizens.
- As a supplement to mapping.
- As a tool and record for kaizen events. One company places kaizen event A3s on the wall near the relevant area for a standard period of twelve months.
- As a supplement to policy deployment.
- As a test to evaluate a new employee.

Further Reading

Cindy Jimmerson, *A3 Problem Solving for Healthcare*, Healthcare Performance Press, 2007. Jimmerson has been a pioneer of A3 use in healthcare.
Jeffrey Liker and David Meier, *The Toyota Way Fieldbook*, McGraw Hill, 2006, Chapter 18

Variation, Queues, and Perishability of Service

Variation is the enemy of Lean but it is a fact of life, particularly in administration and service. Ignore variation at your peril. Beware of 'drowning in a river of average depth one metre'.

In service and administration, it is disastrous to ignore variation.

It is also unwise to assume that demand rates and service rates will be normally distributed. Much research, and common experience, show that the Poisson distribution is a far better assumption, certainly for customer or job arrival rates. The Poisson distribution often has a long tail. Common experience suggests that 'buses arrive in twos' and that service times in queues are unevenly distributed; just as you think the queue is moving steadily, the person immediately in front will inevitably have numerous transactions! Both these situations arise because the distribution is Poisson, not normal. Maintenance work invariably arrives according to a Poisson distribution. Design work also has this characteristic – some small jobs take a very long time.

The Poisson distribution goes from zero to infinity. For instance, in a bank there is no chance of getting less than zero arrivals in an hour, and a small probability of getting 1000 arrivals in an hour. For customer arrivals or product breakdown rates, if there is theoretically an infinite number of arrivals it is a Poisson distribution. If there is a finite maximum number of possible arrivals, it is a Binomial distribution. Arrivals are usually Poisson distributed.

The good news is that the Poisson is characterised by only one figure – the average rate. There is no standard deviation. The average rate can sometimes be found by looking up the records of the number of arrivals or product breakdowns or events per day, week, hour or whatever. With caution you can convert to the required time interval. For example, if you work a six-hour day and usually get 36 calls, you can say that you get six calls per hour provided that calls are more or less uniform throughout the day.

Once you know the average demand rate, then you can predict the probability of a certain number of events in any time period. For instance, if you know that the average product failure rate requiring service is four per day, then, if failures follow Poisson – and they usually will – you can easily calculate the probability of there being exactly 0, 1, 2, 3, 4, 5, 6, etc. failures on any day. This will help to determine the appropriate capacity to service the failures. The probability can be found from the Poisson function on Excel, or by using the formula:

$$P(x) = e^{-\lambda}\lambda^x / (x!)$$

where λ is the average rate of arrivals over the time period in question, e is the base of natural logs (found on most calculators), and x is the number of arrivals in the period. (x! means the number multiplied by all successive numbers below that number to 1, for instance
$$4! = 4 \times 3 \times 2 \times 1 = 24).$$

Many texts on statistics or operations management list the Poisson cumulative distribution – that is, the probability of that number of arrivals or less in the period. For instance, if the average arrival rate is six per hour, the probability of six arrivals or fewer is 0.61, and the probability of twelve arrivals or fewer is 0.99.

Where the average number of arrivals or events per period is greater than 20, the Poisson becomes unwieldy and the normal approximation to the Poisson can be used. This can be done quite easily by taking the mean (μ) of the normal distribution as λ and the standard deviation (σ) as $\sigma = \sqrt{\lambda}$. Thereafter use the usual properties of the normal distribution.

The z value, where $z = (x - \mu) / \sigma$, can be used to calculate any probability.

Of course, for an important process it is worth checking whether the Poisson assumption is valid. For automated processes, such as using an ATM, assuming the Poisson is likely to be incorrect. Note that the exponential distribution, related to the Poisson and also available on Excel, can be used to model the time between events.

For arrivals, the Poisson is generally a good assumption. The Poisson uses the average rate of arrivals, and calculates the probability of the number of arrivals in a time period. The probability of the time between arrivals is given by the related exponential distribution. The average inter-arrival time is the inverse of the arrival rate. So if the average arrival rate is five per hour, the average inter-arrival time is 1/5 = 12 minutes.

Relating the Poisson Distribution to Queues

Queues are widely found in service, so understanding their characteristics is important.

A headache in administration and service is that service capacity usually cannot be stored or inventoried – it is perishable. This is a major reason why it is simply not good enough to provide the average capacity. If there are no customers, service capacity is lost forever. But customers will continue to arrive at the average rate, so a server working at the average rate of arrivals will fall further and further behind.

The ratio of arrival rate to service rate is important for service management. The ratio is known as the utilisation factor ρ (called rho), where $\rho = \lambda / \mu$ and λ is as before the arrival rate – say in customers per hour – and μ is the service rate also in customers per hour. ρ can take on values between 0 and 1. Where ρ is zero there is no queue. As ρ increases, queues grow very slowly at first, then rapidly above a ratio of about 70% or 80%. The lower the variation, the later the 'take off' point. If there is no variation then the queue is zero as long as the arrival rate is less than the service rate, but as soon as the arrival rate exceeds the service rate, even minutely, the queue will grow to infinity. In practice there is always variation, so the queue starts to increase rapidly above, say, 70%.

The shape of the Poisson distribution, particularly at low values, has a long tail. This is in line with everyone's experience of waiting in a queue at a bank or post office: most people have very short transactions, but a few have very long transactions. The same applies to arrivals. See the figure as an example. This is the Poisson distribution for an average of three arrivals during a period of time. So, for example, there is some chance of no arrivals and a very small chance of nine arrivals during any period.

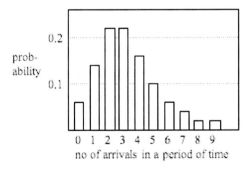

Understanding Variation

An understanding of variation is important for service and administration – particularly in situations involving scheduling or capacity planning decisions.

There are two types of variation.

- **Variation in the arrival rate** λ. Over the short term, little can be done in general about this variation, apart from trying to influence the rate by showing a sign of the expected wait. In the longer term, bookings can be made, and incentives (price and wait time) offered to encourage customers to arrive at a steadier rate. This is worthwhile.
- **Variation in the service rate** μ. This type of variation is more under the control of the organisation. For example, standard work can be used, or automation can be employed. Reducing this type of variation will have an impact on the queue length and hence on the quality of service, so it is also worthwhile.

Hopp and Spearman have written the definitive text on variation in *Factory Physics*. Here we summarise one of the most important formulas, which is applicable in a single-stage queuing process – the most common type and widely experienced by customers. The formula is also referred to in texts on Queuing theory where it is called 'the general system approximation'.

$$\text{Expected Lead time} = \tfrac{1}{2} * t_e * (C_a^2 + C_e^2) * (\rho/(1 - \rho)) + t_e$$

Where

the expected lead time is time from arrival to completion
t_e is the average processing time, or service rate, while serving
t_a is the average inter-arrival time, or arrival rate
ρ is the utilisation factor λ / μ, discussed in the last section
and ρ is also the ration of t_e / t_a
$C_a^2 = \sigma_a^2 / t_a^2$ and $C_e^2 = \sigma_e^2 / t_e^2$
and
σ_a^2 is the variance of the inter-arrival time
σ_e^2 is the variance of the processing time

The mathematics of the formula itself is not really important but the implications are vital for every service manager. Please also refer to the graph shown below. This will assist understanding.

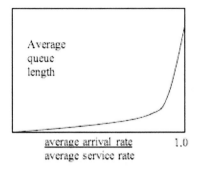

average arrival rate
average service rate   1.0

In the expected waiting time formula you should notice the following:

- The equation is in two parts, the queuing or waiting time and the processing time. The equation applies to the steady state – in other words where sufficient time has elapsed to allow the queue to establish itself.
- Where there is no variation, there is no queue – provided that the utilisation factor is less than 1, and then the expected lead time is equal to the processing time.
- The queue time is highly dependent on the utilisation factor ρ, as discussed in the last section. Where ρ is 1 or more the queue time is infinite, and where ρ is 0 there is no queue because there are no arrivals.
- Both types of variation discussed above are represented. But notice that both types, C_a and C_e, are equally represented. If you are able to reduce the processing time variation to zero (difficult, but may be approached where a machine is used), the lead time will halve. This is a powerful piece of knowledge for service managers.

Most people have experienced sitting in a jam on a highway where it is assumed that there is an accident ahead. Sometimes there isn't one on your carriageway, but drivers are slowing down ('rubber necking') to see what has happened on the other carriageway. This, of course, increases the variance of the inter-arrival times – from fast to slow – and so increases the expected lead time. Traffic engineers know all about these phenomena, and adopt various policies. On the M25 around London there is a variable speed limit that attempts to reduce variation. Other highways try to limit access at peak times, thereby decreasing the utilisation factor. Yet others try, via traffic lights, to allow new entrants onto the highway during gaps in the flow. This smoothes the inter-arrival rate variance.

Hopp and Spearman have developed what they call 'The Laws of Factory Physics'. Two are particularly relevant to service and administration:

- 'If a system increases utilisation without making any other changes, response time will increase in a highly nonlinear fashion.' Referring to the figure in the Capacity section below, it is vital to avoid the part of the curve that starts increasing rapidly above about 80% utilisation. In this region, a very small difference in utilisation can make a very large difference to customer delays and satisfaction. Extra capacity may need to be brought in – as Tesco does by opening up another checkout counter when queues start to build. On the other hand, a small decrease in utilisation (or a small increase in capacity) can lead to a dramatic reduction in queue time.
- 'Increasing variability always increases average response time and inventory levels' (in a factory). So variability reduction, either by working through the provider or server, or by influencing the customer, is most worthwhile.

For an important or expensive resource it may be necessary to model the system using computer simulation. The good news is that this is nowhere near as specialised a task as it was fifteen years ago. Computer simulation is powerful, relatively quick, and can give excellent visualisation.

Tesco is well known for 'pulling' or capacity to manage queues. When a queue builds up more tills are opened. Checkout people have buttons to signal the queue length to store management, and the management responds by reallocating staff. The dramatic effects of increasing the capacity (or reducing the utilisation ratio) can be seen on the graph in the next section. This is good, adaptive practice that can be widely and simply applied.

Dice Games for Service

The phenomena just discussed can be illustrated by some simple dice games.

In all games, there are two players; each rolls a dice simultaneously. One player is all the customers, the other player is the server. The customer dice roll represents the number of customers arriving in a period. The server dice roll represents the capacity, or number of customers that could be served, during the period. A queue results if the arrivals exceed the capacity. In this case the queue is carried over to the next. The queue is recorded at the end of every period. The game should be played over at least 20 periods. 30 periods is better if you have time. Start with zero in the queue. At least half a dozen simultaneous games, each going through all six stages below, should be played to get representative results.

1. In the first stage, the server adds three to the dice roll. Record the queues on each of 20 periods. Calculate the average queue length by dividing by 20. It will generally be very small.
2. In the second stage, the server adds two. Otherwise the same activities.
3. In the third stage, the server adds one. Otherwise the same activities.
4. In the fourth stage, nothing is added.
5. In the fifth stage, reduce the variation of the server by re-rolling if a 1 or 6 is rolled (valid numbers are 2 to 5). Add +1 to the server roll.
6. As for the fifth stage, but the server adds zero.

For games 1 to 4, plot the results on a large sheet with queue length along the vertical axis and the four stages (+3, +2, +1, 0) along the horizontal axis. Draw a line of best fit (by 'eyeball') though the centre of gravity of each set of points. The four stages correspond to 3.5/6.5=54%, 3.5/5.5=64%, 3.5/4.5=78%, and 3.5/3.5=100% utilisation. You should see a clear exponential shape emerge. You will get a graph just like the one shown in the next section on Capacity Management.

For stages 5 and 6, again plot the points but using a different colour. Again draw a line of best fit. This second line will normally be some way below the first line. These last two stages show the effect of reducing variation on the part of the server.

Making Queuing Less Painful

The previous sections have dealt with the statistics of queuing.

Of course, from a Lean perspective you would like to avoid any queue. So this should be the first priority. Try booking. Try scheduling. Try Heijunka. (See other sections on these). Inform customers about capacity. But since variation is so endemic, some queues may be unavoidable. Then the other half of the question is the psychology of queuing, or making queuing less painful. Several researchers have studied this aspect. In general improvement is 'low cost/no cost', once you are aware of the situation.

- Pre-process waits feel longer. It is the time to the first contact which is most important. Once customers feel that they are 'in the system' they relax a little. So, at A&E in a hospital the waiting time to get to the initial point of contact is more important than the subsequent wait to be seen by the doctor. So have an early greeting process, even if subsequent waits are longer. Can this be done in call centres?
- Unoccupied waits feel longer. If people have nothing to do, the wait feels longer. So:
    - Distract: provide reading material, computer games.
    - Provide mirrors so people have something to look at while they are waiting. This works!
    - Amuse: as at Disney.
    - Let them know that they are not forgotten: play music while callers are waiting in a telephone queue, or better still, give a countdown (see next section).
    - Prioritise: allow customers to do other tasks (shopping) by picking up a number and displaying the number of the next customer to be served.
    - Prioritise 2: call restaurant customers on their mobile (cell) phone when their table is ready.
- Uncertain waits feel longer. So:
    - Inform: Disney informs customers of the length of time to get to the ride if you are standing at a particular point – but then also deliberately overestimates the wait time.
    - Keep appointments. The previous section showed the folly of booking to 100% of utilisation. Inevitably there will be delays, so build in buffer time.
- Unfair waits feel longer. The British feel strongly about perceived queue jumpers. But sometimes it is necessary to give priority. So:

- Most important, always try to have a single queue rather than multiple queues. There is generally no excuse for parallel queues.
- Have a separate entrance or queue where there are different priorities.

Capacity Management in Service

Capacity management in service varies with the type of service system – particularly the flexibility of resources and time to acquire or train resources. In some service situations, for instance a supermarket, it may be easy to react to demand by shifting people from shelf-stacking to tills, whenever demand grows. This is capacity management by short-term pull. In other situations non-flexible resources may have to be recruited or trained – or capital resources like aircraft or hotel rooms acquired.

There are some guidelines.

The most important guideline is to decide on the purpose of the service system before deciding on the capacity. In one classic case a government department thought that they were hugely overstretched, only to discover some months later that they had a surplus of staff when the system was redesigned – not by a piecemeal waste reduction exercise, but by a fundamental re-think as to what the process was actually there to do and then asking what would be the best way to do the task.

In another case, when the true requirement of the customer was defined as 'power by the hour' rather than selling engines, the whole business changed, including thinking about the required capacity.

Then ask how much failure demand and waste there is in the process. Failure demand should be eliminated or massively reduced. See the separate section on value and failure demand. Capacity that is there to cope with failure demand may have to be re-deployed. Why are there all those rework loops? How much waste is there in a design office, perhaps doing designs that are subsequently scrapped, or shelved and then substantially re-done? How many service calls are abortive?

Lastly, consider Capacity. A useful figure to have in the background is shown below. See also the section on Queuing Theory.

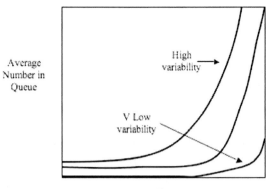

Average Utilization ρ

Note:

- Utilisation (known in Queuing Theory as ρ) is the average arrival rate divided by the average service time. When ρ is 100% the capacity can be considered to be fully loaded. It is the capacity utilisation or load.
- Only with zero variability will throughput be able to equal average capacity. In other words, if you calculate required capacity based on average demand and assuming zero variation, you will not make the schedule and your customers will be disappointed. This is because serving capacity not used is lost and cannot be recovered, but customers continue to arrive at the average rate.
- The greater the variability the longer the queues and the lower the throughput.
- High utilisation has greater uncertainty in queue length – and thus customer satisfaction – because a small change in utilisation makes a huge difference, and utilisation is impossible to predict with precision.
- There is a highly non-linear relation between utilisation and average queue length at higher utilisation levels. Or, a small decrease in utilisation when heavily loaded makes a huge difference in queue time.
- So there are two important factors – variability and utilisation. Toyota calls this Mura and Muri.

So the implications for service capacity management are:

- Opening up another till or server when queues build is smart policy. An extra server will decrease average utilisation, and will have a sharp non-linear effect.

- There is a management decision to be made between high utilisation of resources (for example no-one standing around, everyone working) with longer queues, and lower utilisation (more expensive? more idle time?) with shorter queues. However, if you can continually adjust resources to demand you can have the best of both worlds, even though adjusting may involve more expensive cross training.
- Reduce variation if you can. This is not easy to do in service – if you try to reduce (say) call time variation in a call centre by putting an upper limit on call times, you will almost certainly generate failure demand.
- For a situation where resource flexibility is not possible, aim at designing for a utilisation of around 75% to 85% - this is where the queue line starts to turn up sharply. If you were in the relatively unusual situation in service where you could use takt time, you should design your operation around perhaps 80% of takt. See the next section.

Capacity and Demand

A big differentiator between service and manufacturing is the variability of demand. This is accentuated by the fact that demand, in the form of queues or waits, is often intolerable to customers. Some service demands have to be met on demand or at very short notice, or else failure in the form of defection or dissatisfaction (even death) will result. This is made worse by the fact that 'buffer stock' cannot be kept. Most administrative and service systems experience demand variability from customer to customer, from hour to hour, from day to day, and by season.

John Seddon of Vanguard Consulting suggests that any service analysis begins by determining if the system is 'in control' from a statistical process control point of view. In other words are there 'special causes' at work or is variation 'natural variation'?

Why is this important? Because, if the process is 'out of control' it means there are unpredictable elements at work that disrupt smooth flow of work and lead to poor and erratic customer service. Such out of control elements need different treatment from processes that are in control and where 'common cause' variation is at work. Using a car analogy, the temperature may vary on hot and cold days and when climbing or descending a hill. This is common cause variation in control. But if the fan belt breaks or the radiator springs a leak, this will cause 'special cause' variation and is out of control. If you are trying to improve the performance of the car, you do not want these out of control conditions to be present.

The example shows the time for completion for repairs by a field maintenance service in two regions of the country. The first region is largely in control. Not so the second region. Here there are some unexplained high numbers. We don't know what happened here, but we do know that the variation is too high. There must be some special causes at work. Possibilities are vans going out with the wrong tools or information, untrained staff, confusion over work leading to long delays, or even workers 'goofing off'. Further probing reveals a potential special cause: shortage of parts leading back to the appointment of a new spare-parts manager who was adopting new policies to try and reduce inventories.

To find out if a process or system is in control, first determine the critical customer requirement or measure of the overall end-to-end system response. Examples are

- Order to delivery time
- Number of forms processed per day
- Number of calls handled per day
- Response time for repair
- New product introduction time
- Mortgage approval time
- Ambulance response time.

But note that the measure should be largely under the control of the system, not outside the system. Thus the wait time for a category of patient is a valid parameter, but overall time for a cure is not. The greater the number of events outside the control of the system, the more likely is an 'out of control' signal.

Plot the system response measure on a run diagram. For example, calls per day on the vertical axis against days on the horizontal axis. Calculate mean and upper control limit (UCL) – three standard deviations above the mean. Many statistical packages, such as MiniTab, will do this task. If all plotted points are below the UCL, the system is 'in control' and variation is 'natural'. If there are points above the UCL, these require special examination. Determine the specific circumstances for each. This is just like your car's temperature gauge showing red – you need to stop and investigate. These 'out of control' points are a warning sign of special events which need to be specifically addressed – preferably eliminated but otherwise specially catered for. The 'special causes' above the control limit may be things that can easily be remedied, such as too many people on leave at the same time, but they may also be systemic, such as an inherent flaw in the scheduling system.

Predicting Demand

Demand should be managed, but will still need to be predicted in order to provide the right amount of capacity. Some service organisations believe that demand is difficult or impossible to predict. However, in many situations demand can be predicted by segmenting.

- Graph the total demand. If data is available for a minimum of two cycles – perhaps two years – it should be possible to detect trend and seasonality, if any. Several statistical and forecasting packages are available to assist with this, but do plot the data series before diving into the statistics – there is no substitute for the eye of an experienced manager. If there is trend and seasonality, these effects will have to be removed from the series first so that only the 'noise' remains. Of course, if there is trend or seasonality in the data, the mean and standard deviations are not useful.
- Produce an analysis of demand by events per time segment. Start wide and gradually narrow the time interval. The data series plot is the starting point. Examine this series carefully to identify time groupings. For example, is there usually a difference between the first and last weeks of the month, between Monday and Friday, between morning, lunchtime, and afternoon? Plot the number of events or customer arrivals per day – not as a graph of events against days of the month, but the number of days during the month when there were exactly 0, 1, 2, 3, ... arrivals. Then repeat by

day, for example Wednesday and Friday, or morning and afternoon, depending on what the examination of the data series has revealed. Then (possibly) home in by hour, and so on.

- See if demand follows a Poisson distribution over the various time horizons explored above. If it does – and this is very likely in service and administration for at least one of the time segments – then you have a powerful piece of information which will enable you to design a good, Lean response system and to assess the risk of unmet demand at various staffing levels.
- Classify demand:
  - Predictable, semi-predictable, non-predictable
  - Capable of being influenced, or not capable of being influenced
  - Urgent and non-urgent. A critical activity or event ideally requires an immediate response. It must have priority.

Examples of predictable demand:
  - Routine maintenance
  - Insurance renewals
  - Direct debit instructions
  - Shut down periods
  - Routine events (Christmas, Easter, Thanksgiving)
  - Planned promotions
  - Pre-booked events

Examples of semi-predictable demand
  - Car service distance intervals
  - Events related to the main interval (like brake shoe replacement every second service)
  - Lunchtime demands
  - Service or extension demands related to prior purchases (likelihood of purchasing an upgrade x months after a computer is purchased)
  - Some consumable repurchases
  - Repeat visits by businessmen visiting a hotel (this can be asked for, or an incentive given)
  - Weather-related services (accidents, drinks, leisure)
  - Lagged demands, for instance, after a new house or office is occupied or started to be built, or after the sale of a new car

- Statistical, for example the probability of a bird hit every 1000 flights, or knowing that arrivals follow a Poisson distribution with average rate of y per week.

Examples of demand which can be influenced
- Price incentives
- Warnings of delays
- Upgrade incentives
- Reminders for service

Calculating the Load

Load is the amount of work coming on to a particular resource (person, group, facility) in a time period. Calculating the workload on resources is necessary to identify those resources that are critical from a capacity point of view. In manufacturing this can be relatively easily done by assembling the routings for each product, multiplying the volume of the product by the unit time spent on each resource, and collecting up the sum of the total times spent by all products on the resource. This is generally done ignoring variation. In service, calculating the load is similar in principle and is discussed in the next section.

Calculating load, when done correctly and supportively, can have the added benefit of a time management exercise.

Shared Resources

Some manufacturing value streams and a few administrative and service value streams can get away with ignoring the impact of shared resources. If you are lucky enough to have resources that are dedicated to a value stream full-time, or for a known proportion of time, the problem is considerably simplified. In this case, average load can be determined by volume multiplied by average unit processing time.

The next easiest problem to solve is where there are clear priorities. For example, when an emergency call comes in, all routine tasks are abandoned and the resource is devoted to the value stream. In this case the load is calculated as above, and shared resources can be ignored except where there may be several priority demands from different value streams – for example, a call centre or administrator being shared across more than one value stream. In the latter case, see the next section. It is unwise to ignore other activities that are not part of the value stream in question, but that have an impact nevertheless on the load on a critical resource in a value stream. For example, the call centre or administrator may be subject to seasonal time demands that result from another value stream.

The objective is to get the value stream to flow. But in order to allow flow, the total load on critical resources must be determined because the resource may be a bottleneck, or effectively overloaded – also called 'overburden' by Toyota. We have learned that to load a resource above about 80% of nominal available capacity courts disaster in the form of sharply escalated delays. The 80% figure is a typical guideline dependent on variation both of customer arrivals and of service time.

Assuming that we do not have the simple case and that critical resources are shared between several value streams, it is necessary to estimate the average load:

- Decide on a suitable period. This may be a half-day for a repetitive transactional process such as order picking, making meals, hotel check-in. A day may be suitable for a semi-repetitive administrative or repair process, a week for many office tasks where deadlines are known well in advance or for longer-cycle maintenance, an even longer period for some professional or creative processes.
- List the range of tasks typically undertaken during the period.
- Estimate the length of tasks. This is often done by voluntary recording or tagging. Times for short cycle tasks may be found by direct observation. Tagging is suitable for long cycle tasks – simply have a traveller form going around with the document or ask people to record activities during the day on a piece of paper. Remember to explain the reasons for recording. Short cycle tasks can be recorded by video, but this is undesirable unless the video is made and analysed by the operators themselves, perhaps to be used as a follow-up kaizen activity.
- Estimate the time split between tasks and, crucially, how much the time split varies. Is the resource heavily loaded one week, lighter the next?
- Estimate the likelihood of the resource being overloaded, and under what circumstances. For example, an accountant working in two value streams is heavily loaded by one of the value streams for the last four days of the month. Are the delays on both value streams tolerable, or does capacity need to be adjusted by overtime, temporary work, or secondment?
- Decide on the necessary actions, if any.

Capacity, Takt Time, and the Yamazumi Board

In repetitive service situations – in some offices and warehouses, even if for a part of the day - you may be able to use takt time. What follows applies to repetitive short cycle activities – that is, where most activities take less than (say) fifteen minutes, and are done by a group all doing approximately the same general task. Activities accumulate into jobs, perhaps passed from person to person.

Relevant formulas are:

Takt time = available work time / demand

Cycle time for an office = .8 x takt time

No. of workers required = sum of the activity manual times/cycle time

Applying this:

- Before you even start timing or looking at activities, you need to look at the activities themselves. Are they really necessary from the customer's perspective?
- Do a 'paper kaizen'. That is, take out the ONVA (Organisation Non-Value Added) activities. Redesign for flow using the checklist above. The sum of the activity times should decline sharply, and as the times decline so will the number of resources. Of course, other work will have to be found for the extras (an opportunity to expand customer service).
- And before calculating activity times, the work should be examined for waste and the existence of failure demand. Both should be removed as soon as possible – and as they are removed so the work content will fall and so will the number of workers needed. As this happens, they should be reassigned not fired. A map and a Spaghetti Diagram would be useful.
- The available time is the time available for processing work, after meetings, kaizens, and all breaks. This need not be a full work day – perhaps the task is worked on only in the morning.
- In an office or warehouse with flexible workers who can be moved around, the takt time can be calculated every day and the appropriate number of workers assigned daily. In fact, the number of workers can be altered during the day – if, for example, there is a heavy workload in the mornings but a much smaller workload in the afternoon. Workers could, for instance,

work on order picking in the morning and then some of them could be assigned to work in the dispatch bay in the afternoon.

- Cycle time is taken at 80% of takt because of variation (discussed above). The factor 0.8 is a matter of experience. In practice it may be found too high or too low, but 0.8 is an excellent starting point.
- The sum of the activity times is the total manual work content to complete one piece of work from start to finish in the area – assuming that workers do not stand and watch printers, photocopiers and the like. Of course times will vary and will have to be observed or estimated. The best way is to get the workers themselves (nurses? clerks? engineers?) to time a number of operation cycles. Then exclude any 'way-out' times – high or low – and take the lowest repeated time.
- The 'profile' or histogram of times for an activity is interesting in itself. Refer to the figure below. The lowest observed times should not be taken; they are 'flukes'. There is a strong case for taking the second or third times as the activity time. Perhaps average these two. The distribution is bi-modal. Why is that? Could it be that there are two levels of skill, or that what is regarded as an activity has not been adequately thought through? In either case there is an opportunity for improvement. There are also some 'outliers' on the right – what has happened in these cases could be looked at.

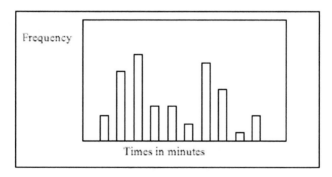

- In the figure above there is evidence of good practice and not so good practice. There is an opportunity to learn from the best. What is it that those recorded on the left are doing differently from those on the right – assuming that they are all doing similar tasks? (By the way, it is not always necessary to time activities to find this out. Let office or service workers study one another.)
- If rates of demand change significantly over the day it is good practice to consider having several takt times over the day.

Perhaps the demand for correspondence is highest in the morning, and invoices have to be completed in the afternoon. Perhaps you can use this takt time calculation for only part of the day – the remainder of the day being given over to less repetitive work.

- If an activity takes longer than 80% of takt it must be done in parallel: for example two people working on an activity that takes twice as long as 80% of takt.
- There is also a concept called the 'Drop-off rate' (not to be confused with the term used in economics or HR hiring). This is useful because it relates to the completion rate – i.e. total demand less failure demand. A completion rate is, of course, the inverse of takt time. This is possibly a better rate to use in future state system design, when the aim is to eliminate as much failure demand as possible. The 'Drop-off' rate time will be greater than takt because the demand is less – so you will need fewer people.
- Then comes the Yamazumi Board or Work Balance board. Refer to the figure below. The idea is to allocate the activities between the workers.

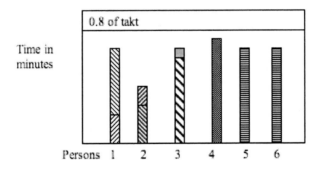

- At the outset the Yamazumi calculation is far looser than the manufacturing equivalent. Take (perhaps) 80% of takt time. Then balance the activities between the people so that 80% of takt is not exceeded. In the figure above persons 1 to 3 both do two jobs. Person 2 is lightly loaded, but for the moment nothing can be done about it. Person 4 does one activity. Persons 5 and 6 do the same activity, but it has an activity time longer than 80% of takt so each person does every second activity. Possibly, if the work content of activity 5/6 could be reduced, or if the work content of person 2 could be reduced, then one person could be saved (reallocated to another group).
- You may be able to use a Heijunka System. Please refer to the later section on Heijunka.

- It is good practice to balance for several rates of work (takt times) while you are about it. Then if or when the rate changes, the appropriate work allocation can follow.
- The calculation for the current resource rate serves as a useful check. It should work out at about the present resource staffing level. If the calculated resources are much more than currently employed, you may have missed some work that is being done or your activity times are loose. If the calculated resources are much less than currently employed, you may have been misled as to amount of work that is being done, or your times are too tight.
- The calculation for the number of workers will probably not yield a nice round number. This is then a judgment call: if the fraction is 0.8 or above probably ignore, if the fraction is 0.6 or below it may be worth considering assigning a worker to work only half the time in the area and the other half on some other activity.

Cells and Bottlenecks: Drum Buffer Rope and FIFO Lanes

Work cells are probably most applicable in repetitive office work, but have wider application in any situation where work is passed from person to person or stage to stage. Refer to the later section on Layout and Cells. In some (all?) cells there is a bottleneck, and in many sequential operations (one stage feeding another) one of the stages may be a bottleneck – or at least heavily loaded.

A bottleneck is a resource, usually a person but possibly a machine, which is very heavily loaded to the extent that it is almost unable to cope. This is not a strict definition of a bottleneck, but it is useful in this context.

Where there is bottleneck stage in (typically but not exclusively) an office operation, Drum Buffer Rope (DBR) and FIFO lanes may assist. DBR is a concept from Eli Goldratt, and amounts to a multi-stage kanban or pull system. The DBR concept has quite wide applicability in sequential service operations.

The Drum is the bottleneck. This is the resource to focus on. To quote Goldratt, 'An hour lost by a bottleneck is an hour lost for the whole system, but an hour lost by a non bottleneck is merely a mirage'. So a bottleneck resource needs to be 'protected' from being under-utilised through waiting for work. That is where the Buffer comes in. The

Buffer protects the bottleneck from running out of work. The Buffer could be a FIFO (first in, first out) lane. This could be an accumulation of files perhaps arranged on a gravity-fed chute, or on a 'lazy susan' that swings around when full. Remember, an in-basket is not a FIFO lane; it is a LIFO arrangement, and not good for flow. The extent of the Buffer – that is, the maximum length of time that work in the Buffer must cover – should be estimated from the likelihood of the Drum running out of work due to problems and variation in the activities between the first operation and the Drum.

The Rope connects the Drum to the first workstation. As each element of work is completed at the Drum, a corresponding element is let in at the first station. This stabilises the lead time through the process. Work that has accumulated in front of the first workstation is immediately apparent.

On the management of bottlenecks, reading Goldratt and Cox's classic novel *The Goal* is recommended for any service manager having sequential tasks, even though it is manufacturing-based.

See also the next section.

More on Capacity: Bottlenecks

As a result of variation in server times, arrival times, and customer requirements, it is vital that capacity be sized accordingly. In other words, there must be a cushion of extra capacity, a cushion of customers or a queue or very short-term flexibility of resources to switch into high load areas. A critical resource generally means a person but could be a machine such as a CAT scanner.

However, it is insulting to assume, by asking customers to wait, that the customer's time is free, particularly when customers observe the critical resource wasting time doing things that should have been done beforehand, or should be done by someone else.

In relation to key resources in particular, there are obligations on the part of the service provider to do the work efficiently but there are also obligations on the part of the customer. In some service and administration situations, equipment is involved. This must also enjoy priority to make sure that it is working when needed. So there may be three components required for effectiveness: the provider, the customer, the equipment. See the section on Overall effectiveness.

In service and administration, as in manufacturing, be guided by Goldratt's five steps:

- Identify the constraint (or critical resource)
- Exploit the constraint
- Subordinate the constraint
- Elevate the constraint
- Do it all again

- **Identify** the constraint means recognising the most heavily loaded or critical resources. The bottleneck is usually the stage in the process that takes the longest time. Note, however, that if more than one person works on the stage, then the time for the stage should be divided by the number of workers. So in fact the longest operation may not be the bottleneck. The bottleneck may also be a skill bottleneck: it may be that someone with unique skills or authority is not available to work all day, so work tends to accumulate in front of the stage. Of course, a bottleneck may also be a machine like a copier that is in constant use. This may sometimes be the case where the machine is a shared resource. In service it is very common for the bottleneck to be 'floating', i.e. not at one single constant point. In this case the following may apply to more than one 'bottleneck':

    There is a fundamental distinction between critical and non-critical resources. <u>A critical resource is one that delays a customer from finishing earlier</u>. When seeking to identify critical resources, bear in mind that a good rule of thumb for administration is to allow 20% extra capacity for administrative activities and 30% extra capacity for service activities for variation.

- **Exploit** means to make best use of the available capacity at those critical resources. Make sure that critical resources are used to good effect. For example:

    - Establish a signalling system to direct customers to the available under-utilised, but critical, resource such as a checkout point, the next available check-in counter at an airport, a just-become-free doctor.
    - Ensure that no time is wasted by the critical resource during the service encounter.
    - Make sure that all work arriving at the bottleneck is defect free (i.e. no 'dirty data'), and complete as

needed. Is the paperwork waiting for you when you need it? Perhaps put in an inspection operation before the bottleneck.

- Protect the bottleneck from running out of work. It should never be idle waiting for work. This may mean establishing a buffer (in-basket? patient queue?) in front of the bottleneck.
- Can the bottleneck work longer hours without incurring extra expense? This may mean arranging the work schedules of existing staff.
- Look at the operational efficiency of the bottleneck resource. Are there 'micro wastes' due to poor layout, poor 5S, or poor access to data?
- For a true bottleneck resource, a time buffer of customers may be appropriate.
- Ensure that customers are adequately briefed before the encounter. This means giving customers adequate notice: 'Have your passport ready for inspection'; 'Remove your coat before you get to the actual airport security point'; 'Make sure your form is completed in every respect before handing it in'; 'Check that all items in your supermarket basket are priced'. Sometimes it is worth having a pre-checker. The manufacturing equivalent is placing the inspection point in front of the critical resource.
- Ensure that the work cannot be done by a non-critical resource: the nurse rather than the doctor (or vice versa!), a junior engineer rather than an experienced, highly creative, design engineer.

To summarise, Stalk and Hout spoke about the Golden Rule of Time-based Competition: 'Never delay a value adding activity by a non-value adding activity'.

- **Subordinate** means that the flow of work to a critical resource should enable that critical resource to work effectively. Thus a surgeon should have everything ready to go before the operation starts. The pit-stop analogy is appropriate: do the maximum amount of preparation before the grand-prix car drives into the pits. It sounds trite to say that it is the critical resource that is critical, but so often the critical resource is held up as a result of failure by non-critical activity. For example, the already-checked-in airline passenger who then delays a flight departure while shopping; or the car service customer who has to return because a part was not available, when the information could have been gleaned at the phone-in stage.

> So, is all accompanying paperwork there on time? Is there batching at a prior operation which means that work arrives at the bottleneck in erratic batches? Can one-piece flow of files or patients be arranged? If room service is the bottleneck, is there an efficient communication system with checkout? Is the anaesthetist there when the surgeon needs to start work?

- **Elevate** means break the constraint. The exploit and subordinate stages are often low cost or no cost. But elevate can cost money. So don't hire an additional critical resource before you have exploited and elevated.

- From a Lean perspective, the ideal is to have flexible capacity that can switch into high load activities at short notice. An example is the British supermarket chain Tesco, which continually monitors checkout queue lengths and opens up extra checkout stations at short notice. The extra checkout staff are drawn from specially trained staff who work in 'back stage' activities such as shelf-packing and who can catch up load in off-peak times. To this end, a table such as a skills matrix can be helpful.
- One company I know uses a combination of flexitime, annualised hours, drawing on other operational staff, and finally drawing on office staff, to address variable capacity requirements.
- Then comes the possible trade-off between extra human resources (in-sourced or out-sourced) and technology such as ATMs or self check-in at an airport, check-in via the internet, or even auto-scan shopping trolleys.
- 'Self' is a powerful word in service. It is both a way to address capacity issues and a way to improve flow and efficiency. Can the customers take on some of the work themselves – for example, via online airline check-in at home? Self-inspect, self-check, self-serve. Sometimes customers really love this aspect of self-service. At other times it is seen as simply offloading work onto the customer. You have to know which of these is the case.

- ***Do it all again. Avoid Inertia.*** When the bottleneck has been broken another bottleneck is likely to arise.

More on Capacity: Forecasting and Adding Capacity Incrementally

If capacity (people, machines such as buses) takes time to acquire, you will need to forecast demand. 'The only thing you know about a forecast is that it will be wrong', and 'a forecast is lucky or lousy'. A forecast is not a prediction, it merely sets out the bounds of uncertainty. So:

- A forecast should be three numbers: average, upper and lower bound. According to Paul Saffro, they form an expanding 'cone of uncertainty'.
- Know at what stage the product or service is in the life cycle. There is much more uncertainty early on, so adapt the forecasting method.
- Use 'Sales and Operations Planning'. In other words, use the collective expertise of sales, marketing, operations and any others.

You can mitigate forecast uncertainty by adopting the good Lean principle of 'small machines'. In other words select the smallest, most simple machine possible. Multiple small machines have multiple advantages over larger machines – not least a reduced risk of oversizing. This principle extends to people too. Beware of a highly specialist person. Consider instead a home-grown multifunction worker who is happy working in several areas.

Be aware, however, of *The Black Swan*. Only white swans were observed for a thousand years or more, and on that basis Europeans believed that all swans were white. Then a black swan was found in Australia. Nassim Taleb in *The Black Swan* quotes Bertrand Russell's 'problem of inductive knowledge' with his story of the chicken that is fed every day and comes to believe that the general rule of life is to be fed regularly and be cared for by humans. Then on the Wednesday before Christmas something unexpected happens. It has huge consequences for the chicken. These 'catastrophic' events are much more common in service than the occasional 9/11 – and because of their huge impact it can be unwise to rely on the comfortable assumption of the normal distribution.

More on Capacity: Influencing and Smoothing Demand

In service there are widely adopted ways of smoothing demand, including price hikes at peak times, discounts and offers during off-peaks, making customers queue at peak times, and informing customers of anticipated delays. In some service businesses, more than might be expected at first glance, it is possible to build ahead of demand, for example by pre-preparing legal documents (see the section on service inventories), and making sure that the customers' path is smoothed by working through the service blueprint ahead of time. Ask at each Moment of Truth, but particularly at bottleneck stages, if and what it is possible to pre-prepare. In general, of course, service is perishable and cannot be stored, but do question this assumption. (See the inventory section.)

Smoothing demand and flow is, of course, the essence of the Toyota system. It is called Heijunka. The ideal system is smoothed end-to-end flow, not erratic batch and queue, stop and start.

Further Reading

Richard Metters *et al*, *Successful Service Operations Management*, Thompson, 2003
Paul Saffro, 'Six Rules for Effective Forecasting', *Harvard Business Review*, July-August 2007.
Eli Goldratt and Geoff Cox, *The Goal*, STG, 1985

Heijunka in the Office

Heijunka means 'level production'. Although it is established in repetitive manufacturing, it is virtually unknown in the office or in service. Essentially the Heijunka system divides the day into equal parcels of time, and divides up the work to fit into the parcels. In the classic Toyota system, a Heijunka card authorises a number of components to be made in each time parcel, called a pitch increment. A typical pitch increment may be fifteen minutes. In each pitch increment, the cell leader or the material handler is authorised to do exactly the work specified on the Heijunka card. Pitch increments are usually short – less than half an hour. So even if the same product is made all day, the day's work is divided into (say) 30 or more segments. Of course, each Heijunka card may authorise a different piece of work in each time parcel or pitch increment. In fact it is usual in a Heijunka schedule to use 'mix model' – that is, to alternate between products. ABCABCABC is preferred to AAABBBCCC because the work is more even, and if a fault is found with an A at least relatively few have been made.

Not all Heijunka systems use cards. Any system that paces the work can be regarded as a Heijunka system – for example an electronic overhead display may be effective. Note that a system that simply counts the number of completed jobs, as in many call centres, is not a Heijunka system. A count display in a call centre may have undesirable consequences like encouraging operators to rush calls to meet the target. In general, a Heijunka system is not suitable where work is triggered in real time. It can be very effective where work can be pre-planned a day or a week ahead.

The advantages are numerous, at least for repetitive operations:

- The work is spread out evenly across the day.
- Workers are assumed to work at a constant speed, neither too fast nor too slow.
- There is visibility of progress at any moment in the day – it is very clear how many time parcels a worker is behind. This allows extra work to be scheduled if necessary, and to give warnings to management and customers.
- The reasons for missing a parcel of work should be recorded – not for blame and punishment, but as a powerful way to surface problems and then to resolve them.
- In a factory, the flow of materials and components to the work area is even and steady throughout the day.

So how can the Heijunka concept be applied in administration and service?

To reiterate, it should be a powerful contender in any fairly repetitive process that can be pre-planned, where the task lengths can be reasonably estimated. Some examples:

In warehousing: order picking can be arranged into time slots, each requiring a number of picks. The picker begins and ends each order pick route at the Heijunka box.

Warehouse Level Loading Example

A warehouse generally knows the demand pattern. Maybe, morning 8-10am, 50%, late afternoon 3-5pm, (30%) high; otherwise 10-3 moderate (20%). A prediction can be made of tomorrow's orders. Then, morning pick cycles per hour required = demand x 50% / 2 hours. Morning pickers required = pick cycles required / takt time for a pick cycle.

Then, on a board, have a column for each picker. The rows are the pick cycles during the first two hours – one row per pick cycle. The cumulative times are shown. As the shift proceeds, each picker writes up the completion time of her pick cycle on the board. If there is a problem the picker writes up an appropriate error code. These error codes accumulate into Paretos. The focus for improvement work is then clear.

During the second period there will be another calculation, with another number of pickers. Excess pickers from the first period should be found other work – for example stacking shelves.

In maintenance: a maintenance schedule – say for aircraft or machines – can be broken down by day and by hour within the day. This will probably require a pre-diagnostic phase. The cards are turned over when the work is complete. Note that a Heijunka system can be used for a time buffer to prevent work starting too early, thereby allowing adequate preparation to be completed. Once the work starts, there should be no delays, rather than starting and stopping.

In a hotel: Room makeup can be scheduled using Heijunka. This has the advantage of pacing the work rather than rushing it and thereby introducing errors, and it also has the advantage of making the programme for the day visible.

In pension fund administration: Some pension fund administrators deal with numbers of new admissions, enquiries, and people going onto pension, each day. Although there is great variety between cases, the work can be paced over the day into segments.

In accounting: Some accounting and finance offices have regular tasks that must be completed every day, every week, every month. Examples are expenses, billing, cash reconciliation, debtors.

In hospitals: A study has found that that the principle reason for waiting lists is temporary mismatches between demand and capacity due to variation. The variation in health service capacity far exceeds variation in demand. The study showed that this was principally due to the way that NHS work was organised. Variation between patients was much less important. So what should be the solution? Answer: Heijunka to smooth capacity!

Further Reading

Kate Silvester and Paul Whalley, 'Preventing the Deficit', *Healthcare Finance Journal*, July-August 2005.
Don Tapping and Tom Shuker, *Value Stream Management for the Lean Office*, Productivity, 2003

Layout, Spaghetti Diagrams, Touches

The layout question is arguably the most pervasive problem in operations management. Every office, business and house makes layout decisions, however cursory. The first and over-riding point to make is that the layout should support the service concept. A layout analysis should follow the Level 1 systems analysis, and be part of the Level 2 analysis, in the case of Transactional, Interactive, and Custom process types.

Most offices are arranged in so-called functional layout: in other words, like functions (accounting, marketing, logistics, etc.) are grouped together. This layout type has the advantages of flexibility and of allowing members of a discipline to learn from and support one another. From a Lean perspective, however, functional layout usually has long lead times, inefficient movement, poor visibility, poor control (from an end-to-end perspective), and, worst of all, many handoffs, with many subsequent rework loops and defects. The value adding time is usually far less than the total lead time. Service cells could well be an answer. These are discussed below, but first some general points.

Spaghetti Diagrams and Service Layout Analysis

The Spaghetti Diagram is useful in any service or administrative system where there are face-to-face interactions between the customer and the provider, or where there is repetitive physical movement of people or documents. It is of no use where transactions are electronic. Spaghetti Diagrams are a useful supplement to many process maps, and fit in very well with the 'servicescape' concept (see below). A Spaghetti Diagram could not be simpler: just draw a diagram of the physical layout and trace the movements of the customer, document or person. The following are useful:

PQRST and AEIOUX: Richard Muther in *Systematic Layout Planning* uses the easy to remember sequences PQRST (Product, Quantity, Routings, Support, Transport), and, for the relative importance of locating areas close to one another, AEIOUX (Absolutely necessary, Especially important, Important, Ordinary, Unimportant, and Undesirable).

PQ is the product/service quantity. Here draw a Pareto as follows:

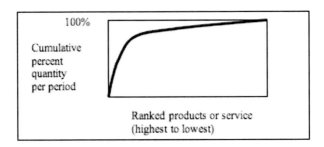

The steepness of the curve will give an indication of layout possibilities – perhaps putting the highest-ranking services into a cell and the remaining in functional layout.

The following is more relevant in repetitive environments – it is much less relevant in custom environments.

R is routings: Do all services follow the same route through the office? Draw the spaghetti. Look for dominant routes.

S is support: What support services are required? Internal or external? How should they best be accessed?

T is transport: the movement routes around the office, hospital, supermarket, etc. Is there a regular 'runner' route where post or medicines are distributed regularly, or do such movements simply take place as required? The Runner is a Lean manufacturing concept that has some use in repetitive service environments. This is a person who goes around a specific route at specific intervals – every two hours, twice a day, whatever. All document and material movement is via the Runner. On each route he picks up and drops off. Thus a regular drumbeat flow of work is established.

For functional layouts or areas only (not cells):

AEIOUX and the REL (or relationship diagram). Each area is set against each other. For example

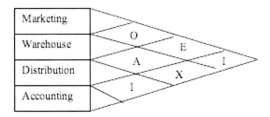

Then connect the area with lines: A: 4 lines; E: 3 Lines; I: 2 lines; O: 1 line; X: a wavy line.

For the current layout, the REL diagram is:

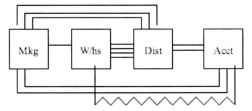

A better layout, seeking to minimise the number of multiple lines over long distances is:

Cell Layout

Cell layout attempts to create the advantages of an efficient assembly line layout while retaining flexibility. The method is simply to line up the functions in process order and, ideally, flow work one at a time. This not only drastically cuts lead time but also improves visibility and problem solving.

Consider the following case.

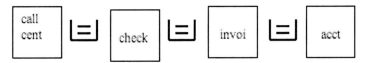

Process time is one minute per file at each stage. Batches of ten are processed before moving.

Time for first file to come out = 40 minutes
Time for last file to come out = 40 minutes.

Now, if files can be moved one at a time:

Time for first file to come out = 4 minutes
Time for last file to come out = 14 minutes.

Here are two examples:

Example 1:

A local authority's plans approval process involves the files moving through the following areas: Town Planning, Building Survey, City Health, Engineers, Water Authority, and Electricity Authority. Each is sited at a separate location. Applications are moved in batches. Overall lead time is between three weeks and six months. Tracing files is difficult. Rework loops result in considerable delay.

So, reorganise into a cell which meets three times per week. Representatives from all the departments and authorities sit in one room, and progress the applications one at a time. Referrals back are dealt with immediately. Lead time is reduced to between two days and one week!

There are, of course, organisational issues to be worked out.

Example 2:

This is a story told by Hal Mather, at the Institute of Operations Management, UK. Six ships arrive together in a port with six cranes. A crane can unload $\frac{1}{6}$ of a ship per day. Time in the port does not generate cash, so the quicker they can get to sea the better. If one crane is allocated per ship, all ships get out of port after six days. Average time in port is six days. Is there a better way?

All cranes work together on ship 1. It leaves after one day. Then all work on ship 2. It leaves after two days. And so on. Average time in port is $(1+2+3+4+5+6)/6 = 3.5$ days.

Moral: cell team working can be much more effective.

Split Tasks and Batches

A highly relevant point to both manufacturing and service cells, but particularly to service cells, is that jobs or tasks need to be broken down into the smallest feasible, sensible element. In Lean manufacturing the dangers of large batches and the advantages of small batches are well appreciated (see above). In service, a large batch is not necessarily a large number of similar jobs – think rather of a large batch as a long sequence of small tasks done by one person before being passed onto the next person. 'Batching' can cause major queues and delays. By contrast, 'levelling' the work means passing on smaller elements of the larger task so that the complete task can be worked on in parallel. This is particularly relevant where there are critical resources, for two reasons:

- The tasks may not all require the skills of the critical resource, thereby freeing up the most valuable constrained time.
- The critical resource is likely to be 'starved' of work less often.
- Alternatively, the critical resource will be level-loaded, rather than work coming in waves.

Three Ways to Reorganise into Service Cells

All the following are much superior to functional layout, but they do have pros and cons.

1   The first is to allocate a <u>caseworker</u>, who works with a client through all stages. This is more personalised for the client, but there are training and expertise issues.
2   Clients are progressed through a cell, moving work one piece at a time between several workers. Workers can focus on areas of expertise. But client personalisation is lost.
3   Virtual cells. This makes use of workflow software that routes files between team members, and monitors any delays, but team members are not required to relocate physically.

Further Issues on Layout and Physical Movement

- **The cost of the last 50 metres**. Tesco has analysed where the costs lie in the distribution chain. Answer: lots of cost in the last 50m. Why? Because that is where there are many touches. Tesco aims to reduce the number of touches on the way to the final location on the supermarket floor. Today several SKU items are taken directly to the point of use on wheeled pallets.

- **Customers can participate.** At Sholdice hospital in Toronto, which specialises in hernia operations, patients who have had their operation show new patients around. This is good systems thinking. Those who have had their operation get fit quicker by walking around. New patients are reassured. Hospital staff can be used more effectively.
- **'Supermarkets'.** 'Supermarket' is a service concept borrowed by manufacturing but in turn it has some utility in repetitive service. A 'supermarket' is a central location where common parts are stored and material handlers or 'runners' 'go shopping'. A service supermarket may contain files, food, or spares.
- **FIFO Lane.** Instead of an in-basket that is often last in, first out, a first in, first out lane maintains the sequence of work. A good FIFO lane has a designated maximum length with visible warnings if it is exceeded. It is possible to use a 'lazy susan', which swings round when full.

Layout and Attention to Detail

Attention to detail in service environments can have a dramatic effect, but it is often not thought of, or given adequate attention. Why not do a mini 'kaizen event', taking just an hour or two to think through a good layout with the team?

Take four 'obvious' examples:

- **Layout of medication carts.** These are the equivalent of the changeover carts found in manufacturing. Include shadow boards. Think what items need to be included. Keep a record of how many times items are used, what items are needed but not included, and what are excluded. Consider what items should be on the top rack, for easy access, and what on the bottom. Is the trolley itself the right size, and does it have the required manoeuvrability?

- **Restaurant layout.** Almost everyone is familiar with the batch and queue buffet process during mealtimes at conference venues. Why does it have to be that way? Consider a Lean or systems solution:
    - Distributing the cutlery at several locations to eliminate backtracking.

- Having several mini-tables rather than one or two large tables that work at the rate of the slowest guest.
- Separating the main foodstuffs within a course – say carvery at one location, cold meats in another, vegetarian at another – all clearly signposted. And don't mix them in with others such as salads – this is to create what is called 'requisite variety' in systems language.
- Using several smaller, separated bowls of a food, rather than one large bowl – distribute the possible bottlenecks.
- Having a kanban-like signalling system that guests can use to show that a replacement bowl is required.
- Mixing dessert, salad and vegetables on the same table, so that queue batches don't 'float' according to course. Have signs to explain this.
- Distributing most dishes directly to eating tables.
- Breaking up the queues by serving the first course directly at the eating tables.
- Continually reviewing the most popular and least popular foods. Keep a tally chart of usage.

- **Layout of the Registration Process**, at a conference or at the start of a university term. This is an aspect that sometimes gets attention. First: are there clear signs of where to go? Of course, delegate labels are prepared. But how are they laid out and grouped: alphabetically, by company/class or by interest group (to foster networking)? Again, have clear signs according to the grouping. What is the queue discipline: multiple queues or a single queue to several parallel servers? If several servers have to be visited, does everyone have to follow a strict sequence – and if not, can a checklist be provided on whom to visit? Should delegate packs be collected with the name badges or separately? How many servers are required, and can they move from queue to queue? Is some pre-registration or label printing possible, like online check-in at an airport? There is surely a 'one best way' for any registration…

- **Layout of stationery cupboards**. This is straightforward 5S – but are locations clearly labelled? Re-order points apparent? Frequently used items in the most convenient locations? And are these reviewed? Do you really need to have drawers and doors?

The Benihana Case is a famous Harvard Business School case study illustrating a systems approach to layout for a fast turn around, but fun, dining experience. Guests congregate in the bar where they are assembled into table-sized groups – but they also spend money while waiting. They move in a group to a U-shape hotplate table where the chef is already waiting in the middle. A group means that intimate, romantic but long conversations are minimised. Also there are minimal wasted vacant seats. Cooking takes place at the table so unproductive kitchen space is minimised. The chef bows and gives out the limited menus. The limited menu means efficient inventory control with reduced waste. The chef cuts meat while guests make up their selections – but the chef distributes small delicacies while selection is proceeding. Each waitress serves a limited number of tables. Cooking begins as soon as the selections are made. The chef puts on an entertaining knifework and cooking display. There are no delays while waiting for service. Dessert is offered and served almost immediately after the main course. It is ice cream. Why? Because it melts near the hotplate so the guests have to eat fast. After dessert and coffee, the chef bows and begins to clean the hotplate. Guests get the message. The show is over. They should be moving on. A fun experience with good food is had by all. In fact, the Benihana concept starts long before the meal, by understanding the customer and offering comfortable Western food (steak) in Oriental surroundings. What could be better than an Oriental evening but with your favourite food?

Servicescape

Zeithaml and Bitner believe that the 'Servicescape' affects service delivery by influencing both customers and employees. Their framework is useful. The 'inputs' are ambience (temperature, humidity, noise), layout (arrangement, relative locations, visibility, ease of movement) and artefacts (signs, furniture, etc.). These inputs produce responses in customers and employees: Cognitive (beliefs, impressions), Emotional (mood, attitude) and Physiological (comfort, convenience).

Further Reading

Richard Muther, *Systematic Layout Planning*, Richard Muther and Associates, New York

W Earl Sasser, *Benihana of Tokyo*, Harvard Business School Case No. 9-673-057

Valerie Zeithaml, Mary Jo Bitner and Dwayne Gremler, *Services Marketing*, 4th edition, McGraw Hill, 2006, Chapter 11 on Servicescape

Nancy Hyer and Urban Weemerlov, *Reorganizing the Factory*, Productivity Press, 2002, Section 5, Extending the Concept – Cells in the Office

Michel Baudin, *Lean Assembly*, Productivity Press, 2002. A manufacturing book but one which has many lessons for service.

The Kano Model

Dr Noriaki Kano is a Japanese quality expert who is best known for his excellent 'Kano model'. The Kano Model has emerged as one of the most useful and powerful aids to product and service design and improvement. It is included here because of its relevance to QFD, the design process and R&D.

The Kano model relates three factors, which Kano argues are present in every product or service, to their degree of implementation or level of implementation, as shown in the diagram. Kano's three factors are Basic (or 'must be'), Performance (or 'more is better'), and Delighter (or excitement). The degree of customer satisfaction ranges from 'dissatisfaction', through neutrality, to 'delight'.

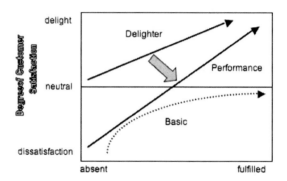

A Basic factor is something that a customer simply expects to be there. If it is not present the customer will be dissatisfied or disgusted, but if it is fully implemented or present it will merely result in a feeling of neutrality. Examples are clean sheets in a hotel, a station tuner on a radio, or windscreen washers on a car. Note that there may be degrees of implementation: sheets may be clean but blemished. Basic factors should not be taken for granted, or regarded as easy to satisfy; some may even be exceptionally difficult to identify. One example is course handouts, which a lecturer may regard as trivial but the audience may regard as a basic necessity. If you don't get the basics right, everything else may fail. To this extent it's like Maslow's Hierarchy of Needs: it's no good thinking about self-esteem needs unless survival needs are catered for. Market research is of limited value for Basics because they are simply expected. A service provider therefore needs to build up a list by accumulating past experience, by observation, and by organised feedback.

A Performance factor can cause dissatisfaction at one extreme, but if fully implemented it can result in 'delight'. This factor is also termed 'more is better' but it could also be 'faster is better' or 'easier is better'. Performance factors are usually in existence already, but they are neutral, causing neither 'dissatisfaction' nor 'delight'. It is not so much the fact that the Performance factor exists, but how it can be improved, which is important. The challenge is to identify it, and to change its performance. Examples are speed of check-in at a hotel, ease of tuning on a radio, or fuel consumption. Performance factors represent a real opportunity to designers and to R&D staff. They may be identified through market research, but observation is also important, especially in identifying those which are causing dissatisfaction. Creativity or process redesign is often required to deliver the factor faster or more easily, and information support may play a role, as in the 'one minute' check-in at some top hotels. The 'cycle of service' (see separate section) is a useful starting point to identify Performance factors.

Finally, a Delighter is something that customers do not expect, but may increase delight. Examples are flowers and wine awaiting guest arrivals in some hotel rooms, or a radio tuner that retunes itself when moving out of range of a transmitter. Identifying true Delighters requires the study of early adopters. By definition, market research is of little use here, at least ahead of time: you cannot ask the customer, 'What don't you expect?' Once again, it is creativity, based on an appreciation of (latent) customer needs, which can provide the breakthrough.

We should also note that the Kano factors are not static. What may be a Delighter this year may migrate towards being a Basic in a few years' time. And also, what may be a Delighter in one part of the world may be a Basic in another. Thus it is crucial to keep up to date with changing customer expectations. Benchmarking may be a way to go. From Kano we also learn that a reactive quality policy, reacting to complaints, or Dissatisfiers, will at best lead to neutrality, but proactive action is required to create 'delight'. As Schneider and Bowen state, 'If you dissatisfy customers by not meeting their expectations you can still recover', but 'If you dissatisfy customers by not meeting their basic needs you will lose them'. In a time when customer retention is increasingly important to profitability, the Kano concepts are therefore key.

The Kano Model works well with Quality Function Deployment. Basics should be satisfied, and Delighters can be explicitly traded off in the 'roof' of the QFD matrix. For example, fuel consumption may suggest a lighter car, but safety a stronger one - so the quest is to find material that is light, strong, and inexpensive.

Further Reading

John Bicheno and Phil Catherwood, *Six Sigma and The Quality Toolbox*, PICSIE Books, 2004
Readings in English are difficult to obtain, but an excellent article is Hofmeister, Walters, Gongos, 'Discovering Customer WOW's', *Annual Quality Congress*, ASQC, May 1996, pp 759-770
Lou Cohen, *Quality Function Deployment*, Addison Wesley, Reading MA, 1995, pp 36-41

Loyalty and Retention

Customers need to be acquired and retained. Building loyalty is a key to both. But the lock for the key is good operations.

Loyalty and retention have become big issues in service and manufacturing, since the evidence has mounted that loyal customers buy more products and services over time and become ever more profitable. Witness the growth of loyalty cards during the 1990s. Loyal customers are less expensive to reach by advertising, are early adopters of new products and services, and tend to give an increasing share of their business to their preferred suppliers. Loyal customers are also the source of word-of-mouth advertising, which is highly effective, and free! However, the concepts are not without their critics. There is a need to distinguish between truly loyal customers and, for example, those who use the service because it is convenient or those who are locked in by contract.

For service operations it is necessary to understand that there are at least two categories of loyalty: to the brand, and to the service provider. These are inter-related. For example, a car dealership and maintenance centre may have customers who are loyal to the car brand or to the dealership or both. Research has shown that:

- The operations part of the service can destroy loyalty to the brand – as has frequently happened with car dealerships.
- Where there is loyalty both to the service operation and to the brand there are powerful synergistic effects.

While brand loyalty is not the subject of this book, the building of loyalty through service operations is central. Lean service operations therefore play an important and synergistic role with marketing.

Assael, reproduced in Keiningham *et al*, has proposed a useful framework for thinking about loyalty. The Assael framework is redrawn and adapted below for comparison with the service mapping typology used in this book.

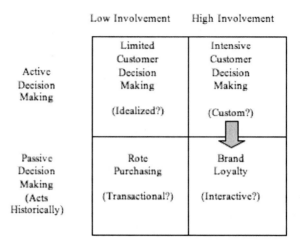

	Low Involvement	High Involvement
Active Decision Making	Limited Customer Decision Making (Idealized?)	Intensive Customer Decision Making (Custom?)
Passive Decision Making (Acts Historically)	Rote Purchasing (Transactional?)	Brand Loyalty (Interactive?)

Of course there is not supposed to be any one-on-one mapping between the mapping typology matrix and the matrix given above, but the parallels are clear.

The point is that high involvement customers begin with active decision making, and migrate towards the bottom right hand corner as successful purchases are made and the risk is seen to decline. There are interesting implications for service operations here: build up the positive experiences early on and then customers do less evaluation of other products and services as they become used to good service. But this does not mean that you can rely on such 'loyalty', because customers will still experiment with other service providers.

This can be compared with Stauss and Neuhaus, who suggest 'five quality levels of satisfaction'.

	Demanding Satisfied	Stable Satisfied	Resigned Satisfied	Stable Dissatisfied	Demanding Dissatisfied
Feeling	Optimism	Faith	Ignorance	Disappointment	Protest
Repurchase	Definitely	Probably	Maybe	Unlikely	No way

Measuring Loyalty

Reichheld, Sasser and others at Harvard originally established the principle of the lifetime value of a customer. The lifetime value can be estimated by multiplying the average spend per period by the estimated period of retention. Additional purchases and profits made from referrals can be added to this, and the savings made by not advertising to established customers can be subtracted.

By contrast, Reichheld suggests (1996) that a company may lose 50% of its customer base by not managing retention, and he therefore suggests that retention is as important a measure as profit or ROI.

Reichheld then proposed 'the ultimate question': 'How likely is it that you would recommend company x to a friend or colleague?' This 'ultimate question', Reichheld believes, captures both 'head' dimensions such as price, quality, ease of use and so on but also 'heart' dimensions or feel-good factors: the sense that the organisation understands, listens, and shares the customer's principles. The ultimate question is answered on a scale of 0 to 10, where answers between 0 to 6 are 'detractors', answers of 7 or 8 are 'passive', and answers of 9 or 10 are 'promoters'. Then the net promoter score (NPS) is the percentage of 'promoters' minus the percentage of 'detractors'. A positive score is the minimum acceptable. This is a good way of measuring the effectiveness of a service process.

Riechheld now believes that a lifetime value needs to distinguish between promoters and detractors – because promoters defect to other providers at lower rates, are less price-sensitive, increase their spend over time more rapidly, and are likely to use word-of-mouth promotion more widely.

TARP, a Boston based consultancy, has produced an often-quoted set of findings (Goodman). These are:

- Problems decrease customer loyalty by 15% to 30%.
- Most customers encountering problems do not complain to the company but many of them will tell their friends – hence the importance of actively soliciting complaints.
- Quality of service can affect loyalty – perhaps a 50% gain in some industries. Customers who are completely satisfied with the resolution of a problem exhibit no less loyalty and sometimes more. 'Mollified' complainants,

by contrast, are only slightly more loyal than dissatisfied complainants.

- Service can affect word-of-mouth behaviour. Customers who are dissatisfied tell twice as many people about their experiences as do satisfied customers.

Reichheld identifies three categories of loyalty: customer, employee, and investor. Loyal employees are increasingly seen as being necessary for loyal customers. A prerequisite.

Zeithaml and Bitner suggest that there are four types of retention strategy:

1. **Financial bonds**, for example, loyalty cards, pricing, and bundling.
2. **Social bonds**, created by building personal relationships – these are more common in professional services.
3. **Customisation bonds**, whereby the provider seeks to understand the detailed requirements of customers through anticipation and customer knowledge – for example books provided with customised covers.
4. **Structural bonds**, where the service is designed specifically for the customer – for example by joint investment and in the book example by adapting the contents to specific company requirements.

These four levels may be seen as successive, with Level 2 building on Level 1 for example.

Reichheld (2001) also suggests that really to win loyal customers requires very senior managers to 'walk that talk'. He proposes six principles:

1. **Preach what you practise**: The leader must articulate his views as well as practise them.
2. **Win-win**: Build loyalty by making sure that both the company and the customer win – it's no win if you take advantage.
3. **Be picky**: Choose the customers to work with, don't accept everyone just for short term gains.
4. **Keep it simple**: Decentralise and delegate real authority to make service decisions rapidly.
5. **Reward the right results**: Make sure that loyalty is rewarded, not short term gains.

6   **'Listen hard, talk straight'**: 'Seek first to understand then to be understood'. This is really a restatement of one of Stephen Covey's seven principles.

Is Loyalty worth pursuing for all Customers?

Apparently not. Some financial institutions now differentiate customers on a Pareto (ABC) basis. 'A' class customers are cultivated with great attention, but 'C' class are just not worth the effort. Worse, paying attention to 'terrorist' customers may divert attention from good prospects. Some institutions have actively tried to discourage some customers from running high transaction, low balance accounts. This may be sensible and pragmatic, but remember that some of the C class customers may eventually turn into A class. Dimensions other than current return are necessary.

The Opportunity Box concept may be useful here. See separate section.

The Myth of Loyalty?

How much of the theory on loyalty is a myth? Henry warns of six common flaws about loyalty (NB retention is not the same as loyalty).

1   There may be many reasons for retention hiding under the heading of loyalty (i.e. geographically locked in, no alternative, switching costs, risk avoidance, other incentives such as frequent flyer schemes).
2   Profitability may be ascribed to loyalty when in fact superior business design drives both.
3   Managerial complacency.
4   Lifetime value is overstated.
5   A competitor's apparently loyal customers discourage effort.

Keiningham *et al* give a list of an amazing 53 myths about loyalty grouped into six categories concerning, for instance, myths about customers, about loyalty programmes, about employees, and about goals and profitability.

Further Reading

John Goodman, Pat O'Brien and Eden Segal, 'Turning CFOs into Quality Champions', *Quality Progress*, March 2000, pp 47-54
Timothy Keiningham *et al*, *Loyalty Myths*, Wiley, 2005
Frederick Reichheld, *The Loyalty Effect*, Harvard Business School Press, 1996
Frederick Reichheld and W Sasser, 'Zero Defections: Quality Comes to Services', *Harvard Business Review*, Sept-Oct 1990, pp 105–111
Frederick Reichheld, 'Lead for Loyalty', *Harvard Business Review*, July-August 2001, pp 76–84
Frederick Reichheld, *The Ultimate Question*, Harvard Business School Press, 2006
Christopher Lovelock and Lauren Wright, *Principles of Service Marketing and Management*, Prentice Hall, New York, 1999
Craig Douglas Henry, 'Is Customer Loyalty a Pernicious Myth?', *Business Horizons*, July-August 2000, pp 13-16

Reference

W. Biemans, 'Satisfaction vs. Loyalty', Lecture Notes of University of Groningen, Holland, 2000

Activity Sampling

Activity sampling is a long-established way to determine the relative time split between activities. It simply involves taking a number of random observations over a representative period of time and recording and categorising what is done at that particular moment of observation. Around 200 observations are required for reasonable validity. Formulas are available in workstudy/time and motion texts which give the number of observations required to obtain a given level of confidence, allowing for variation in the data. But these are seldom necessary. 200 is a good number, spread over a representative period in line with the chosen suitable period mentioned earlier.

Activity sampling is easy and powerful, but it has fallen into disrepute because of alienation between worker and management where it was seen as a means to spy or cut jobs. Today we hope that there is more trust. Activity sampling is best done by the area supervisor or by the workers themselves, in the full knowledge of what the data will be used for – to improve flow, service, and resource allocation with a guarantee of no job losses through an improvement activity. Activity sampling is efficient because it can be done part-time and it can observe several tasks at once.

A random observation needs to be random. One way to do this is simply to decide on the number of observations per hour, pull the appropriate number from a hat containing numbers one to sixty to determine the minute, and then make the observation exactly on the minute.

Classify the activities and record them against 'bar and gate'.

Activity sampling can be a most useful tool to quantify value adding time, the types of waste and necessary non-value added activities.

Begin by making a list of likely wastes, and then for (say) 200 random observations accumulate the type of activity (value added or waste type). You can often make multiple observations at almost the same random moment by observing several workers.

You may like to add notes to the observations - for example whether the office was busy or not.

Recording activity times can also be done in the same manner. Here, you would be interested in the distribution of times, not just the average time. Often the lowest repeatable time will be a good basis for capacity planning, although you will have to factor in breaks - say ten minutes in each hour.

Communications Board

In virtually all service situations, a Communications Board is a major device for improvement. It links directly with Lean philosophy, as it is a means of

- Communicating purpose, and ensuring consistency
- Problem surfacing and resolution
- Waste reduction
- Teamworking.

The Communications Board becomes the focal point for communication, review and problem solving. Every morning there is a meeting around the Communications Board. Communication is two-way – from the group leader to the group and from the group to the group leader. A meeting should take less than fifteen minutes, and often less than ten. An excellent user of Communications Boards in offices is Unipart, Oxford, UK.

Charts shown on the board may include:

- **The Policy Deployment matrix**: This shows the aims, projects, measures and results for the area. It should also show how the area's activities relate to the wider organisational aims and projects.
- **Concern, Cause, Countermeasure (3C) chart**: Any concerns should be raised and entered, and all outstanding concerns discussed at the daily meeting. Each stage of each concern should be dated. A standard methodology such as A3 could be used with the Communications Board showing the overall status. A3s relating to concerns could be displayed in an area next to the board.
- **Performance charts**: Linked to productivity measures such as throughput. It is important that these are a source of problem identification and NOT a means of blame or competition.
- **Quality chart**: Tracking problem areas, complaints, errors. Also a means for improvement not blame.
- **Management audits**: Where different levels of management are expected to visit the area at appropriate frequencies – for instance CEO once per year, appropriate director quarterly, departmental managers monthly, section managers weekly, team leaders daily. Each turns over a magnetic counter from red to green when the visit

is complete. The re-set dates (green to red) are stated. The set of activities that each is supposed to cover is kept on a clipboard next to the board.

- **Total Productive Maintenance/OPE** in the office charts. See the separate section on this topic.
- **Progress charts**: These are usually related to the stages of the regular work cycle.
- **A skills matrix**: Showing stages of development (learner, can do under instruction, can do working alone, instructor) against each skill category. These are often shown in a PDCA format cycle with the quadrants coloured in as the skill level is attained. A skills matrix is not just a 'factory thing'; it has many uses in professional environments, from lecturer to engineer, to accountant.
- **A task allocation chart**: Who is working on what projects.
- **A leave roster**.
- **General company notices**.

Each chart has a designated person responsible for chart maintenance and updating. This must be done by a designated time, before the daily meeting. But the Communications Board is to be used by the entire team.

Don't forget simple things like having a marker attached to a string and using a prominent location.

The RATER Dimensions and Service Gaps

Zeithaml, Parasuraman and Berry (or PZB as they are sometimes known) have developed over several years a well-researched and tested methodology for the 'dimensions' of service and the 'gaps' that exist between the service that customers expect and their perception of the service they have received.

The Dimensions

The PZB dimensions or determinants of service are known by the mnemonic RATER (easy to remember: how do you rate the service?).

R: Reliability: The ability to perform the service dependably and accurately. That is, doing what they say they will do, reliably and accurately. Understandably, surveys have found this to be the most important dimension. If your bank transactions are incorrect you don't care what the bank looks like or how friendly they are.
A: Assurance: The possession of the required knowledge, the skill to perform the service, and the ability to convey trust, confidence and security.
T: Tangibles: The physical appearance of the place, dress of the staff, stationery, signs, and equipment. The appeal of the facilities.
E: Empathy: The ability to understand the customer's needs and to provide an individual, sympathetic, caring, listening service.
R: Responsiveness: The willingness to help and respond quickly to individual requirements.

Together these are known as SERVQUAL, a registered phrase widely known in service. SERVQUAL is an instrument for measuring customer perceptions of service quality. The SERVQUAL instrument is available in PZB's book, *Delivering Service Quality*. It was developed from a large number of dimensions mentioned in customer interviews and reduced to five by statistical analysis. Of course, like many theories, the prime research was done in the USA and does not necessarily apply worldwide. For example, research by Mahesh at the University of Buckingham shows that Far East Airline passengers value respect above reliability.

The Gaps

Related to SERVQUAL is the very useful and widely known Gaps Model. Gap analysis helps to identify the causes of service quality shortfalls in each of the five RATER dimensions. The model is shown in the next figure.

According to PZB, customers build an expectation of the service to be received depending on four factors:

- Word of mouth communication – the most powerful
- Personal needs
- Past experience
- Communications put out by the service provider which create their own expectations.

Gap 1 results from the difference between what customers expect and what management perceives these expectations to be. This can occur, for example, as a result of management not undertaking sufficient research, or from communications failures between the front line staff who actually hear the customer's complaints and requirements, and management. It could be that management fails to 'Go to Gemba', in Lean speak.

The Gaps Model
Adapted from
Zeithaml, Parasuraman and Berry
'Delivering Service Quality', Free Press, 1990

Gap 2 results from the difference between management perceptions of what customers expect and the specifications that management draws up, or fails to draw up, spelling out what service delivery actions are required. This can be the result of inadequate management commitment or interest, a perception that the staff already know what is required, a perception that it is impossible to convey the requirements, or a failure in the way in which the company sets its goals in relation to its customers.

This last point amounts to a failure in the Policy Deployment process, as described in a later section.

Gap 3 results from a mismatch between the service delivery specifications required by management and the actual service delivered by front line staff. There are many possible reasons for this gap. They include inappropriate training, poor teamwork, and inappropriate standards. A big reason, discussed several times in this book, is inappropriate targets or measures – for example inappropriate productivity targets in a call centre.

Gap 4 results from the difference between the actual service that is delivered and communications that are put out to customers about what to expect. Perhaps a misleading Service Level Agreement or a glossy brochure portraying an idyllic holiday resort. There is a common 'propensity to over-promise' which is distinct from a marketing puff that many would forgive. Better to under-promise and over-deliver, than the reverse.

Gap 5 is the overall gap resulting from all the other 'provider' gaps. This is the gap between the expected service and the perceived service experience. Notice the word 'perceived'. It means that service quality is relative, not absolute, and different customers may perceive the same service in different ways. It is the customer who has 'all the votes', not the service provider.

Of significance to Lean service mapping and process improvement is that Gap 1 more or less corresponds to Purpose, Gap 2 to process design, and Gap 3 to process implementation and execution. Gap 4 is not explicitly covered but is obviously important. PZB provide a survey instrument in their book, which enables the 'antecedents' of the various gaps to be identified. This is clearly a very useful addition to the improvement of any process.

Grönroos, in his usual thoughtful way, cautions about using measurement instruments that are based on comparisons between expectations and experiences:

- If expectations are measured after the experience, what is being measured is not really expectation.
- Measuring expectations before the experience also has its problems because expectations may change during the experience.

Grönroos suggests seven criteria of good perceived service quality. These are

- Professionalism and skills
- Reputation and credibility
- Servicescape
- Attitudes and behaviour
- Accessibility and flexibility
- Reliability and trustworthiness
- Service recovery

Professionalism is related to outcome, and reputation is related to image. The first two criteria may therefore prove unsatisfactory irrespective of the mechanical process. Servicescape is discussed under Interactive Mapping.

However, as Kano points out, the last four criteria are process-related and therefore of great relevance to this book.

Further Reading

Valerie Zeithaml, Mary Jo Bitner and Dayne Gremler, *Services Marketing*, 4th edition, McGraw Hill, Boston, 2006, Chapter 4
Valerie Zeithaml, A Parasuraman and Leonard Berry, *Delivering Quality Service*, Free Press, 1990
Christian Grönroos, *Service Management and Marketing*, 3rd edition, Wiley, 2007, Chapter 4

Mapping the Flow of Customer Feedback and Complaints

What happens when customers complain or give feedback? This can be as important as mapping the forward flows. The following steps are required:

- Is there a person who has responsibility for feedback and complaints (F&C)? If it is everyone's job, it will probably be nobody's. Appoint a person with F&C responsibility. This person is not responsible for taking the action – actions must often be taken very quickly by someone at the lowest and most immediate level – but he does have the responsibility for making sure that the processes work.
- Identify the prime points at which customers complain or give feedback – typically front line staff, but also correspondence, internet, or telephone. Every Moment of Truth interaction is a potential point of feedback or complaint.
- Does every front line employee or person likely to encounter F&C have a standard procedure? Five immediate actions and two medium-term actions are generally required: apology, acknowledgement, thanks, resolution, and communication immediately; improvement and prevention in the medium term.
- What employee empowerment or authority is appropriate for short-term resolution? Levels of seriousness in particular should be considered.
- Is the path of communication clear, unambiguous, and immediate?
- Who is responsible for improvement and prevention?
- Where does the information accumulate?

Goldratt Analysis: The Evaporating Cloud and Current Reality Tree

One of the most useful sets of tools in service operations management, which we have used several times, is Eli Goldratt's evaporating Cloud and Current Reality Tree. Here, only an overview is attempted and the reader is recommended to read the excellent guide by Dettner or to attend one of the courses offered by the Goldratt Institute.

Goldratt believes that there are three questions fundamental to change. For each, Goldratt has developed one or more tools.

The three questions are:

- What to Change?
- What to Change To?
- How to Change?

The 'Current Reality Tree' addressed the first question. The 'Evaporating Cloud' helps to expose current conflicts and to break deadlocks and is therefore relevant to questions two and three. Goldratt has other tools too, but these are not discussed here. Together these are known as the Thinking Process.

There are a number of conventions used in drawing Thinking Process diagrams, and the reader is advised to become familiar with these in the Dettmer reference.

Current Reality Tree

The Current Reality Tree begins by collecting a list of symptoms of 'undesirable effects' (UDEs) - usually between five and ten. The next step is to connect any UDEs that appear to be causally related. Beware, however: in the strict version each connection needs to be 'scrutinised' using Goldratt's 'Categories of Legitimate Reservation', preferably with the help of an outside validator or neutral third party. The potential relationship should be stated as 'if A then B'. The validator may express a legitimate reservation, from a list of tests.

Construction of a Current Reality Tree fits in very well with the Check Stage (Level 1) or the mapping process (Level 2) described in this book. The undesirable effects come out of the 'Wastes and System Conditions' as described under Transactional Mapping.

Then, proceed to connect all other UDEs, once again scrutinising the links. Stop when they have all been connected. Then read the diagram from the bottom up, once again scrutinising. Expand or trim the tree if necessary. Finally, identify the point of entry which contributes to most UDEs (at least to 70% either directly or indirectly is considered satisfactory). A partial example is given – there are other 'off-page connectors' to other causal factors and undesirable effects.

The Goldratt procedure is very rigorous, but experience has shown that the exercise of drawing out the Current Reality Tree leads to much valuable discussion.

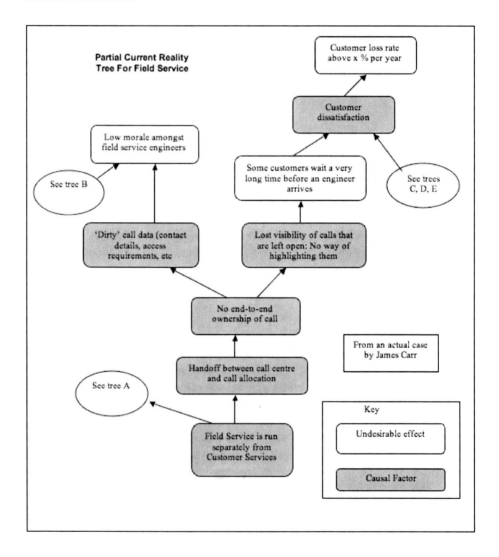

Further Reading

William Dettmer, *Goldratt's Theory of Constraints*, ASQ Quality Press, 1997
Lawrence Leach, *Lean Project Management: Eight Principles for Success*, Advanced Projects, 2005

Policy Deployment

Policy Deployment is just that: it is an effective way of deploying policy – making sure that everyone is not only swimming in the same direction, but is fully committed and bought in to the steps that need to be taken. In essence Policy Deployment (or Hoshin Kanri) is about 'Nemawashi' (consensus building) and 'Ringi' (shared decision making).

Policy Deployment has become a well-accepted way of planning and communicating quality and productivity goals throughout a Lean organisation. Some Hoshin Kanri work (e.g. by Jackson, and by Hines) is very strongly strategy-related. Others accept that strategies are made by some other process, and that policy deployment is about deployment. This section concentrates on deployment.

Here we will use 'Hoshin' and 'Policy Deployment' interchangeably. Strict Japanese-style Hoshin is hugely bureaucratic and form-intensive, so 'Policy Deployment' is a preferable phrase to distinguish it from the rather non-Lean 'Hoshin'.

Some writers and consultants include Strategy in Policy Deployment. Others do not. In any case it is the deployment process that should be central. To quote Pfeffer, 'What is extremely difficult to copy – and what therefore does provide competitive advantage – is the way a company implements and executes its strategy'. Anyone can talk about being the technology leader or providing outstanding customer service, but few organisations can actually make good that promise. That's why Wells Fargo CEO Richard Kovacevich once said he could leave the company's strategic plan on a plane and it wouldn't make any difference: 'Our success has nothing to do with planning. It has to do with execution'.

Hope and Fraser attack the wastefulness and dysfunctional behaviour that the traditional budget process engenders. The internal competitive behaviour that is frequently generated is the very antithesis of the cooperative systems approach advocated throughout this book. 'So long as the budget dominates business planning, a self-motivated workforce is a fantasy, however many cutting-edge techniques a company embraces.' So don't begin with the financial, and issue top-down command and control edicts. Instead, begin with the processes which can create the aims and therefore bring about financial results. This is what Policy Deployment enables you to do.

At the outset we should say that Policy Deployment can be used in two ways. First (undesirable) is to use it in a 'command and control' way: top-down objective setting with little discussion, starting with the financial or other results in mind. This can and will encourage all the 'game playing' and pseudo-measurement practices that are so common in many command and control organisations. Second (much more preferable) is to use it in a systems way: understanding the needs of the system and then developing more detailed participative plans to meet the system requirements. Results come out of the process, not the other way around.

Policy Deployment is in fact the PDCA cycle applied on an organisational level. Witcher and Butterworth talk about the FAIR model beginning with the Act stage: Focus (act), Alignment (plan), Integration (do), and Responsiveness (check).

Cowley and Domb provide a useful visual metaphor. This shows a road leading from the present position (the current state) to the destination (the vision or future state). The road is the plan or action plan. Along the road are scattered small rocks and large boulders which are obstacles or problems. PD is used to remove the boulders one at a time. Kaizen is used to remove the smaller rocks, although this is not what we are concerned with here. Also, there are boulders which are off the road and which should not be tackled. PD is about focusing on the 'vital few'. The vision must be shared, level by level. What not to do must be agreed. And alternatives must be developed. The road metaphor is even more useful when used with Maps – current and future state.

A 'Hoshin' is a word that is increasingly being heard in Western companies, to mean those few breakthroughs or Aims which have to be achieved to meet the overall plan. At the top level there may be only three to five Aims. But at lower levels, the Hoshins form a network or hierarchy of activities that lead to the top level Hoshins. They are developed by consultation. Hoshin objectives are customer focused, based on company wide information, and measurable.

Imagine a tree deployment process. At the top you have the broad aim: for example, to improve conference facilities at a hotel. This means that the hotel marketing, hotel facilities, hotel catering, hotel HR, and hotel operations all have roles to play. These departments need to cooperate on integrated projects: for example guest comfort, speaker requirements, and promotion. Then within each project there may be yet more detailed activities.

A good concept, with applications far beyond PD, is to use the Toyota concept of requiring all plans or projects to be written up as an A3. See separate section.

PD starts with the concept of homing in on the 'vital few'. Where there is little change in operating conditions, a company still needs to rely upon departmental management, and top management planning is not required. However, where there is significant change, top management must first understand the purpose of the system. Debate what the system requires. This involves strategic planning for future alignment (to identify the vital few strategic gaps), strategy management for change, and cross-functional management to manage horizontal business processes.

Departmental management should be relied upon for 'kaizen' (i.e. incremental) improvements, but breakthrough improvements, which often involve cross-functional activities and top level support, should be the focus for PD planning.

An important aspect is Learning. The future is uncertain, although the destination is clear. Treat every unexpected event as an opportunity to learn and to adapt.

There are various Learning loops. The projects that are thought necessary to achieve the aims are in fact hypotheses – they are not certain. So the correct spirit of Policy Deployment is one of experimentation. At the end of the year you need to look back and ask whether the hypotheses were correct, and what can be learned. Also, the Policy Deployment process itself needs to be specifically reviewed. This is very unlike the traditional planning/budgeting cycle, where every year new plans are made without ever looking back at past plans and the fifth year out always looks brilliant!

'Nemawashi' and Catchball

Once the vital few strategic gaps have been identified by top management, employees and teams at each level are required to develop plans as to how to close the gaps. The premise is that insights and ideas are not the preserve of management. Moreover, commitment is built by participation. This requires employees to have access to adequate up-to-date information, thus breaking down 'confidentiality' barriers found in many Western organisations. There must be a clear link, or cause-and-effect relationship, between the organisational aims, projects, delivery, and results. The employees themselves propose measures, including checkpoints. At each level, Deming's Plan, Do, Check, Act cycle operates. And there is also there is strong use of A3 methodology.

The main stages explained by Cowley and Domb, are: 'What do we need to do?', 'How should we do it?', and 'How are we doing?' The first stage is strongly linked with the strategy process, but benefits from feedback from later stages ('What did we learn from the last time?'). This stage also involves the identification of Hoshins and other actions that are delegated to 'Daily Management'. In the second stage the nemawashi and catchball process then deploys the Hoshins. 'Catchball' is a phrase from basketball which indicates throwing the ball among team members before scoring. There is both vertical and horizontal catchball. Another analogy is the knockup in tennis where players hit the ball to each other, but without winners or losers. As deployment proceeds a group meeting takes place at each level. Ideas flow from all directions, and agreement is arrived at by consensus and negotiation, not authority. If a goal is really not feasible the upper tier is informed. The Japanese word for this system is 'Ringi'. Much use is made of affinity diagrams and post-it notes. The process can and should be tied in with the Future State and Action Plans developed under Value Stream Mapping.

PD uses the 'outcome, what, how, how much, and who' framework. A Policy Matrix is useful here. See the figure below. At board level, a visioning process covers the key questions of what is required from the system (the Purpose and the design), what is to be achieved (e.g. reductions in lead time), how is it to be done (e.g. by extending Lean manufacturing principles), and by how much (e.g. all areas on 5S by year end). Specific quality and productivity goals are established. Then, the 'who' are discussed. Normally there will be several managers responsible for achieving these objectives. Appropriate measures are also developed.

The PD plans are cascaded in a Tree Diagram form. This cascading process is also different from most traditional models. In traditional models, cascading plans come down from the top without consultation, and there is little vertical and even less horizontal alignment. In PD, the people who must implement the plan also design the plan. The means, not just the outcomes, must be specified. And there are specific and ongoing checks to see that local plans add up to overall plans. The matrix is used to assure horizontal alignment.

As the plans are cascaded, projects at one level become the aims at the lower level.

A final stage in the cycle is the Hoshin Review where achievements against plan are formally rolled up the organisation. This uses visual results where possible. Exceptions are noted and carried forward. Hewlett Packard does this very formally once per quarter, by 'flagging up' problem areas with yellow or red 'flags'. Intel uses a classification against each Hoshin, showing highlights, lowlights, issues, and plans. Again, root causes are identified. At Unipart in the UK, a policy deployment matrix like the one shown below can be seen in each work area. Staff are able to reconcile what they are doing with the wider organisation's aims.

So PD is in essence an expanded form of 'team briefing' but it requires written commitment, identification of goals, the setting of measures, and discussion at each level. In Western companies, top management sometimes spends much time on corporate vision but then fails to put in place a mechanism to translate the vision into deliverables and measures at each level in the organisation. Hoshin may go some way to explaining why in better Japanese companies the decision making process is slower, but implementation is much faster and smoother.

Correlation between Aims and Projects	What projects are needed to achieve the Aims?	Correlation between Projects and Deliverables
What are the Strategic Objectives?	Projects / Aims · Delivery / Results	What are the project deliverables?
Correlation between Results and Aims	What financial and other benefits are expected?	Correlation between Deliverables and Results

Further Reading

Y Akao, Hoshin Kanri, *Policy Deployment for Successful TQM*,
Productivity Press, Portland, 1991
Michael Cowley and Ellen Domb, *Beyond Strategic Vision: Effective
Corporate Action with Hoshin Planning*, Butterworth Heinemann, 1997
Pascal Dennis, *Getting the Right Things Done*, LEI, 2006
Thomas Jackson, *Hoshin Kanri for the Lean Enterprise*, Productivity
Press, 2006
Jeremy Hope and Robin Fraser, 'Who Needs Budgets', *Harvard
Business Review*, February 2003
Jeffrey Pfeffer, *What Were They Thinking?*, Harvard Business School
Press, 2007, Chapter 25

References

Ellen Domb, *Hoshin Planning*, Material presented at Cardiff Business
School seminar, 2005
Peter Hines, *Policy Deployment*, Material presented during MSc Lean
Ops, Cardiff Business School, 2006
Michele L Bechtell, *The Management Compass: Steering the
Corporation Using Hoshin Planning*, AMA Management Briefing, New
York, 1995
Unipart, *Policy Deployment*, Material presented by Unipart staff during
MSc Lean Ops modules, Cardiff Business School, 200

Index

Books and Games from PICSIE Books

The Buckingham Lean Game

An ideal game to learn about Lean Manufacturing. Unlike other Lean games this game includes several products, changeover, quality and right size machines. Can be adapted to multiple environments. Over 300 games have been sold.

The Buckingham Service Operations Game

Built around an actual situation, this game demonstrates several lean service concepts including service mapping, failure demand, 5S in service, and customer interactions.

Fishbone Flow   John Bicheno   2006 A5 122 pages

This book is an extensive revision of the bestselling booklet 'Cause and Effect Lean'. Lean is explained in over 50 fishbone diagrams and supporting text. The framework used is a development of the powerful 'Thinkflow' model of Creating Flow, Maintaining Flow, and Organising for Flow that has won many accolades. From this high level concept, several levels of detail are developed, resulting at the lowest levels in specific guidance. A feature of the new book is the integration of three other world-class concepts of Six Sigma, TPM, and TRIZ.

Six Sigma and the Quality Toolbox
Bicheno and Catherwood   152 pages

This book is a companion volume to **The *New* Lean Toolbox** but focuses specifically on Six Sigma methodology and a large range of tools for quality improvement and problem solving. The book also includes a section on the theories of the major quality gurus and a section on tools and concepts relevant to service operation – whether in a specific service company or as part of the product service bundle. The book has been reprinted by the Welsh Development Agency and is also widely used by consultants and prescribed by several universities. The down-to-earth, snappy style of former editions of the book has attracted wide non-solicited acclaim.

The New Lean Toolbox (2004) is a more general book on Lean operations with a strong manufacturing slant. It will be superceded by the 4th edition of **The Lean Toolbox** (publication date summer 2008) .

Printed in the United Kingdom
by Lightning Source UK Ltd.
127035UK00002B/51-500/P